GUY DEBORD

COMPLETE CINEMATIC WORKS

Revised and Expanded Edition

Translated and edited by Ken Knabb

PM PRESS

The original French edition of Guy Debord's film scripts, *Oeuvres Cinématographiques Complètes*, was published in 1978 by Éditions Champ Libre and reissued in 1994 by Éditions Gallimard (Paris). Copyright 1994 by Éditions Gallimard.

Guy Debord's *Complete Cinematic Works*, translated and edited by Ken Knabb, was originally published in 2003 by AK Press. The present edition, published in 2026 by PM Press, is a revised and expanded version of that 2003 edition.

ISBN: 979-8-887441-55-9
ISBN (ebook): 979-8-887441-56-6
Library of Congress Control Number: 2025936233

Book and cover design: Jeanne Smith

PM Press
PO Box 23912
Oakland, CA 94623
www.pmpress.org

Printed in USA.

Contents

INTRODUCTION

If we ever get out of this mess and manage to create a sane, liberated society, future generations will look back on Guy Debord as the person who contributed to that liberation more than anyone else in the twentieth century.

Guy Debord (1931–1994) was the most influential figure in the Situationist International, the notorious group that played a key role in catalyzing the May 1968 revolt in France. The impact of his writings has been profound, and sufficiently evident for those who know how to look behind surface appearances. His equally remarkable films, however, have been much less well known, at least until now.

This is due to the fact that they have scarcely been accessible. The first three films were rarely shown, although the first one provoked a few brief scandals in the 1950s. The three later ones were shown somewhat more extensively in Paris in the 1970s and early 1980s, but few people elsewhere ever had a chance to see them. Then in 1984 Debord's friend and publisher Gérard Lebovici (who had also financed his last three films) was assassinated. Angered by the response of the French press, which spread rumors about Lebovici's supposed "shady associates" and in some cases even hinted that Debord himself might have had something to do with the murder of his friend, Debord withdrew all of his films from circulation. Except for a few private showings no one saw any of them again until January 1995, when two of the films (along with a recently completed video) were broadcast on a French cable channel shortly after Debord's death. Pirated video copies of those three works have circulated since that time, but the actual films remained inaccessible until 2001, when Debord's widow Alice began the process of rereleasing them.

Technically and aesthetically, Debord's films are among the most brilliantly innovative works in the history of the cinema. But they are really not so much "works of art" as subversive provocations. In my opinion, they are the most important radical films ever made, not just because they express the most profound radical perspective of the last century, but because they have had no real cinematic competition. Many films have exposed this or that aspect of modern society, but Debord's are the only ones that embody a consistent critique of the whole global system. Many radical filmmakers have given lip service to Brecht's notion of provoking spectators to think and act for themselves rather than sucking them into passive identification with heroes or plots, but Debord is virtually the only one who has actually achieved this goal. With the partial exception of a few distinctly lesser Debord-influenced works, his films are the only ones that have made a coherent use of the situationist tactic of *détournement:* the diversion of already existing cultural elements to new subversive purposes. Détournement has been widely imitated, but usually only in confused and half-conscious ways or for purely humoristic ends. It does not mean merely randomly juxtaposing incongruous elements, but (1) creating out of those elements a new coherent whole that (2) criticizes both the existing world and its own relation to that world. Certain artists, filmmakers, and even ad designers have used superficially similar juxtapositions, but most are far from fulfilling (1), much less (2).

Debord's works are neither ivory tower philosophical discourses nor knee-jerk militant protests, but ruthlessly lucid examinations of the most fundamental tendencies and contradictions of the society we live in. This means that they need to be reread (or in the case of the films, reseen) many times, but it also means that they remain as pertinent as ever while countless radical and intellectual fads have come and gone. In the decades since the original publication of *The Society of the Spectacle* (1967), the spectacle has become more pervasive than ever, to the point of repressing virtually any awareness of pre-spectacle history or anti-spectacle possibilities. "Spectacular domination has succeeded in raising an entire generation molded to its laws" (*Comments on the Society of the Spectacle*).

As a result of this new development, statements by Debord that used to be dismissed as extravagant or incomprehensible are now with equal superficiality dismissed as trite and obvious; people who used to claim that the obscurity of situationist ideas proved their insignificance now claim that their notoriety demonstrates their obsolescence. But those who think that the situationists have been co-opted because a few fragments of their works have been displayed in museums, dissected in universities, or discussed in the media probably haven't bothered to reread them lately.

> Our agitators disseminated ideas that a class society *cannot stomach*. The intellectuals in the service of the system—themselves even more obviously in decline than the system itself—are now cautiously investigating these poisons in the hope of discovering some antidotes; but they won't succeed. They used to try just as hard to ignore them—but just as vainly, so great is the power of a truth spoken in its time. . . . Don't ask now what good our weapons were: they remain in the throat of the reigning system of lies. [*In girum*]

I venture to say that the same will prove true with Debord's films, despite all attempts to neutralize them.

As the most penetrating diagnostician of the present age, it is hardly surprising that Debord has become increasingly notorious, nor that this notoriety consists so largely of hostile rumors about his personal life and ludicrous misconceptions about his projects and perspectives. Fortunately, he is quite capable of explaining and defending himself, so I don't believe there is any need here for me to try to do so in his place.

I will, however, take the liberty of quoting him one more time in order to refute one of the most gross and prevalent falsifications, which presents him as an artist or literary stylist who passed through a radical phase but supposedly later became disillusioned and resigned:

> From the very beginning I have devoted myself to overthrowing this society, and I have acted accordingly. I took this position at a time when almost everybody believed that this despicable society (in its bourgeois or bureaucratic version) had the most promising future. And since then I have not, like so many others, changed my views one or several times with the changing of the times; it is rather the times that have changed in accordance with my views. This is one of the main reasons I have aroused such animosity on the part of my contemporaries. [*In girum*]

Even those who complain about Debord's "obscurity" should be able to understand that statement easily enough.

I do not claim that Debord is beyond criticism, merely that most of the criticisms made of him thus far have been erroneous or irrelevant. It should go without saying that passively venerating him is contrary to everything he stood for. The point is to assimilate what he has to say, use what seems pertinent, and ignore what does not. The real issue posed in these films is not what Debord did with his life, but what you are going to do with yours.

* * *

The original French edition of these film scripts contains no notes or other texts. For the present edition I have added some documents (all by Debord) and other related material. Although I have generally refrained from interpretive commentary, I have included relatively full informational notes, including the sources of most of the references and détournements that I am aware of, and all of Debord's own annotations to *In girum*. I would appreciate hearing about any errors or omissions in the notes and receiving suggestions for improving the translations.

The French edition presents the scripts in a rather complex inter-linear manner. For technical reasons I have rearranged them into two separate columns. The left column presents the main voice-over text (usually spoken by Debord himself). The right column describes the corresponding images as well as occasional other material (music, sub-titles, text frames, passages from other films). An image or sequence of images begins during the line of spoken text directly across from its first line and continues until another image is indicated. The illustra-tions, located at the end of each film script, are the same ones selected by Debord for the French edition.

These translations will also be used for subtitling the films. As this book goes to press the timing and other specifics of the subtitling and distribution have yet to be determined, but if all goes well it is likely that English-subtitled versions of the films will be available sometime in 2004. Up-to-date information can be found at my website: www.bopsecrets.org/SI/debord.films.

Thanks to Alice Debord, who made the welcome decision to re-release the films and who did me the honor of asking me to translate them; to Michèle Bernstein, James Brook, Daniel Daligand, Alice Debord, and Mateusz Kwaterko, who provided information, criticisms, and suggestions; to Jeanne Smith for the superb book and cover design and for technical assistance in implementing the script layout; and to the folks at AK Press for taking on what has turned out to be an unusu-ally challenging (though exciting) project. A salute also to the previous translators and others who helped disseminate the scripts and video copies when the films were unavailable and virtually unknown.

Ken Knabb
April 2003

* * *

Note for the 2026 PM Press edition:

In the original edition of this book (AK Press, 2003) I translated only the six film scripts included in Debord's *Oeuvres Cinématographiques Complètes*. For this new edition I have added the one-hour video that Debord (in collaboration with Brigitte Cornand) made shortly before his death: *Guy Debord: His Art and His Time*.

Apart from that, the rest of the book remains largely the same as the original edition, except that I have corrected a few typos, added a few more notes, and made a number of minor revisions in my translations (mostly very minute stylistic tweaks).

Thanks to the folks at PM Press for their enthusiastic collaboration; and once again special thanks to Jeanne Smith for her excellent design work and immensely helpful technical assistance.

KK

Howls for Sade

Voice 1: *Howls for Sade,* a film by Guy-Ernest Debord.

Voice 2: *Howls for Sade* is dedicated to Gil J Wolman.

Voice 3: Article 115. If a person has ceased to appear at his place of residence and nothing has been heard concerning him for four years, interested parties may petition the civil court to officially recognize the absence of said person.

Voice 1: Love is valid only in a prerevolutionary period.

Voice 2: Those girls don't *all* love you, you liar! Arts begin, grow, and disappear because dissatisfied people break through the world of official expressions and go beyond its festivals of poverty.

Voice 4: Tell me, did you sleep with Françoise?

Voice 1: What a springtime! Crib sheet for the history of film: 1902: *A Trip to the Moon.* 1920: *The Cabinet of Doctor Caligari.* 1924: *Entr'acte.* 1926: *Potemkin.* 1928: *An Andalusian Dog.* 1931: *City Lights.* Birth of Guy-Ernest Debord. 1951: *Treatise on Slime and Eternity.* 1952: *The Anticoncept. Howls for Sade.*

Voice 5: "Just as the projection was about to begin, Guy-Ernest Debord was supposed to step onto the stage and make a few introductory remarks. Had he done so, he would simply have said: 'There's no film. Cinema is dead. No more films are possible. If you wish, we can move on to the discussion.' "

Voice 3: Article 516. Property is either real or personal.

Voice 2: In order never to be alone again.

Voice 1: She is ugliness and beauty—like everything we love today.

Voice 2: The arts of the future can be nothing less than disruptions of situations.

VOICE 3: In the cafés of Saint-Germain-des-Prés!

VOICE 1: You know, I like you a lot.

VOICE 3: A sizable commando of some thirty lettrists, all wearing the filthy uniform that is their only really original trademark, showed up at Cannes determined to provoke a scandal that would draw attention to themselves.

VOICE 1: Happiness is a new idea in Europe.

VOICE 5: "I know people only by their actions. In other respects they are indistinguishable from each other. In the final analysis, we are differentiated only by our works."

VOICE 1: And their revolts became conform-isms.

VOICE 3: Article 488. The age of adulthood is 21 years; a person of that age is capable of all acts of civil life.

TWO MINUTES OF SILENCE
DURING WHICH THE SCREEN
REMAINS DARK.

VOICE 4: She constantly reappeared in his memory, in a flash like sodium fireworks on contact with water.

VOICE 1: He was well aware that nothing of his exploits would remain in a town that revolves with the Earth, as the Earth revolves within a galaxy that is only an insignificant part of a tiny island endlessly receding from us.

VOICE 2: Totally dark, eyes closed to the enormity of the disaster.

ONE MINUTE OF SILENCE DURING WHICH THE SCREEN REMAINS DARK.

VOICE 1: A science of situations needs to be created, which will incorporate elements from psychology, statistics, urbanism, and ethics. These elements must be focused on a totally new goal: the conscious creation of situations.

THIRTY SECONDS OF SILENCE DURING WHICH THE SCREEN REMAINS DARK.

VOICE 1: Lines from a 1950 newspaper: "Young Radio Actress Throws Herself Into the Isère. Grenoble. Twelve-and-a-half-year-old Madeleine Reineri, who under the stage name 'Pirouette' starred in the Alpes-Grenoble radio program *Happy Thursdays,* threw herself into the Isère River Friday afternoon after having placed her schoolbag on the bank."

VOICE 2: Little sister, we're not a pretty sight. The river and the misery continue. We're powerless.

ONE MINUTE AND THIRTY SECONDS
OF SILENCE DURING WHICH THE
SCREEN REMAINS DARK.

VOICE 4: But no one talks about Sade in this film.

VOICE 1: The cold of interstellar space, thousands of degrees below freezing point or the absolute zero of Fahrenheit, Centigrade or Réaumur: the incipient intimations of proximate dawn. The rapid passage of Jacques Vaché through the wartime sky, his overwhelming sense of urgency, the catastrophic haste that led him to destroy himself; the whipcracking spirit of Arthur Cravan, who vanished in the Gulf of Mexico around that same time . . .

VOICE 3: Article 1793. When an architect or contractor contracts with a landowner to construct a building in accordance with an agreed plan and for a specified payment, he cannot demand any increase in that payment on any grounds, whether because of an increase in the work force or materials or because of any changes or additions made to the plan, unless such changes, additions, or increases have been authorized in writing and the new payment has been agreed to by the landowner.

VOICE 2: The perfection of suicide lies in its ambiguity.

FIVE MINUTES OF SILENCE
DURING WHICH THE SCREEN
REMAINS DARK.

VOICE 2: What is a one and only love?

VOICE 3: I will answer only in the presence of my attorney.

ONE MINUTE OF SILENCE
DURING WHICH THE SCREEN
REMAINS DARK.

VOICE 1: Order reigns but does not govern.

TWO MINUTES OF SILENCE
DURING WHICH THE SCREEN
REMAINS DARK.

VOICE 2: The first marvel is to come before her without knowing how to talk to her. The imprisoned hands move no faster than race horses filmed in slow motion as they touch her mouth and breasts; in all innocence the ropes become water and we roll together toward dawn.

VOICE 4: I don't think we'll ever see each other again.

VOICE 2: The lights of the winter streets will end near a kiss.

VOICE 4: Paris was real fun because of the transportation strike.

VOICE 2: Jack the Ripper was never caught.

VOICE 4: Telephones, they're funny.

VOICE 2: What a love-challenge, as Madame de Ségur said.

VOICE 4: I'll tell you some real scary stories from my part of the country, but they have to be told at night.

VOICE 2: My dear Ivich, unfortunately there are fewer Chinatowns than you think. You are fifteen years old. One of these days you'll stop wearing such gaudy colors.

VOICE 4: I already knew you.

VOICE 2: Continental drift carries you farther away each day. The virgin forest is less virgin than you.

VOICE 4: Guy, one more minute and it'll be tomorrow.

VOICE 2: Gun Crazy. You remember. That's how it was. No one was good enough for us. Nevertheless . . . The hailstones on the banners of glass. We won't forget this cursed planet.

FOUR MINUTES OF SILENCE
DURING WHICH THE SCREEN
REMAINS DARK.

VOICE 2: They'll be famous someday, you'll see! I will never accept the outrageous and scarcely credible fact that there is such a thing as a police force. Several cathedrals have been erected in memory of Serge Berna. Love is valid only in a prerevolutionary period. I made this film while there was still time to talk about it. Jean-Isidore, in order to escape this ephemeral crowd. On Place Gabriel-Pomerand when we've grown old. In the future all these little jokers will be studied in the high schools and colleges.

THREE MINUTES OF SILENCE
DURING WHICH THE SCREEN
REMAINS DARK.

VOICE 2: There are still many people who aren't moved to laugh or to scream by the word "morality."

VOICE 3: Article 489. An adult who is usually in a state of imbecility or dementia or who has frequent fits of rage must be kept in protective custody even if he has intervals of lucidity.

VOICE 2: So close, so gently, I lose myself in the hollow archipelagos of language. I bear down on you, you're as open as a cry, it's so easy. A hot stream. A sea of oil. A forest fire.

VOICE 1: That sounds like the movies!

VOICE 3: The Paris police are equipped with 30,000 billy clubs.

FOUR MINUTES OF SILENCE
DURING WHICH THE SCREEN
REMAINS DARK.

VOICE 2: "Poetic worlds close in on themselves and are forgotten." In a corner of the night sailors are making war; ships in bottles are for you who loved them. You rolled over into the sand as into hands more loving than the rain, the wind and the thunder slip under your dress every evening. Life is wonderful at Cannes in the summertime. Rape, which is forbidden, becomes banalized in our memories. "When we were on the Shenandoah." Yes. Of course.

VOICE 1: And the silting up of those faces, which once bore flashes of desire like ink splattered on a wall, which were like shooting stars. Gin, rum, brandy—down the hatch like the Grand Armada. So much for the funeral oration. But all those people were so commonplace.

FIVE MINUTES OF SILENCE
DURING WHICH THE SCREEN
REMAINS DARK.

VOICE 1: We had a narrow escape.

VOICE 2: The most beautiful is still to come. Death would be a steak tartare; wet hair on the scalding beach of our silence.

VOICE 1: But he's a Jew!

VOICE 2: We were ready to blow up all the bridges, but the bridges let us down.

FOUR MINUTES OF SILENCE DURING WHICH THE SCREEN REMAINS DARK.

VOICE 1: Twelve-and-a-half-year-old Madeleine Reineri, who under the stage name "Pirouette" starred in the Alpes-Grenoble radio program *Happy Thursdays,* threw herself into the Isère River.

VOICE 2: Mademoiselle Reineri of the Europe Quarter, you still have your wonderstruck face and that body, the best of promised lands. Like neon lights, the dialogues repeat their definitive truths.

VOICE 1: I love you.

VOICE 4: It must be terrible to die.

VOICE 1: See you later.

VOICE 4: You drink far too much.

VOICE 1: What are childhood loves?

VOICE 4: I don't understand you.

VOICE 1: I knew it. And there was a time when I regretted it very much.

VOICE 4: Would you like an orange?

VOICE 1: The beautiful breakups of volcanic islands.

VOICE 4: In the past.

VOICE 1: I have nothing more to say to you.

VOICE 2: Once again, after all the untimely answers and the aging of youth, night falls from on high.

THREE MINUTES OF SILENCE DURING WHICH THE SCREEN REMAINS DARK.

VOICE 2: Like lost children we live our unfinished adventures.

TWENTY-FOUR MINUTES OF SILENCE DURING WHICH THE SCREEN REMAINS DARK.

On the Passage of a Few Persons Through a Rather Brief Unity of Time

VOICE 1: This neighborhood was designed for the wretched dignity of the petty bourgeoisie, for respectable occupations and intellectual tourism. The sedentary population of the upper floors was sheltered from the influences of the street. The neighborhood itself has remained the same. It was the external setting of our story, where a few people put into practice a systematic questioning of all the works and diversions of a society, a total critique of its notion of happiness.

These people also scorned "subjective profundity." The only thing that interested them was a satisfactory concrete expression of their own lives.

Façades of buildings in the Saint-Germain-des-Prés neighborhood. **SUBTITLE: Paris, 1952.**

Young people pass by.

Handel: "Thème cérémonieux des aventures." Photograph of two couples drinking wine at a café table, shot from different angles in the style of an art film.

VOICE 2: Human beings are not fully conscious of their real lives. Groping in the dark, overwhelmed by the consequences of their acts, at every moment groups and individuals find themselves faced with outcomes they had not intended.

The music breaks off.

VOICE 1: They said that oblivion was their dominant passion. They wanted to reinvent everything each day; to make themselves the masters and possessors of their own lives.

Other faces.

Just as we do not judge an individual by what he thinks about himself, we cannot judge such a period of transformation by its own consciousness. On the contrary, this consciousness must be understood as reflecting the contradictions of material life, the conflict between social conditions and the forces of social production.

The Pope and other churchmen.

Advances in the harnessing of nature were not yet matched by a corresponding liberation of everyday life. Youth passed away among the various controls of resignation.

Girls coming out of a high school.

French police in the street.

Our camera has captured for you a few glimpses of an ephemeral microsociety.

Café tables in Saint-Germain-des-Prés, filmed in news-report style.

Knowledge of empirical facts remains abstract and superficial as long as it is not concretized by being related to the whole situation—the only method that enables us to supersede partial and abstract problems and get to their *concrete essence,* and thus implicitly to their meaning.

This group lived on the margins of the economy. It tended toward a role of pure consumption, particularly the free consumption of its own time. It thus found itself directly involved in qualitative divergences from ordinary life, but deprived of any means to influence those divergences.

The group ranged over a very small area. The same times brought them back to the same places. No one wanted to go to bed early. Discussions continued on the meaning of it all. . . .

Les Halles at night.

Pan shot across a lively and crowded intersection in Les Halles at night.

VOICE 2: "Our life is a journey, in winter and night. We seek our passage . . ."

VOICE 1: The literature they had abandoned nevertheless exerted a delaying influence, expressed in some affective formulations.

Several views of dawn over Les Halles.

VOICE 2: There was the fatigue and the cold of morning in this much-traversed labyrinth, like an enigma that we had to resolve. It was a *trompe-l'oeil* reality through which we had to discover the potential richness of what was really there.

On the bank of the river evening began again; and the caresses; and the importance of a world without importance. Just as the eyes have a blurred vision of many things and can clearly see only one, so the will can strive only imperfectly toward diverse objects and can completely love only one at a time.

Delalande: "Noble and Tragic Theme" (bassoon solo from Caprice #2). Paris: eastward view of the Seine. Piles of bricks on the Quai Saint-Bernard.

A young woman.

The music fades out.

Inside the labyrinth of bricks.

VOICE 3: No one counted on the future. It would never be possible to be together later, or anywhere else. There would never be a greater freedom.

Police vans depart.
Île Saint-Louis at dusk.
Two teenage couples dance on a beach beside a guitar player.

VOICE 1: The refusal of time and of growing old automatically limited encounters in this narrow and contingent zone, where what was lacking was felt as irreparable. The extreme precariousness of their methods for getting by without working was at the root of this impatience which made excesses necessary and breaks irrevocable.

Scenes between Place Saint-Sulpice and Rue Mazarine.

VOICE 2: We can never really challenge any form of social organization without challenging all of that organization's forms of language.

THE SCREEN BECOMES BLANK WHITE.

VOICE 1: When freedom is practiced in a closed circle, it fades into a dream, becomes a mere image of itself. The ambiance of play is by nature unstable. At any moment "ordinary life" may prevail once again. The geographical limitation of play is even more striking than its temporal limitation. Every game takes place within the boundaries of its own spatial domain.

Delalande: Court Music Allegro (from Caprice #2). Tracking shot in a café. The camera's movement is arbitrarily interrupted by TEXT FRAMES: "Passions and parties of a violent age" . . . "In the process of movement and consequently by their ephemeral side" . . . "The most gripping suspense!"

Outside the neighborhood, beyond its fleeting and continually threatened changelessness,

TEXT FRAME: "In the prestigious decor constructed specifically for this purpose."

stretched a half-known city where people met only by chance, losing their way forever.

The girls who found their way there, because they were legally under the control of their family until the age of eighteen, were often re-captured by the defenders of that detestable institution. They were generally locked up under the custody of those creatures who among all the bad products of a bad society present the most ugly and repugnant appearance: nuns.

What makes most documentaries so easy to understand is the arbitrary limitation of their subject matter. They confine themselves to depicting fragmented social functions and their isolated products. In contrast, imagine the full complexity of a moment that is not resolved into a work, a moment whose development contains interrelated facts and values and whose meaning is not yet apparent. This confused totality could be the subject matter of such a documentary.

Voice 2: The era had attained a level of knowl-edge and technologies that made possible, and

People passing along Boulevard Saint-Michel in foggy weather. *The music fades out.*

A couple at a café table.

In Japan several hundred helmeted police come into view, running.

Outer wall of the Chevilly-Larue reformatory.

THE SCREEN BECOMES BLANK WHITE.

Violent confrontations between Japanese workers and police.

increasingly necessary, a *direct* construction of all the aspects of an emotionally and materially liberated way of life. The appearance of these superior means of action, though they remained unused because of the delays in the project of abolishing the commodity economy, had already revealed the obsolescence of all aesthetic activity, whose ambitions and powers had both dwindled away. The decay of art and of all the old codes of conduct had formed our sociological background. The ruling class's monopoly on the instruments we needed in order to implement the collective art of our time had left us completely outside the official cultural production, which was devoted to illustrating and repeating the past. An art film on this generation can only be a film about its lack of real creations.

Others unthinkingly followed the paths learned once and for all, to their work and their home, to their predictable future. For them duty had already become a habit, and habit a duty. They did not see the deficiency of their city. They thought the deficiency of their life was natural.

A series of medium-long shots of the same event. The police slowly gain ground.

THE SCREEN BECOMES BLANK WHITE.

People passing by the railings in front of the Cluny Museum.

We wanted to break out of this conditioning, in search of different uses of the urban landscape, in search of new passions. The atmosphere of a few places gave us intimations of the future powers of an architecture it would be necessary to create in order to provide the setting for less mediocre games. We could expect nothing of anything that we ourselves had not altered. The urban environment proclaimed the orders and tastes of the ruling society just as violently as the newspapers. Man unifies the world, but man has extended himself everywhere. People can see nothing around them that is not their own image; everything speaks to them of themselves. Their very landscape is animated. Obstacles were everywhere. And they were all interrelated, maintaining a unified reign of poverty. Since everything was connected, it was necessary to *change everything* through a unitary struggle, or nothing. It was necessary to link up with the masses, but we were surrounded by sleep.

Repeat of the Handel theme. Windows lit by night on Rue des Écoles and Rue Montagne-Saint-Geneviève.

The music breaks off.

Some houses in Paris.

English police, on foot and horseback, drive back demonstrators.

THE SCREEN BECOMES BLANK WHITE.

VOICE 3: The dictatorship of the proletariat is a relentless struggle, bloody and bloodless, violent and peaceful, military and economic, educative and administrative, against the forces and traditions of the old society.

VOICE 1: But in this country it is once again the forces of law and order who have rebelled and reinforced their power. They have been allowed to aggravate the grotesqueness of the ruling conditions according to their will, embellishing their system with the funereal ceremonies of the past.

Demonstration of French colonists in Algiers, May 1958. General Massu and General Salan. A company of paratroopers marches toward the camera.

De Gaulle speaks at a podium, pounding it with his fist.

VOICE 2: Years, like a single instant prolonged to this moment, come to an end.

THE SCREEN BECOMES BLANK WHITE.

VOICE 1: What was directly lived reappears frozen in the distance, engraved in the tastes and illusions of an era and carried off with it.

The star of an advertisement for Monsavon brand soap. The face of a young woman.

A cavalry charge through the streets of a town.

VOICE 2: The appearance of events that we have not created—events that others have in fact created against us—now obliges us to assess the passage of time and its results and to envisage the transformation of our own desires into events. What differentiates the past from the present is precisely its out-of-reach objectivity.

THE SCREEN BECOMES BLANK WHITE.

The face of another young woman.

There is no more should-be; being has been consumed to the point of ceasing to exist. The details are already lost in the dust of time. Who was afraid of life, afraid of the night, afraid of being taken, afraid of being kept?

A starlet taking a bath.

Film of a solar flare. Tracking shot of the bathing starlet. Continuation of the solar flare.

VOICE 3: What should be abolished continues, and we continue to wear away with it. We are engulfed. Separated from each other. The years pass and we haven't changed anything.

In Japan a dozen policemen with helmets and gas masks continue to slowly advance across a large space that has been cleared, launching tear-gas canisters.

VOICE 2: Once again, morning in the same streets. Once again the fatigue of so many similarly passed nights. It's a journey that has lasted a long time.

Repeat of Delalande's "Noble and Tragic Theme." Daybreak over a Paris bridge. Slow pan shot across Place des Victoires at dawn.

The music fades out.

VOICE 1: Really hard to drink more.

THE SCREEN BECOMES BLANK WHITE.

VOICE 2: Of course one might make a film about it. But even if such a film succeeded in being as fundamentally incoherent and unsatisfying as the reality it dealt with, it could never be more than a re-creation—as impoverished and false as this botched tracking shot.

The film crew, grouped around a camera.

The previously seen tracking shot (across the café) is repeated, this time with the worst take, without any cuts, and with a succession of defects—people intruding into the field of vision, lens reflections, camera shadows—ending with a swish pan shot.

VOICE 3: There are now people who pride themselves on being authors of films, as others were authors of novels. They are even more backward than the novelists because they are unaware of the decomposition and exhaustion of individual expression in our time, unaware that the arts of passivity are over and done. They are sometimes praised for their sincerity since they dramatize with more personal depth the conventions of which their life consists. There is talk about "liberating the cinema." But what does it matter to us if one more art is liberated to the point that every Tom, Dick, and Harry can use it to complacently express their servile sentiments? The only interesting venture is the liberation of everyday life, not only in a historical perspective, but for us, right now. This project implies the withering away of all the alienated forms of communication. The cinema, too, must be destroyed.

VOICE 2: In the final analysis, stars are not created by their talent or lack of talent, or even by the film industry or advertising. They are created by the need we have for them. A pathetic

THE SCREEN BECOMES BLANK WHITE.

A car stops. Tracking shot of the Monsavon star as she emerges from it.

Two images of the present film's clapboard signaling two already viewed shots.

need, arising out of a dismal and anonymous life that would like to enlarge itself to the dimensions of cinematic life. The imaginary life on the screen is the product of this real need. The star is the projection of this need.

Ladies riding horses in the Bois de Boulogne.

The advertisements during intermissions are the truest reflection of an intermission from life.

The advertising starlet shows how much she likes the soap, and smiles to the audience.

To really describe this era it would no doubt be necessary to show many other things. But what would be the point?

THE SCREEN BECOMES BLANK WHITE AND REMAINS SO UNTIL TWENTY SECONDS AFTER THE LAST WORD.

The point is to understand all that has been done, and what remains to be done. Not to add more ruins to the old world of spectacles and memories.

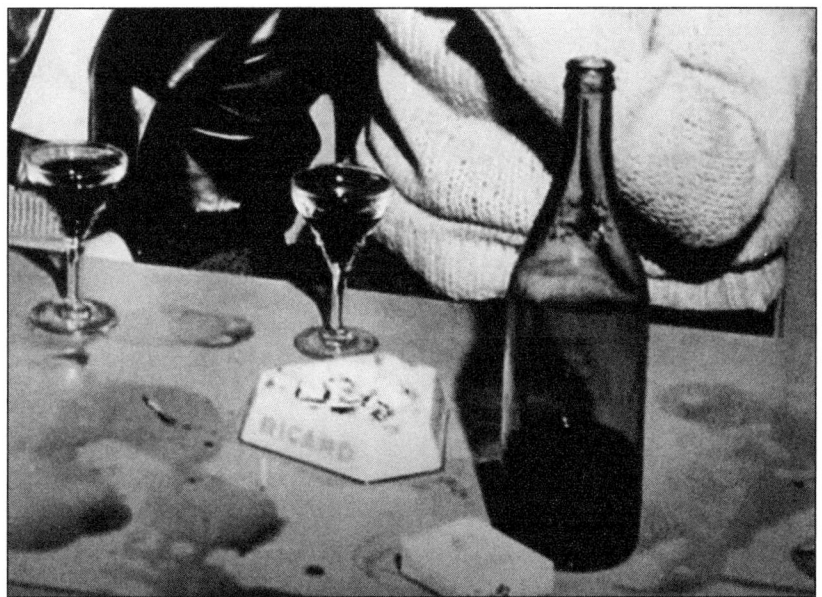

Human beings are not fully conscious of their real lives. Groping in the dark, overwhelmed by the consequences of their acts . . . [p. 14]

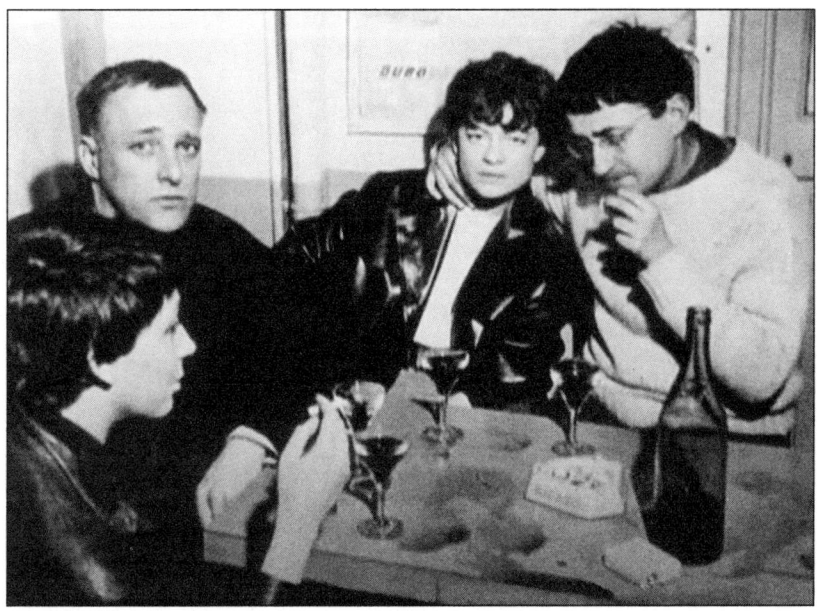

. . . at every moment groups and individuals find themselves faced with outcomes they had not intended. [p. 14]

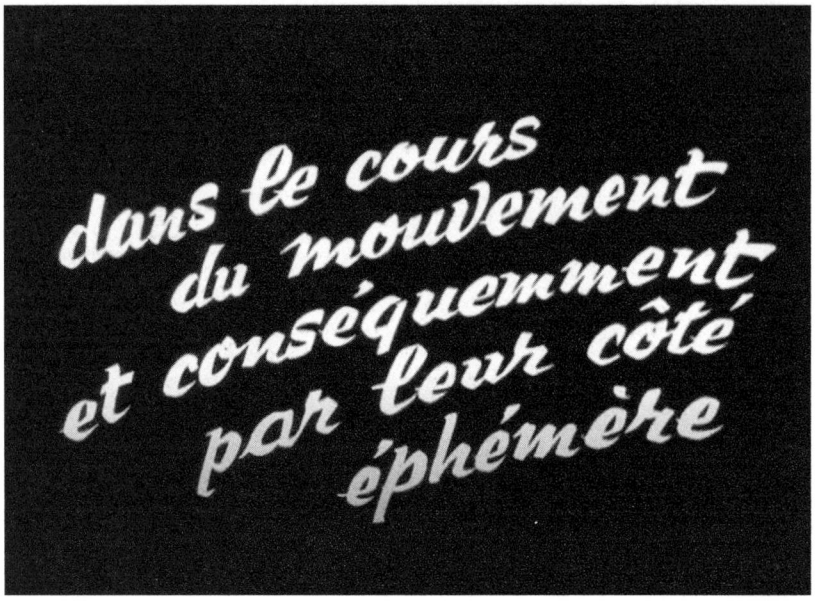

The ambiance of play is by nature unstable. At any moment "ordinary life" may prevail once again. [p. 17]

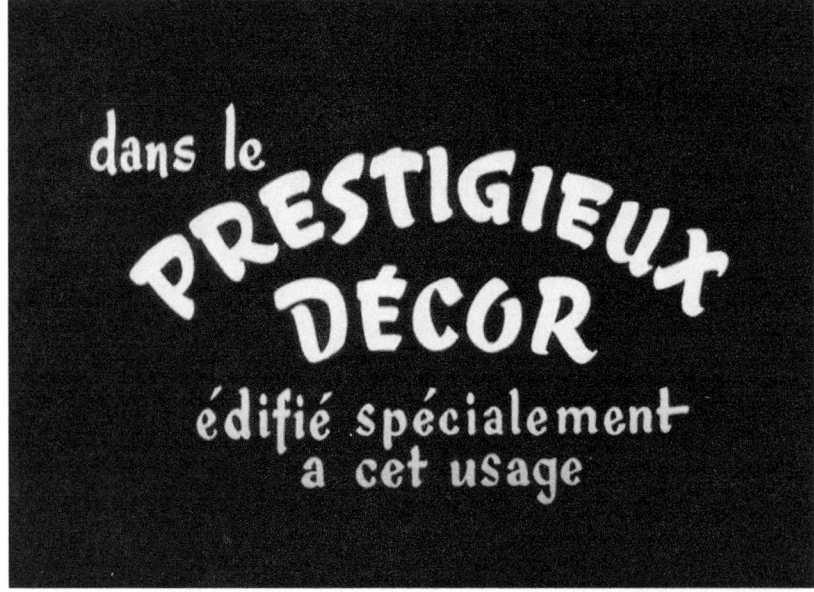

Outside the neighborhood, beyond its fleeting and continually threatened changelessness, stretched a half-known city where people met only by chance . . . [pp. 17–18]

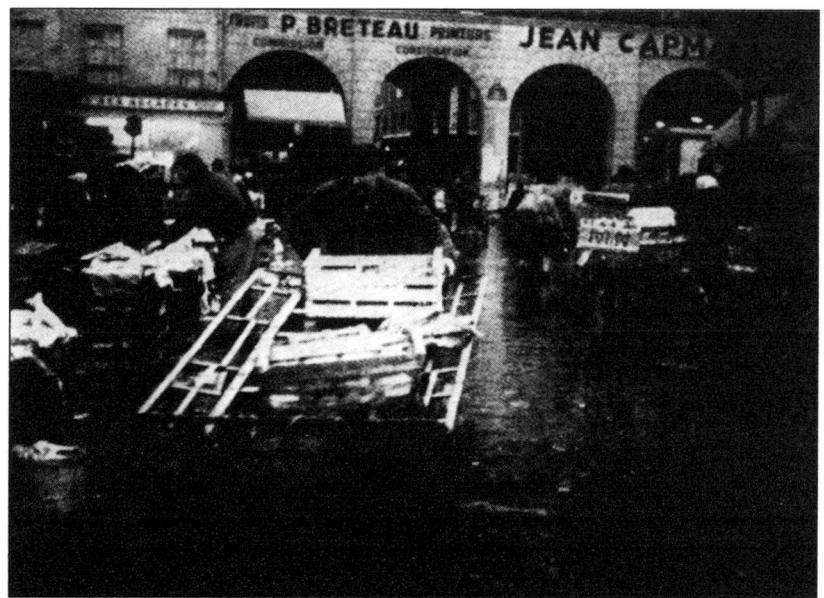

"Our life is a journey, in winter and night. We seek our passage . . ." [p. 16]

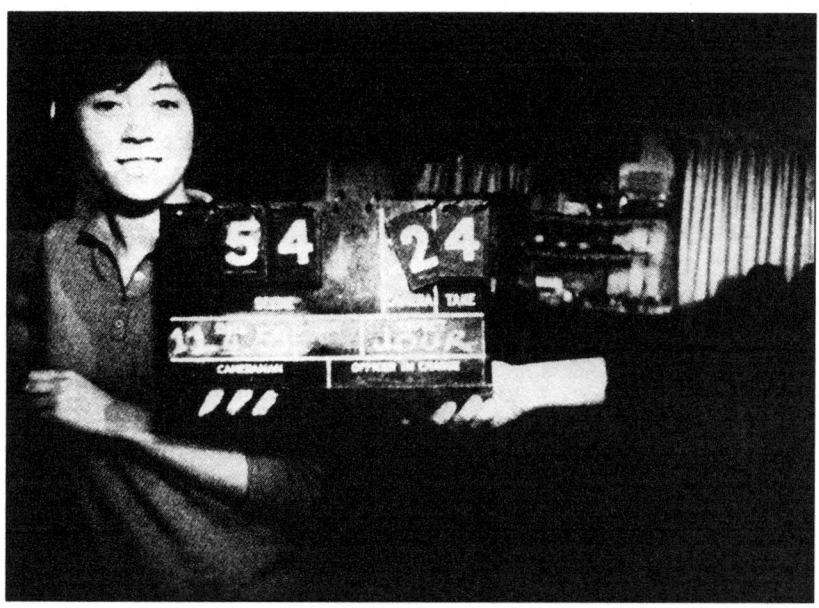

Stars are created by the need we have for them. A pathetic need . . . [pp. 23–24]

CRITIQUE OF SEPARATION

We don't know what to say. Sequences of words are repeated; gestures are recognized. Outside us. Of course some methods are mastered, some results are verified. Often it's amusing. But so many things we wanted have not been attained, or only partially and not like we imagined. What communication have we desired, or experienced, or only simulated? What real project has been lost?

The cinematic spectacle has its rules, its reliable methods for producing satisfactory products. But the reality that must be taken as a point of departure is dissatisfaction. The function of the cinema, whether dramatic or documentary, is to present a false and isolated coherence as a substitute for a communication and activity

Tracking shot of a group of people on a café terrace. The camera, hand-held as in a news report, zeroes in on Debord talking to a young brunette.

Medium-long shot of the two of them walking together.
Another young woman, this one a blonde.

Comic strip: Tired-looking young blonde. Caption: "But she failed. The jeep was stuck too deeply in the mud of the swamp. . . ."

Couperin: "March of the Regiment of Champagne." 360-degree pan shot from the center of Plateau Saint-Merri. **Subtitles: Midway on the journey of our life . . . I found myself in a dark forest . . . where the right way was lost.**

that are absent. To demystify documentary cinema it is necessary to dissolve its "subject matter."

The music ends.

A well-established rule is that any statement in
a film that is not illustrated by images must be
repeated or else the spectators will miss it. That
may be true. But this same type of miscommu-
nication constantly occurs in everyday encounters. Something must be specified, but there's
not enough time, and you're not sure you have
been understood. Before you have said or done
what was necessary, the other person has already
gone. Across the street. Overseas. Too late for any
rectification.

Comic strip: A deep-sea diver thinks: "With no air and no lifeline, I won't last long. If only I could free myself from these weights . . ."

High-angle shot of a bar. A couple enter, shut the door, and continue forward.

Still from a film: A U.S. Navy radiotelegrapher; behind him stand an officer and the heroine. **Subtitle: Do you read me? Do you read me? Answer me, answer me . . . Over!**

After all the empty time, all the lost moments,
there remain these endlessly traversed postcard
landscapes; this distance organized between each
and everyone. Childhood? It's right here—we've
never emerged from it.

Helicopter view of Place de la Concorde.
The Seine, in the center of Paris.

Our era accumulates powers and imagines itself
as rational. But no one recognizes these powers
as their own. Nowhere is there any entry to
adulthood. The only thing that happens is that

Close-up of a rocket launching.

Distant view of a rocket launching.

this long restlessness sometimes eventually evolves into a routinized sleep. Because no one ceases to be kept under guardianship. The point is not to recognize that some people live more or less poorly than others, but that we all live in ways that are out of our control.

A pilot equipped for the stratosphere. An officer with a drawn sword.

The cover of a science-fiction book.

At the same time, it is a world that has taught us how things change. Nothing stays the same. The world changes more rapidly every day; and I have no doubt that those who day after day produce it against themselves can appropriate it for themselves.

A ball moving in a pinball machine.

The only adventure, we said, is to contest the totality centered on this way of living, where we can test our strength but never use it. No adventure is directly created for us. The adventures that are presented to us form part of the mass of legends transmitted by the cinema or in other ways; part of the whole spectacular sham of history.

Bodin de Boismortier: Allegro from Five-Part Concerto in E Minor (Opus 37). Film still: A king and knights at a Round Table. **SUBTITLE: To give every person the social space essential for a fulfilling life.**

Two situationists.

One knight challenges another in a Hollywood still.
A situationist drinking a glass of wine.

Full view of a group sitting at a table in a Montagne-Saint-Geneviève café. **SUBTITLES: If man is shaped by circumstances, it is necessary to create human**

circumstances. . . .
Comrades: Unitary urbanism is dynamic, that is, it is directly interrelated with modes of behavior.

Until the environment is collectively dominated, there will be no real individuals—only specters haunting the objects anarchically presented to them by others. In chance situations we meet separated people moving randomly. Their divergent emotions neutralize each other and reinforce their solid environment of boredom. As long as we are unable to make our own history, to freely create situations, our striving toward unity will give rise to other separations. The quest for a unified activity leads to the formation of new specializations.

Other situationists.
SUBTITLES: Passions have been interpreted enough. The point now is to discover new ones. . . . The new beauty will be a beauty of situations.

The young woman from the opening shots passes by. Aerial pan shot of the center of Paris.

And only a few encounters were like signals emanating from a more intense life, a life that has not really been found.

The music fades out.
The quarreling knights.
The same young woman.

What cannot be forgotten reappears in dreams. At the end of this type of dream, half asleep, the events are still for a brief moment taken as real. Then the reactions they give rise to become clearer, more distinct, more reasonable; like in so

Tracking shots: the face of the young woman alternates with an airplane flying into the distance as it fires on a snow-covered landscape.

many mornings the memory of what you drank the night before. Then comes the awareness that it's all false, that "it was only a dream," that the new realities were illusory and you can't get back into them. Nothing you can hold on to. These dreams are flashes from the un-resolved past, flashes that illuminate moments previously lived in confusion and doubt. They provide a blunt revelation of our unfulfilled needs.

Here we see daylight, and perspectives that now no longer have any meaning. The sectors of a city are to some extent decipherable. But the personal meaning they have had for us is incommunicable, as is the secrecy of private life in general, regarding which we possess nothing but pitiful documents.

Repeat of Bodin de Boismortier's Allegro. Pan shot of the Quai d'Orléans seen from the Left Bank. Close-up of a detail from the same quai. Pan shot of trees shaken by a tornado. Aerial photo of the Allée des Cygnes in Paris.

The music fades out.

Official news is elsewhere. Society broadcasts to itself its own image of its own history, a his-tory reduced to a superficial and static pageant of its rulers—the personages who embody the apparent inevitability of whatever happens. The world of the rulers is the world of the spectacle.

United Nations Security Council. Khrushchev in a room with de Gaulle at his side.

Eisenhower welcomes de Gaulle.

Patriotic ceremony at the Arc de Triomphe; de Gaulle and Khrushchev stand at attention.

The cinema suits them well. Regardless of its subject matter, the cinema presents heroes and exemplary conduct modeled on the same old pattern as the rulers.

Eisenhower talks with the Pope.

Eisenhower embraced by Franco.

But this dominant equilibrium is brought back into question each time unknown people try to live differently. But it was always far away. We learn about it through the papers and newscasts. We remain outside it, relating to it as just another spectacle. We are separated from it by our own nonintervention, and end up being rather disappointed. At what moment was choice postponed? When did we miss our chance? We have not found the arms we needed. We've let things slip away.

A riot in the Congo; soldiers disperse the crowd with blows from their rifle butts.

Photograph of Djamila Bouhired in a police station. Also in the field of view are the hands of the paratrooper-journalist Lartéguy.

Tracking shot toward the prisoner's face.

I have let time slip away. I have lost what I should have defended.

Repeat of Couperin's "March of the Regiment of Champagne." The young woman seen earlier talks and laughs.

This general critique of separation obviously contains, and conceals, some particular memories. A less recognized pain, a less explainable feeling of shame. Just what separation was it?

How quickly we've lived! It is to this point in our haphazard story that we now return.

The music breaks off.

Everything involving the sphere of loss—including what I have lost of myself, the time that has gone; and disappearance, flight; and the general evanescence of things, and even what in the prevalent and therefore most vulgar social sense of time is called wasted time—all this finds in that strangely apt old military term, *lost children,* its intersection with the sphere of discovery, of the exploration of unknown terrains, and with all the forms of quest, adventure, avant-garde. This is the crossroads where we have found ourselves and lost our way.

In a tracking shot the camera passes quickly across the façade of the Saint-Lazare train station, then up Rue du Havre as numerous cars approach down the same street.

A squad of Republican Guards pass in the distance. **SUBTITLE: In face of all the directions of the possible, converging so quickly on this moment, our only friend, our bitter enemy.**

It must be admitted that none of this is very clear. It is a completely typical drunken monologue, with its incomprehensible allusions and tiresome delivery. With its vain phrases that do not await response and its overbearing explanations. And its silences.

Parade of West Point cadets in equally old-fashioned uniforms.

The poverty of means is intended to evoke the scandalous poverty of the subject matter.

A squad on maneuvers.

The events that occur in our individual existence as it is now organized, the events that really concern us and require our participation, generally merit nothing more than our indifference as distant and bored spectators. In contrast, the situations presented in artistic works are often attractive, situations that would merit our active participation. This is a paradox to reverse, to put back on its feet. This is what must be realized in practice. As for this idiotic spectacle of the filtered and fragmented past, full of sound and fury, the point is not to transform or "adapt" it into another neatly ordered spectacle that would play the game of neatly ordered comprehension and participation. No. A coherent artistic expression expresses nothing but the coherence of the past, nothing but passivity.

It is necessary to destroy memory in art. To undermine the conventions of its communication. To demoralize its fans. What a task! As in a blurry drunken vision, the memory and language of the film fade out simultaneously. At the extreme, miserable subjectivity is reversed into a

Continuation of the pinball's trajectory. SUBTITLES: **Who would wish to have for a friend a man who talks in such a manner? Who would choose him among others to discuss his affairs? Who would turn to him in times of tribulation? What useful purpose in life could he serve?** Rebellious prisoners repressed in the courtyard of an American prison. The pinball disappears. Tracking shot over a mass of parked cars. SUBTITLES: **Disrupt the existing false dialogue everywhere. . . . Already farther away than India or China.**

A couple kiss on the street. Teenagers at a café table. Two of the "lost children" of Saint-Germain-des-Prés. SUBTITLES: **A poor rebellion, without language but not without a cause. The program will take its own shape. . . . Partisans of the power of oblivion.**

A prison guard in a watchtower.

THE SCREEN BECOMES DARK. SUBTITLE: **Besides, it's less a matter of forms than of traces of forms, impressions, memories.**

SUBTITLE: **We are faced with a world that is relentlessly falling apart.**

certain sort of objectivity: a documentation of the conditions of noncommunication.

For example, I don't talk about her. False face. False relation. A real person is separated from the interpreter of that person, if only by the time passed between the event and its evocation, by a distance that continually increases, a distance that is increasing at this very moment. Just as a conserved expression remains separate from those who hear it abstractly and without any power over it.

The spectacle as a whole is nothing other than this era, an era in which a certain youth has recognized itself. It is the gap between that image and its consequences; the gap between the visions, tastes, refusals, and projects that previously characterized this youth and the way it has advanced into ordinary life.

THE SCREEN REMAINS DARK, WITHOUT EITHER SUBTITLES OR COMMENTARY.

The young woman we have already seen so much of.

SUBTITLE: **The truth about a phony society.** Pan shot across sentence fragments: "The production also shows the marks of youth" . . . "Its dreadful, magnificent, and desperate disorder" . . . "It has all the elements of an American detective novel—violence, sex, cruelty— but the scene . . ."

Swimmers filmed underwater.

Photos of some situationists.

Repeat of Couperin's "March of the Regiment of Champagne."

We have invented nothing. We are adapting ourselves, with a few variations, into the network of
possible itineraries. We get used to it, it seems.

A group at a café counter.

Comic strip: A man holding a glass thinks: "The die is cast. Now she has to say yes to me, soon, very soon . . ." **SUBTITLE: How many bottles since then? In how many glasses, in how many bottles has he hidden himself alone since then?**

No one returns from an enterprise with the
ardor they had upon setting out. Fair companions, adventure is dead.

The cover of a detective novel titled *Imposture*. A woman in profile; farther back, a man with a glass in his hand.

A young blonde.

Trees in a tornado.

A napalm explosion.

The path cut by the tornado.

The same young blonde.

The music ends.

Pan shot across the sentence fragment: "The wine of life is drawn; in this cellar of vanity only the dregs remain."

Who will resist? It is necessary to go beyond this
partial defeat. Of course. And how to do it?

Continuation of the Congo riot.

Two already-seen photos of situationists alternate with a single subtitle that represents the conversation they are having. **SUBTITLE: It is only to be expected that a film about private life would consist entirely of private jokes.**

This is a film that interrupts itself and does not come to an end.

The young blonde. SUBTITLE: **I didn't understand all of it.**

All conclusions remain to be drawn; everything has to be recalculated.

Asger Jorn. SUBTITLE: **One could make a series of documentaries like this, a sort of serial lasting three hours.**

The problem continues to be posed—in continually more complicated terms. We have to resort to other measures.

Debord. SUBTITLE: **The "Mysteries of New York" of alienation.**

Just as there was no profound reason to begin this formless message, so there is none for concluding it.

Asger Jorn. SUBTITLE: **Yes, that would be better: more boring, more meaningful.**

I have scarcely begun to make you understand that I don't intend to play that game.

Debord; the camera moves away from him. SUBTITLE: **More convincing.**

SUBTITLE: **(To be continued.)**

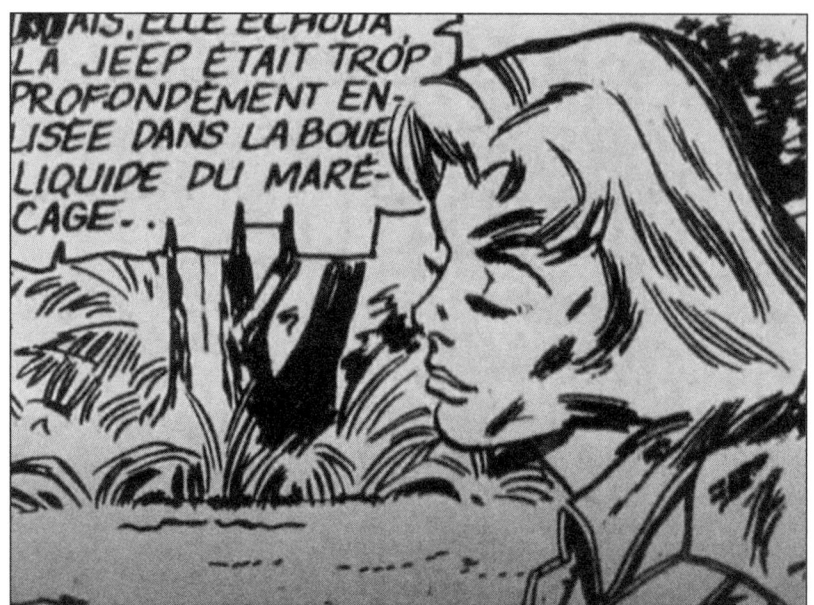

What communication have we desired, or experienced, or only simulated? What real project has been lost? [p. 29]

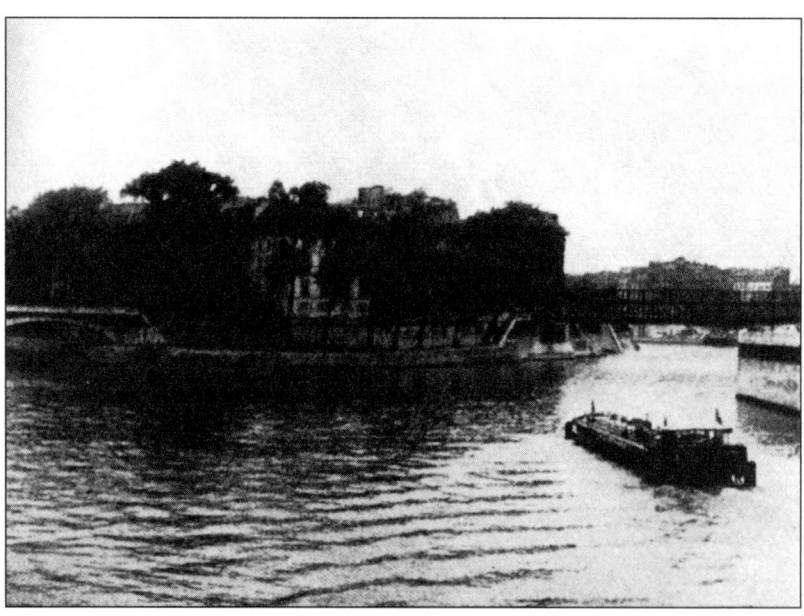

There remain these endlessly traversed postcard landscapes; this distance organized between each and everyone. Childhood? It's right here—we've never emerged from it. [p. 30]

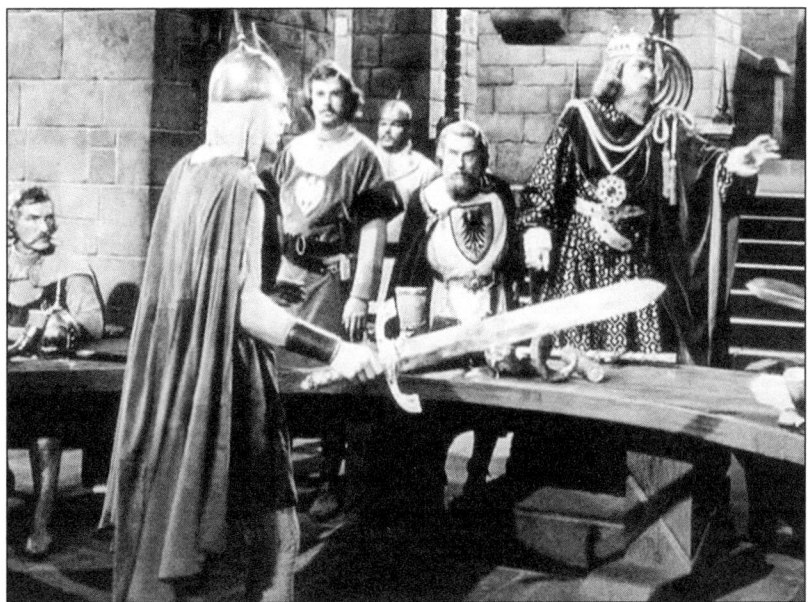

No adventure is directly created for us. The adventures that are presented to us form part of the mass of legends transmitted by the cinema or in other ways; part of the whole spectacular sham of history. [p. 31]

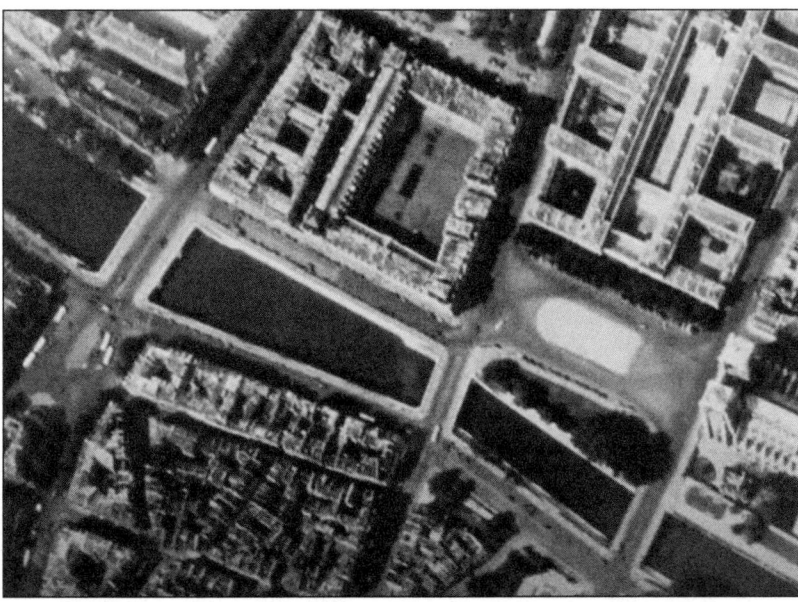

Their divergent emotions neutralize each other and reinforce their solid environment of boredom. [p. 32]

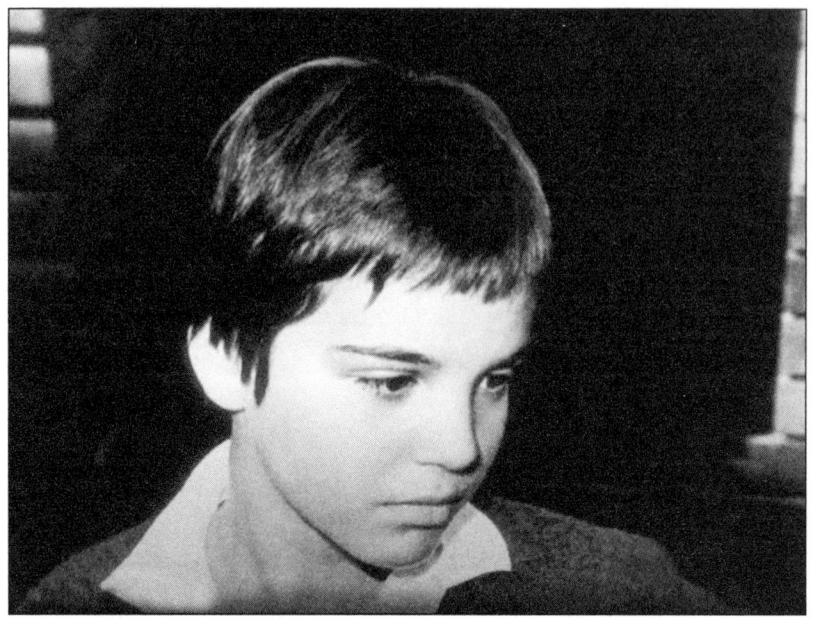

These dreams are flashes from the unresolved past, flashes that illuminate moments previously lived in confusion and doubt. [p. 33]

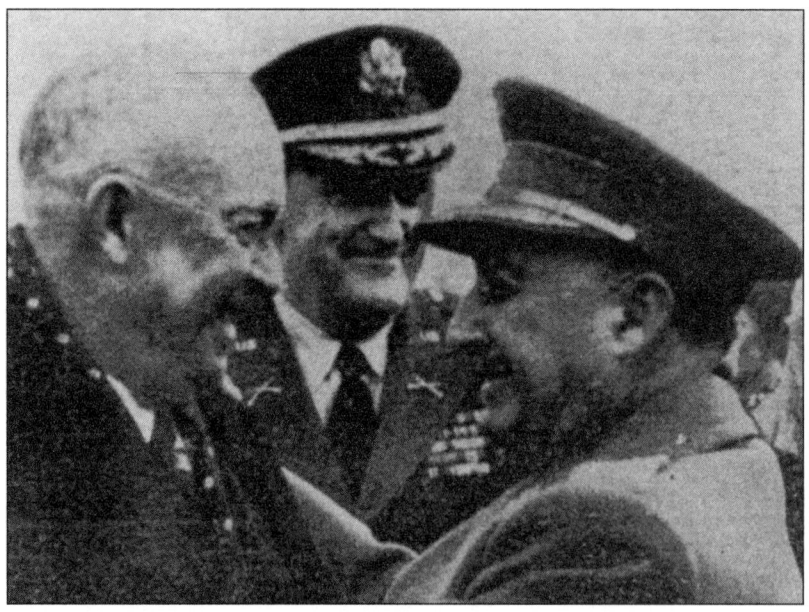

Regardless of its subject matter, the cinema presents heroes and exemplary conduct modeled on the same old pattern as the rulers. [p. 34]

The Society of the Spectacle

Michel Corrette: Sonata in D Major for Cello and Harpsichord.

Sequence on Alice.
SUBTITLES: **Since each particular feeling is only a part of life and not life in its entirety, life yearns to spread into the full diversity of feelings so as to rediscover itself in the whole of this diversity. . . . In love, the separate still exists, but it exists as unified, no longer as separate: the living meets the living. . . . THIS FILM IS DEDICATED TO ALICE BECKER-HO.**

The music ends.

In societies where modern conditions of production prevail, life is presented as an immense accumulation of *spectacles*. Everything that was directly lived has receded into a representation. [1]

The Earth, filmed from a space rocket, recedes into the distance. An astronaut moves around in space.

A long striptease.

The images detached from every aspect of life merge into a common stream in which the unity of that life can no longer be recovered. *Fragmented* views of reality regroup themselves into a new unity as a *separate pseudoworld* that can only be looked at. The specialization of images of the world has culminated in a world of autonomized images where even the deceivers are deceived. The spectacle is a concrete inversion of life, an autonomous movement of the nonliving. [2]

The spectacle presents itself simultaneously as society itself, as a part of society, and as a *means of unification.* As a part of society, it is ostensibly the focal point of all vision and all consciousness. But due to the very fact that this sector is *separate,* it is in reality the domain of delusion and false consciousness, and the unification it achieves is nothing but an official language of universal separation. [3]

Closed-circuit television screens in the Paris police headquarters, monitoring streets and subway stations.

Lee Harvey Oswald, the alleged assassin of Kennedy, surrounded by Dallas police. A patriotic informer rushes forward and shoots him "live" in front of millions of television viewers.

A speech by Giscard d'Estaing.

Another by Servan-Schreiber.

Near the end of May 1968 the bureaucrat Séguy, reporting to the Renault workers on the "Grenelle Accords" he has just signed, brazenly declares: "At the conclusion of these deliberations we accepted what was positive while making it clear that there was still much to be done." The workers listen in silence.

The spectacle is not a collection of images; it is a social relation between people that is mediated by images. [4]

The workers show their discontent and contempt.

Understood in its totality, the spectacle is both the result and the project of the present mode of production. It is not a mere supplement or decoration added to the real world, it is the heart of this real society's unreality. In all its particular manifestations—news, propaganda, advertising, or consumable entertainment—the spectacle is the *model* of the prevailing way of life. It is the omnipresent affirmation of the choices that have *already been made* in the sphere of production and in the consumption implied by that production. [6]

A fashion show presented by the designer Courrèges.

Separation is itself an integral part of the unity of this world, of a global social practice split into reality and image. The social practice confronted by an autonomous spectacle is at the same time the real totality which contains that spectacle. But the split within this totality mutilates it to the point that the spectacle seems to be its goal. [7]

Workers on assembly lines in various factories.

Brightly lit shops recently installed on Paris subway platforms to enable the public to kill time while waiting.

In a world that has *really been turned upside down,* the true is a moment of the false. [9]

A young woman stands up on a beach. Photo of another lying on a beach.

Considered in its own terms, the spectacle is an *affirmation* of appearances and an identification of all human social life with appearances. But a critique that grasps the spectacle's essential character reveals it to be a visible *negation* of life— a negation that has taken on a *visible form.* [10]

Nuclear submarines maneuvering through a sea of ice floes.

The spectacle presents itself as a vast, inaccessible reality that can never be questioned. Its sole message is: "What appears is good; what is good appears." The passive acceptance it demands is already effectively imposed by its monopoly of appearances, its manner of appearing without allowing any reply. [12]

Fidel Castro speaks to television cameras, then to an assembled crowd.

The spectacle is able to subject human beings to itself because the economy has already totally subjugated them. It is nothing other than the economy developing for itself. It is at once a faithful reflection of the production of things and a distorting objectification of the producers. [16]

An aircraft carrier aims missiles in all directions and fires them.

When the real world is transformed into mere images, mere images become real beings—figments that provide the direct motivations for a hypnotic behavior. [18]

Aerial bombardments in Vietnam.

As long as necessity is socially dreamed, dreaming will remain necessary. The spectacle is the bad dream of a modern society in chains and ultimately expresses nothing more than its wish for sleep. The spectacle is the guardian of that sleep. [21]

The fact that the practical power of modern society has detached itself from that society and established an independent realm in the spectacle can be explained only by the additional fact that that powerful practice continued to lack cohesion and had remained in contradiction with itself. [22]

Astronauts on the moon with a flag. Another astronaut propels himself out the door of his spacecraft, remaining attached to it by a cable.

The root of the spectacle is that oldest of all social specializations, the specialization of *power*. The spectacle plays the specialized role of speaking in the name of all the other activities. It is hierarchical society's ambassador to

Frenetic stockbrokers on the trading floor of the Paris Stock Exchange.

itself, delivering its messages at a court where no one else is allowed to speak. The most modern aspect of the spectacle is thus also the most archaic. [23]

The social separation reflected in the spectacle is inseparable from the modern *state*—that product of the social division of labor that is both the chief instrument of class rule and the concentrated expression of all social divisions. [24]

Riot police advance.

A mounted policeman repeatedly clubs a young man sitting on a bench.

In the spectacle, a part of the world *represents itself* to the world and is superior to it. The spectacle is simply the common language of this separation. Spectators are linked solely by their one-way relationship to the very center that keeps them isolated from each other. The spectacle thus reunites the separated, but it reunites them only *in their separateness.* [29]

A striptease by two professionals.

A couple stretched out on a sofa-bed watching television.

Workers do not produce themselves, they produce a power independent of themselves. The *success* of this production, the abundance it generates, is experienced by the producers as an *abundance of dispossession.* As their alienated prod-

Immigrant workers at the foot of the tower blocks they are building in Paris's new suburb, La Défense; pan shot up and across the summits of their work.

ucts accumulate, all time and space become *foreign* to them. The forces that have escaped us *display themselves* to us in all their power. [31]

Though separated from what they produce, people nevertheless produce every detail of their world with ever-increasing power. They thus also find themselves increasingly separated from that world. The closer their life comes to being their own creation, the more they are excluded from that life. [33]

The spectacle is *capital* accumulated to the point that it becomes image. [34]

Critical theory must *communicate itself* in its own language—the language of contradiction, which must be dialectical in both form and content. It must be an all-inclusive critique and it must be grounded in history. It is not a "zero degree of writing," but its reversal. It is not a negation of style, but the style of negation. [204]

The Earth filmed from the Moon.

TEXT FRAME: "Some cinematic value might be acknowledged in this film if the present rhythm were to continue; but it will not continue."

During the Russian Civil War a detachment of Red partisans faces a regiment of White Guards—former Czarist officers now serving as mere foot soldiers. Despite the partisans' machine-gun fire, the Whites advance in parade formation, flags flying before them, without firing back.

The very style of dialectical theory is a scandal and abomination to the prevailing standards of language and to the sensibilities molded by those standards, because while it makes concrete use of existing concepts it simultaneously recognizes their rediscovered *fluidity* and their inevitable destruction. [205]

The partisans joke about the old-fashioned military style of their adversaries: "What elegance!" says one. "Intellectuals!" concludes another.

Despite their losses, the White Guards continue to advance in good order, bayonets fixed on their rifles.

This style, which includes a critique of itself, must express the domination of present critique *over its entire past.* Dialectical theory's mode of exposition reveals the negative spirit within it. "Truth is not like some finished product in which one can no longer find any trace of the tool that made it." This theoretical consciousness of a movement whose traces must remain visible within it is manifested by the *reversal* of established relationships between concepts and by the *détournement* of all the achievements of earlier critical efforts. [206]

Ideas improve. The meaning of words plays a part in that improvement. Plagiarism is neces-

Shaken by the enemy's determination, a few of the partisans show signs of

sary. Progress depends on it. It sticks close to an author's phrasing, exploits his expressions, deletes a false idea, replaces it with the right one. [207]

hesitation, then begin to retreat from the line of fire.

The routed partisans run back in panic, shouting "Retreat!" and "We've lost!" The political commissar stands in their way and commands: "Halt! Cowards! You've abandoned your comrades. Follow me! Forward!" The partisans take up their position again.

Détournement is the flexible language of anti-ideology. It appears in communication that knows it cannot claim to embody any inherent or definitive certainty. It is language that cannot and need not be confirmed by any previous or supracritical reference. On the contrary, its own internal coherence and practical effectiveness are what validate the previous kernels of truth it has brought back into play. Détournement has grounded its cause on nothing but its own truth as present critique. [208]

The Czarist regiment, still in perfectly formed ranks, is on the verge of reaching the Reds' line, but many of its men are cut down by machine-gun fire.

The element of *overt* détournement in formulated theory refutes any notion that such theory is durably autonomous. By introducing into the theoretical domain the same type of *violent subversion* that disrupts and overthrows every existing order, détournement serves as a reminder that theory is nothing in itself, that it can realize itself only through historical action and through the *historical correction* that is its true allegiance. [209]

Three partisans throw grenades. The White ranks waver. The commanding officer falls, then the standard-bearer. The regiment breaks into retreat.

TEXT FRAME: "What the spectacle has taken from reality must be taken back from it. The spectacular expropriators must be expropriated in their turn. The world has already been filmed. The point now is to change it."

The point is to actually participate in the community of dialogue and the game with time that up till now have merely been *represented* by poetic and artistic works. [187]

Two harbors at sunset painted by Claude Lorrain.

When art becomes independent and paints its world in dazzling colors, a moment of life has grown old. Such a moment cannot be rejuvenated by dazzling colors, it can only be evoked in memory. The greatness of art only emerges at the dusk of life. [188]

Some beautiful female faces.

In Vienna's saloon at night, Johnny Guitar drinks alone. Vienna appears and asks: "Having fun, Mr. Logan?" Johnny replies: "I couldn't sleep." Vienna: "That stuff help any?" Johnny: "Makes the night go faster. What's keeping you awake?" She: "Dreams. Bad dreams." He: "Yeah, I get 'em sometimes too. Here, this'll chase 'em away." Vienna refuses the drink: "I've tried that. Didn't seem to help me any." He: "How many men have you forgotten?" She: "As many women as you've remembered." (The whole scene is accompanied by the *Johnny Guitar* theme, which gradually becomes louder.)

TEXT FRAME: "Thus, just as the direct practice of art ceased to be the most eminent activity and that preeminence shifted to theory as such, theory is in turn losing its preeminence to the holistic post-theoretical practice that is now developing, a practice whose primary mission is to be the foundation and fulfillment of both art and philosophy." (August von Cieszkowski, *Prolegomena to Historiosophy*)

The official thought of the social organization of appearances is itself obscured by the generalized *subcommunication* that it has to defend. It cannot understand that conflict is at the origin of everything in its world. The specialists of spectacular power—a power that is absolute within its realm of one-way communication—are absolutely corrupted by their experience of contempt and by the success of that contempt, because they find their contempt confirmed by their awareness of how *truly contemptible* spectators really are. [195]

The Stalinist Marchais speaks at an election rally, with Mitterrand at his side. They applaud each other. Servan-Schreiber also speaks. Marchais on a television screen.

A crowd lined up to get into a movie theater.

In the spectacle's basic practice of incorporating into itself all the *fluid* aspects of human activity so as to possess them in a congealed form, and of *inverting* living values into purely abstract values, we recognize our old enemy *the commodity*, which seems at first glance so trivial and obvious, yet which is actually so complex and full of metaphysical subtleties. [35]

The camera pulls back from a photo of a nude young woman, then pans across another.

President Pompidou visiting an automobile showroom; he admires the latest model, which turns on a revolving platform.

The fetishism of the commodity—the domination of society by "imperceptible as well as perceptible things"—attains its ultimate fulfillment in the spectacle, where the perceptible world is replaced by a selection of images which is projected above it, yet which at the same time succeeds in making itself regarded as the perceptible par excellence. [36]

A series of cover girls in swimsuits.

The world at once present and absent that the spectacle *holds up to view* is the world of the commodity dominating all living experience. The world of the commodity is thus shown for *what it is*, because its development is identical to people's *estrangement* from each other and from their total production. [37]

As long as the economy's role as material basis of social life was neither noticed nor understood—remaining unknown precisely because it was so familiar—the commodity's dominion over the economy was exerted in a covert manner. In societies where actual commodities were few and far between, money was the apparent master, serving as plenipotentiary representative of the greater power that remained unknown. With the Industrial Revolution's manufactural division of labor and mass production for a global market, the commodity finally became fully visible as a power that was *occupying* all social life. It was at that point that political economy established itself as the dominant science, and as the science of domination. [41]

The spectacle is a never-ending opium war designed to force people to equate goods with commodities and to equate satisfaction with a survival that expands according to its own laws. Consumable survival must constantly expand because it never ceases to *include privation*. If augmented survival never comes to a resolution, if

A factory in Marghera polluting the air of Venice. Smoke from factories and cars polluting Mexico City. Piles of rubbish outside the Saint-Nicolas-des-Champs church in Paris. Filthy water of the Seine.

Extensive footage from the Watts riot: fires, the forces of order in action, arrests.

there is no point where it might stop expanding, this is because it is itself stuck in the realm of privation. It may gild poverty, but it cannot transcend it. [44]

Exchange value could arise only as a representative of use value, but the victory it eventually won with its own weapons created the conditions for its own autonomous power. By mobilizing all human use value and monopolizing its fulfillment, exchange value ultimately succeeded in *controlling use*. Use has come to be seen purely in terms of exchange value, and is now completely at its mercy. Starting out like a *condottiere* in the service of use value, exchange value has ended up waging the war for its own sake. [46]

Use value was formerly understood as an implicit aspect of exchange value. Now, however, within the upside-down world of the spectacle, use value must be explicitly proclaimed, both because its actual reality has been eroded by the overdeveloped commodity economy and because it serves as a necessary pseudojustification for a counterfeit life. [48]

With the achievement of *economic* abundance, the concentrated result of social labor becomes visible, subjecting all reality to the appearances that are now that labor's primary product. Capital is no longer the invisible center governing the production process; as it accumulates, it spreads to the ends of the earth in the form of tangible objects. The entire expanse of society is its portrait. [50]

French national riot police being trained in street fighting.

The spectacle, like modern society itself, is at once united and divided. The unity of each is based on violent divisions. But when this contradiction emerges in the spectacle, it is itself contradicted by a reversal of its meaning: the division it presents is unitary, while the unity it presents is divided. [54]

More riot police training: Police costumed as radicals raise a barricade and wave black flags. Their colleagues easily take the barricade.

Although the struggles between different powers for control of the same socioeconomic system are officially presented as fundamental antagonisms, they actually reflect that system's fundamental unity, both internationally and within each nation. [55]

The sham spectacular struggles between rival forms of separate power are at the same time real, in that they express the system's uneven and conflictual development and the more or less contradictory interests of the classes or sections of classes that accept that system and strive to carve out a role for themselves within it. By invoking any number of different criteria, the spectacle can present these oppositions as totally distinct social systems. But in reality they are nothing but particular sectors whose fundamental essence lies in the global system that contains them, the single movement that has turned the whole planet into its field of operation: capitalism. [56]

In paternal fashion Mao Zedong welcomes President Nixon in Beijing.

Behind the glitter of spectacular distractions, a tendency toward *banalization* dominates modern society the world over, even where the more advanced forms of commodity consumption have seemingly multiplied the variety of roles and objects to choose from. The vestiges of religion and of the family (the latter is still the primary mechanism for transferring class power from one generation to the next), along with the

Vietnam: helicopters machine-gun anything on the ground that moves.

A priest blesses a British nuclear submarine.

vestiges of moral repression imposed by those two institutions, can be blended with ostentatious pretensions of worldly gratification precisely because life in this particular world remains repressive and offers nothing but pseudogratifications. Complacent acceptance of the status quo may also coexist with purely spectacular rebelliousness—dissatisfaction itself becomes a commodity as soon as the economy of abundance develops the capacity to process that particular raw material. [59]

An urban traffic jam.

Johnny Hallyday sings and the audience screams with delight; he rolls on the floor.

Stars—spectacular representations of living human beings—project this general banality into images of permitted roles. As specialists of *apparent life,* stars serve as superficial objects that people can identify with in order to compensate for the fragmented productive specializations that they actually live. The function of these celebrities is to act out various lifestyles or sociopolitical viewpoints in a free and uninhibited manner. They embody the inaccessible results of social *labor* by dramatizing the by-products of that labor which are magically projected above it as its ultimate goals: *power*

The Beatles, emerging from an airplane, are welcomed by enthusiastic teenagers; cameras flash. Eddy Mitchell sings to applause. Dick Rivers sings.

Marilyn Monroe at the time of her last, unfinished film.

and *vacations*—the decision-making and consumption that are at the beginning and the end of a process that is never questioned. On one hand, a governmental power may personalize itself as a pseudostar; on the other, a star of consumption may campaign for recognition as a pseudopower over life. But the activities of these stars are not really free and they offer no real choices. [60]

François Mitterrand.

Several more shots of Marilyn Monroe.

Spectacular oppositions conceal the *unity of poverty*. If different forms of the same alienation struggle against each other in the guise of irreconcilable antagonisms, this is because they are all based on real contradictions that are repressed. The spectacle exists in a *concentrated* form or a *diffuse* form, depending on the requirements of the particular stage of poverty it denies and supports. In both cases it is nothing more than an image of happy harmony surrounded by desolation and horror, at the calm center of misery. [63]

German workers leaving their factory shortly after the Nazis' rise to power. Illegal leaflets are thrown to them from a skylight. The workers pick them up and read them.

A convoy of vans delivers French riot police to where they're needed.

Vietnamese troops comb the ground and take prisoners.

The concentrated spectacle is primarily associated with bureaucratic capitalism, though it may

The camera follows Hitler as he marches past the ranks of his followers and mounts a monumental platform.

also be imported as a technique for reinforcing state power in more backward mixed economies or even adopted by advanced capitalism during certain moments of crisis. Bureaucratic property is itself concentrated, in that the individual bureaucrat takes part in the ownership of the entire economy only through his membership in the community of bureaucrats. And since commodity production is less developed under bureaucratic capitalism, it too takes on a concentrated form: the commodity the bureaucracy appropriates is the total social labor, and what it sells back to the society is that society's wholesale survival. The dictatorship of the bureaucratic economy cannot leave the exploited masses any significant margin of choice because it has had to make all the choices itself, and any choice made independently of it, whether regarding food or music or anything else, thus amounts to a declaration of war against it. [64]

Brezhnev and other leading bureaucrats on a platform in Moscow. Their subjects march past them.

During a NATO exercise a large tank demonstrates its full range of maneuvers.

The diffuse spectacle is associated with commodity abundance, with the undisturbed development of modern capitalism. Here each

Lines of cars in a traffic jam. Spectacularly presented food. An old painting. Modern furnishings. Exotic young women in cages. A train arriving at a subway station.

individual commodity is justified in the name of the grandeur of the total commodity production, of which the spectacle is a laudatory catalog. Irreconcilable claims jockey for position on the stage of the affluent economy's unified spectacle, and different star commodities simultaneously promote conflicting social policies. The automobile spectacle, for example, strives for a perfect traffic flow entailing the destruction of old urban districts, while the city spectacle needs to preserve those districts as tourist attractions. The already dubious satisfaction alleged to be obtained from the *consumption of the whole* is thus constantly being disappointed because the actual consumer can directly access only a succession of fragments of this commodity happiness, fragments which invariably lack the quality attributed to the whole. [65]

Disintegrating statues on the roof of a Venice church.

Two Tahitian women on a sailboat.

Pan shot across a typical modern living room, homing in on the television set that is the room's focal point.

Each individual commodity fights for itself. It avoids acknowledging the others and strives to impose itself everywhere as if it were the only one in existence. The spectacle is the epic poem of this struggle, a struggle that no fall of Troy can bring to an end. The spectacle does not sing

A series of nude or scantily clad pin-up girls.

of men and their arms, but of commodities and their passions. In this blind struggle each commodity, by pursuing its own passion, unconsciously generates something beyond itself: the globalization of the commodity (which also amounts to the commodification of the globe). Thus, as a result of the *cunning of the commodity,* while each *particular* manifestation of the commodity eventually falls in battle, the general commodity-form continues onward toward its absolute realization. [66]

The image of blissful social unification through consumption merely *postpones* the consumer's awareness of the actual divisions until his next disillusionment with some particular commodity. Each new product is ceremoniously acclaimed as a unique creation offering a dramatic shortcut to the promised land of total consummation. But as with the fashionable adoption of seemingly aristocratic first names which end up being given to virtually all individuals of the same age, the objects that promise uniqueness can be offered up for mass consumption only if they are numerous enough

The latest car models presented to a respectful crowd.

to have been mass-produced. The prestigious-
ness of mediocre objects of this kind is solely
due to the fact that they have been placed, however briefly, at the center of social life and hailed
as a revelation of the unfathomable purposes of
production. But the object that was prestigious
in the spectacle becomes mundane as soon as it
is taken home by its consumer—at the same time
as by all its other consumers. Too late it reveals
its essential poverty, a poverty that inevitably
reflects the poverty of its production. Meanwhile,
some other object is already replacing it as justification of the system and demanding its own
moment of acclaim. [69]

Assembly-line manufacture of cream cakes.

The fraudulence of the satisfactions offered by
the system is exposed by this continual replacement of products and of general conditions of
production. In both the diffuse and the concentrated spectacle, entities that have brazenly
asserted their definitive perfection nevertheless
end up changing, and only the system endures.
Stalin, like any other outmoded commodity, is
denounced by the very forces that originally promoted him. Each *new lie* of the advertising

Race cars speeding around a track.

Mao Zedong with his "closest comrade-in-arms," Lin Biao.

industry is an *admission* of its previous lie. And with each downfall of a personification of totalitarian power, the *illusory community* that had unanimously approved him is exposed as a mere conglomeration of loners without illusions. [70]

Stalin on a platform, applauded by a monolithic Party Congress. People marching past his successors in Red Square. A huge portrait of Lenin at the same celebration.

The things the spectacle presents as eternal are based on change, and must change as their foundations change. The spectacle is totally dogmatic, yet it is incapable of arriving at any really solid dogma. Nothing stands still for it. This instability is the spectacle's natural condition, but it is completely contrary to its natural inclination. [71]

Budapest 1956: insurrectionary workers demolishing a huge statue of Stalin; only his boots remain.

Pan shot across a young woman, ending at her smiling face.

The unreal unity proclaimed by the spectacle masks the class division underlying the real unity of the capitalist mode of production. What obliges the producers to participate in the construction of the world is also what excludes them from it. What brings people into relation with each other by liberating them from their local and national limitations is also what keeps them apart. What requires increased rationality is also what nourishes the irratio-

Operations in a packaging factory.

nality of hierarchical exploitation and repression. What produces society's abstract power also produces its concrete *lack of freedom.* [72]

Michel Corrette: Sonata in D Major for Cello and Harpsichord. Close-up of Buenaventura Durruti. TEXT FRAME: "Fellow proletarians, are we really living? This age in which we count our time and in which everything we count on is no longer ours, can this be called a life? Can we fail to recognize how much we keep losing with each passing year?" Close-up of a revolutionary sailor from *Ten Days That Shook the World* as he shakes his head. Durruti looks at the sailor. The sailor again shakes his head. TEXT FRAME: "Rest and food, are they not feeble remedies for the constant malady that afflicts us? And what we call 'the final affliction,' is it anything other than a final, more intensive attack of the malady we bear from the moment of our birth?" The Petrograd sailor shakes his head in agreement.
The music fades out.

Capitalist production has unified space, breaking down the boundaries between different societies. This unification is at the same time an extensive and intensive process of *banalization.* Just as the accumulation of commodities mass-produced for the abstract space of the market shattered all regional and legal barriers and all the Medieval guild restrictions that maintained

Battleships on the high seas. French, then English marines disembark at Shanghai. An American marine checks the IDs of Chinese. French soldiers push back a crowd. English soldiers on patrol. Barbed wire protecting the boundary of the Concession, guarded by French colonial infantry.

the *quality* of craft production, it also undermined the autonomy and quality of *places*. This homogenizing power is the heavy artillery that has battered down all the walls of China. [165]

The *free space of commodities* is constantly being modified and rebuilt in order to become ever more identical to itself, to get as close as possible to motionless monotony. [166]

While eliminating geographical distance, this society produces a new internal distance in the form of spectacular separation. [167]

British soldiers closing a gate into the Concession.

Tourism—human circulation packaged for consumption, a by-product of the circulation of commodities—is the opportunity to go and see what has been banalized. The economic organization of travel to different places already guarantees their *equivalence*. The modernization that has eliminated the time involved in travel has simultaneously eliminated any real space from it. [168]

Touristic sightseeing boats on the Seine, with guides commenting on the sights.

TEXT FRAME: "A society based on the expansion of alienated industrial labor naturally becomes as thoroughly unhealthy, noisy, ugly, and filthy as a factory."

The society that reshapes its entire surroundings has evolved its own special technique for molding its very territory, which constitutes the material underpinning for all the aspects of this project. Urbanism—"city planning"—is capitalism's method for taking over the natural and human environment. Following its logical development toward total domination, capitalism now can and must refashion the totality of space into *its own particular decor.* [169]

Modern high-rises.

TEXT FRAME: "Man is beginning to live in caves once again. . . . But the worker has only a precarious right to inhabit these modern caves: they are alien dwellings from which he can be evicted at any moment if he fails to pay. Yes, he actually has to pay to live in these catacombs." (Marx, *Manuscripts of 1844*)

While all the technical forces of capitalism contribute toward various forms of separation, urbanism provides the material foundation for those forces and prepares the ground for their deployment. It is the very *technology of separation.* [171]

French riot police on the terrain produced by modern urbanism.

In all previous periods architectural innovations were designed exclusively for the ruling classes. Now for the first time a new architecture has

Photos and scale models of modern vacation resorts— "seaside" decors which may be located in the mountains as well as by the sea.

been specifically designed *for the poor*. The aesthetic poverty and vast proliferation of this new experience in habitation stem from its *mass* character, which character in turn stems both from its function and from the modern conditions of construction. The obvious core of these conditions is the *authoritarian decision-making* which abstractly converts the environment into an environment of abstraction. Urbanism is one of the most glaring expressions of the contradiction between the growth of society's material powers and the continued *lack of progress* toward any conscious control of those powers. [173]

La Défense, the new suburb being built west of Paris.

TEXT FRAME: "The environment that is being reconstructed more and more hastily and carelessly for profit and repressive control is at the same time becoming more fragile, thus inciting more vandalism. Capitalism in its spectacular stage rebuilds everything with shoddy material and breeds arsonists. Its decor is becoming as inflammable as a French school."

The history that threatens this twilight world could potentially subject space to a directly experienced time. Proletarian revolution is this *critique of human geography* through which individuals and communities could create places

The cruiser *Aurora* moves up the Neva River just before dawn. As day breaks it brings the soldiers it is carrying to the shore.

and events commensurate with the appropriation no longer just of their work, but of their entire history. The ever-changing playing field of this new world and the freely chosen variations in the rules of the game will regenerate a diversity of local scenes that are independent without being insular, thereby reviving the possibility of authentic *journeys*—journeys within an authentic life that is itself understood as a journey containing its whole meaning within itself. [178]

The Tower of Babel.

Buildings and landscapes in an early Italian painting.

Riding through a sandstorm in a Western landscape, Johnny Guitar arrives at an extravagant saloon located marvelously in the middle of a desert. He goes in. There are no other customers, but two croupiers stand ready to accept his bets at a roulette wheel. He goes to the counter and orders a drink.

In *The Shanghai Gesture* a European man shows a young woman around the casino, describing those present: "Javanese, Sumatrans, Hindus, Chinese, Portuguese, Filipinos, Russians, Malayans . . . what a witches' sabbath!" The woman says: "If anyone saw us coming in here, I'd say witches' sabbath! That other place is like a kindergarten compared with this. The smell is so incredibly evil. I didn't think such a thing existed except in my own imagination. It has a ghastly familiarity, like a half-remembered dream. Anything could happen here, at any moment."

The time of production—commodified time—is an infinite accumulation of equivalent intervals. It is irreversible time made abstract, in which each segment need only demonstrate by the clock its purely quantitative equality with all the others. It has no reality apart from its *exchangeability*. [147]

Workers in a tire factory.

This general time of human nondevelopment also has a complementary aspect—a *consumable* form of time based on the present mode of production and manifesting itself in everyday life as a *pseudocyclical time*. [148]

Long sequence of a holiday crowd at Saint-Tropez.

Pseudocyclical time is associated with the consumption of modern economic survival—the augmented survival in which everyday experience is cut off from decision-making and subjected no longer to the natural order, but to the pseudonature created by alienated labor. It is thus quite *natural* that it echoes the old cyclical rhythm that governed survival in preindustrial societies, incorporating the natural vestiges of cyclical time while generating new variants: day and night, work and weekend, periodic vacations. [150]

Consumable pseudocyclical time is spectacular time, both in the narrow sense as time spent consuming images and in the broader sense as image of the consumption of time. The time spent consuming images (images which in turn serve to publicize all the other commodities) is both the particular terrain where the spectacle's mechanisms are most fully implemented and the general goal that those mechanisms present, the focus and epitome of all particular consumptions. As for the social image of the consumption of time, it is exclusively dominated by leisure time and vacations—moments portrayed, like all spectacular commodities, *at a distance* and as desirable by definition. These commodified moments are explicitly presented as moments of real life, whose cyclical return we are supposed to look forward to. But all that is really happening is that the spectacle is displaying and reproducing itself at a higher level of intensity. What is presented as true life turns out to be merely a more *truly spectacular* life. [153]

While the consumption of cyclical time in ancient societies was consistent with the real labor of

Couples sitting in front of their televisions and stereo systems.

More views of the Saint-Tropez crowd, including several topless women.

Planes taking off from an aircraft carrier and relanding on it.

those societies, the pseudocyclical consumption of developed economies contradicts the abstract irreversible time implicit in their system of production. Cyclical time was the really lived time of unchanging illusions. Spectacular time is the illusorily lived time of a constantly changing reality. [155]

The production process's constant innovations are not echoed in consumption, which presents nothing but an expanded repetition of the past. Because dead labor continues to dominate living labor, in spectacular time the past continues to dominate the present. [156]

The lack of general historical life also means that individual life as yet has no history. The pseudoevents that vie for attention in spectacular dramatizations have not been lived by those who are informed about them; and in any case they are soon forgotten due to their increasingly frenetic replacement at every pulsation of the spectacular machinery. Conversely, what is really lived has no relation to the society's official version of irreversible time,

Women lovers, as memories.

and clashes with the pseudocyclical rhythm of that time's consumable by-products. This individual experience of a disconnected everyday life remains without language, without concepts, and without critical access to its own past, which has nowhere been recorded. Uncommunicated, misunderstood, and forgotten, it is smothered by the spectacle's false memory of the unmemorable. [157]

Johnny Guitar, Vienna, and her lover the Dancing Kid in the same saloon. The mood is very tense. Vienna says to the Dancing Kid: "That's the way it goes: lose one, find one." Turning to Johnny, she says: "Play something for me, Mr. Guitar." Johnny: "Anything special?" Vienna: "Just put a lot of love in it." The Kid exclaims: "He ain't gonna play so good all stretched out on the crap table!" Unperturbed, Johnny asks: "What's eating the fancy man?" Vienna: "I don't know." To the Kid: "What's your trouble, Kid?" The Kid replies angrily: "I'm in no trouble, he is. Fooling with a strange woman can bring a man a lot of grief." Johnny asks Vienna: "Are you a strange woman?" She replies: "Only to strangers." The Kid says indignantly: "What's going on with you two?" Johnny: "Just what you see, friend." The Kid: "Oh, you picked the wrong place to come to, mister!" Johnny: "The lady sent for me, not you." The Kid pulls a coin out of his pocket: "Heads I'm going to kill you, mister; tails, you can play her a tune." He flips the coin. Vienna plucks it from midair and asks Johnny to play something. He starts to strum the *Johnny Guitar* theme. Vienna listens dreamily for a moment, then stops him and says curtly: "Play something else."

The spectacle, considered as the reigning society's method for paralyzing history and memory and for suppressing any history based on historical time, represents a *false consciousness of time*. [158]

In the mountains of Spain (*For Whom the Bell Tolls*) a Francoist cavalry patrol, and then an entire squadron, slowly pass by the partisans' hidden machine-gun.

Behind the *fashions* that come and go on the frivolous surface of the spectacle of pseudo-cyclical time, the *grand style* of an era can always be found in what is governed by the secret yet obvious necessity for revolution. [162]

Michel Corrette: Sonata in D Major for Cello and Harpsichord.

In the Winter Palace, soon to be attacked, a little automated owl in a clock turns its head. TEXT FRAME: "Midnight approaches." The bird of Minerva moves again.

Debord. SUBTITLE: **And therefore, since I cannot prove a lover to entertain these fair well-spoken times, I am determined to prove a villain and spoil the idle pleasures of these days.**

The music fades out.

In the *Shanghai Gesture* bar an old Chinese man introduces the young woman to Doctor Omar, who is dressed in Arab garb. "This is my very best friend, Omar." After the Chinese man leaves, the woman asks: "Are you an Egyptian comprador?" "No, a doctor—Doctor Omar of Shanghai . . . and Gomorrah." "Any relation to the poet Omar? 'A book of verses underneath the bough . . .' " He continues the quotation: " '. . . a loaf of bread, a jug of wine, and thou beside me singing in the wilderness . . .' " She asks: "You said 'Doctor' Omar . . . doctor of what?" He replies urbanely: "Doctor of Nothing, Miss Smith. It sounds important and hurts no one, unlike most doctors." She: "And your burnoose, is it real? Where were you born?" He: "My birth took place under a full moon on the sands near Damascus. My father was an Armenian tobacco dealer and was far away. And my mother—the less said about her, the better. She was half French and the other half is lost in the dust of time. In short, I am a thoroughbred mongrel. I'm related to all the Earth and nothing human is foreign to me." With a smile, she asks: "Then perhaps you can explain how our friends suddenly vanished." He replies: "We were alone since I first saw you."

Pan shot over an Italian astronomical chart titled "Revolution of the Earth."

Machiavelli.

Detail from Uccello's *The Battle of San Romano.*

Examining history amounts to *examining the nature of power*. Greece was that moment when power and changes in power were first debated and understood. It was a *democracy of the masters of society*—a total contrast to the despotic state, where power settles accounts only with itself, within the impenetrable obscurity of its inner sanctum, by means of *palace revolutions,* which are beyond the pale of discussion whether they fail or succeed. [134]

Brezhnev and other leading bureaucrats at their stand in Moscow, with Red Army marshals.

TEXT FRAME: "In the chronicles of the North men act in silence; they make war, they conclude peace, but they themselves do not say (nor do the chronicles explain) why they make war or for what reasons they make peace. In the city or at the ruler's court nothing is heard, all is silent. They assemble behind closed doors and deliberate among themselves; the doors open, men come out and appear on the stage. Whatever action they have decided on, they carry it out in silence." (Soloviev, *A History of Russia from the Earliest Times*)

The dry, unexplained chronology that a deified authority offered to its subjects, who were supposed to accept it as the earthly fulfillment of mythic commandments, was destined to be transcended and transformed into conscious history. But for this to happen, extensive groups of people had to have experienced real participation in history. Out of this practical communication between those who have *recognized each other* as possessors of a unique present,

On the deck of the battleship *Potemkin:* the members of the firing squad refuse to execute their mutinous comrades.
In a "coming attractions" clip, English schoolgirls show their enthusiastic approval.

who have experienced a qualitative richness of events in their own activity, and who are at home in their own era, arises the general language of historical communication. Those for whom irreversible time truly exists discover in it both the *memorable* and the *threat of oblivion:* "Herodotus of Halicarnassus here presents the results of his researches, so that time will not abolish the deeds of men. . . ." [133]

A cavalry regiment draws sabers and prepares to charge.

Paris, May 1968: revolutionary assemblies in occupied buildings.

General Sheridan rides into a frontier fort where several of his squadrons are stationed. He is welcomed by a colonel who served under him during the Civil War. Sheridan briefs him on a dangerous campaign against the Indians and concludes: "If you fail in your mission, I can assure you that the court-martial that judges you will be composed of the men who rode with us down at Shenandoah. I'll hand pick them myself." The old colonel, lost in thought, says: "Shenandoah . . ." Sheridan, also thinking back on the old days, says: "I wonder what history will say about Shenandoah."

The victory of the bourgeoisie is the victory of a *profoundly historical* time, because it is the time corresponding to an economic production that continuously transforms society from top to bottom. As long as agrarian production remained the predominant form of labor, the cyclical time

The "Tennis Court Oath."

A ceremonious Chinese banquet in the International Concession of Shanghai.

that remained at the base of society reinforced the joint forces of *tradition,* which tend to hold back any historical movement. But the irreversible time of the bourgeois economy eradicates those vestiges throughout the world. History, which until then had seemed to involve only the actions of individual members of the ruling class, and which had thus been recorded as a mere chronology of events, is now understood as a *general movement*—a relentless movement that crushes any individuals in its path. By discovering its basis in political economy, history becomes aware of what had previously been unconscious; but this basis remains unconscious because it cannot be brought to light. This blind prehistory, this new fate that no one controls, is the only thing that the commodity economy has democratized. [141]

Professionals of values in frantic action at the Paris Stock Exchange.

The bourgeoisie has thus made irreversible historical time known and has imposed it on society, but it has prevented society from *using* it. "Once there was history, but not any more," because the class of owners of the economy, which is inextricably tied to *economic history,*

Recent street fighting in the Netherlands, Ireland, and England.

must repress every other irreversible use of time because it is directly threatened by them all. The ruling class, made up of *specialists in the possession of things* who are themselves therefore possessed by things, is forced to link its fate with the preservation of this reified history, that is, with the preservation of a new immobility *within history*. Meanwhile the worker at the base of society is for the first time not materially *estranged from history*, because the irreversible movement is now generated from that base. By demanding to *live* the historical time that it produces, the proletariat discovers the simple, unforgettable core of its revolutionary project; and each previously defeated attempt to carry out this project represents a possible point of departure for a new historical life. [143]

With the development of capitalism, irreversible time has become *globally unified*. Universal history becomes a reality because the entire world is brought under the sway of this time's development. But this history that is everywhere simultaneously the same is as yet nothing but an intrahistorical rejection of history. What appears

Three Black women dancing.

the world over as *the same day* is merely the time of economic production, time cut up into equal abstract fragments. This unified irreversible time is the time of the *global market,* and thus also the time of the global spectacle. [145]

The irreversible time of production is first of all the measure of commodities. The time officially recognized throughout the world as the *general time of society* actually only reflects the specialized interests that constitute it, and thus is *merely one particular type of time.* [146]

A hovercraft at sea. A plane taking off from an airport.

The class struggles of the long *era of revolutions* initiated by the rise of the bourgeoisie have developed in tandem with the dialectical *thought of history*—the thought which is no longer content to seek the meaning of what exists, but which strives to comprehend the dissolution of everything that exists, and in the process breaks down every separation. [75]

The Earth's rotation filmed from space.

This historical thought is still a consciousness that always arrives too late, a consciousness that can only formulate *retrospective* justifications of what has already happened. It has thus gone beyond separation *only in thought*. Hegel's paradoxical stance—his subordination of the meaning of all reality to its historical culmination while at the same time proclaiming that his own system represents that culmination— flows from the simple fact that this thinker of the bourgeois revolutions of the seventeenth and eighteenth centuries sought in his philosophy only a *reconciliation* with the results of those revolutions. [76]

Hegel.

When the proletariat demonstrates through its own actions that this historical thought has not been forgotten, its refutation of that thought's *conclusion* is at the same time a confirmation of its method. [77]

Facing artillery fire, a detachment of Kronstadt sailors attack with fixed bayonets while singing "The Internationale."

Proletarians during the revolutionary days in Barcelona and Petrograd.

The weakness of Marx's theory is naturally linked to the weakness of the revolutionary struggle of the proletariat of his time. The German working class failed to inaugurate a permanent revolution in 1848; the Paris Commune

A long battle in the American Civil War.

was defeated in isolation. As a result, revolutionary theory could not yet be fully realized. [85]

The theoretical shortcomings of the *scientific* defense of proletarian revolution, both in its content and in its form of exposition, all ultimately result from identifying the proletariat with the bourgeoisie *with respect to the revolutionary seizure of power.* [86]

1917 map of the Winter Palace upon which lines of attack have been penciled in.

1792 map of the Tuileries Palace.

During the Spanish Civil War a partisan who has made it through the lines brings last-minute news that the Francoists have been warned about the imminent republican offensive against them, and await the republicans in force. General Golz, a Russian officer in the service of the Republic, speaks on the telephone from a trench near the front: "Do you read me? . . . What? . . ." He watches a wave of bombers fly over his position, which is the signal for launching the attack, and says into the phone: "Too late. That means we're done for. This time we fail. Too bad. Yes, too bad."

The only two classes that really correspond to Marx's theory, the two pure classes that the entire analysis of *Capital* brings to the fore, are the bourgeoisie and the proletariat. These are also the only two revolutionary classes in history, but operating under different conditions.

Continuation of the American Civil War battle.

The bourgeois revolution has been accomplished. The proletarian revolution is a yet-unrealized project, born on the foundation of the earlier revolution but differing from it qualitatively. If one overlooks the *originality* of the historical role of the bourgeoisie, one also tends to overlook the specific originality of the proletarian project, which can achieve nothing unless it carries its own banners and recognizes the "immensity of its tasks." The bourgeoisie came to power because it was the class of the developing economy. The proletariat cannot embody its own new form of power except by becoming the *class of consciousness*. The growth of productive forces will not in itself guarantee the emergence of such a power—not even indirectly by way of the increasing dispossession which that growth entails. Nor can a Jacobin-style seizure of the state be a means to this end. The proletariat cannot make use of any *ideology* designed to disguise partial goals as general goals, because the proletariat cannot preserve any partial reality that is truly its own. [88]

This ideologically alienated theory was then no longer able to recognize the practical verifica-

The Kronstadt sailors continue their attack to the point of victory.

tions of the unitary historical thought it had betrayed when such verifications emerged in spontaneous working-class struggles; instead, it contributed toward repressing every manifestation and memory of them. Yet those historical forms that took shape in struggle were precisely the practical terrain that was needed in order to validate the theory. They were what the theory needed, yet that need had not been formulated theoretically. The *soviet*, for example, was not a theoretical discovery. And the most advanced theoretical truth of the International Working Men's Association was its own existence in practice. [90]

The storming of the Winter Palace.

Michel Corrette: Sonata in D Major for Cello and Harpsichord.

The Vendôme Column pulled down.

Marx. Bakunin. Marx again.
SUBTITLE: You will learn how bitter is the taste of foreign bread, and how hard it is to climb another's stairs. And the heaviest burden in that valley of exile will be finding yourself condemned to such foolish and unpleasant company. But later it will be to your honor that you had the courage to stand alone and form a party of one.

The music ends.

The historical moment when Bolshevism triumphed *for itself* in Russia and social democracy fought victoriously *for the old world* marks the inauguration of the state of affairs that is at the heart of the modern spectacle's domination: the *representation of the working class* has become an *enemy* of the working class. [100]

Red Army infantry on parade.

Trotsky.

TEXT FRAME: "Those who strive to set up a totalitarian bureaucratic state capitalism without crushing the councils will not last long; nor will those who try to abolish class society without condemning all labor unions and specialized hierarchical parties."

Continuation of the Red Army parade: tanks, artillery, rockets.

The Stalin era revealed the bureaucracy's ultimate function: continuing the reign of the economy by preserving the essence of market society: commodified labor. It also demonstrated the independence of the economy: the economy has come to dominate society so completely that it has proved capable of recreating the class domination it needs for its own continued operation; that is, the bourgeoisie has created an independent power that is capable of maintaining itself even without a bourgeoisie. The totalitarian bureaucracy was not "the last owning class in history" in Bruno Rizzi's sense; it was merely a

On the Odessa steps Czarist troops fire on the crowd of demonstrators.

substitute ruling class for the commodity economy. A faltering capitalist property system was
replaced by a cruder version of itself—simpli-
fied, less diversified, and *concentrated* as the
collective property of the bureaucratic class.
This underdeveloped type of ruling class is also
a reflection of economic underdevelopment,
and it has no agenda beyond overcoming this
underdevelopment in certain regions of the
world. The hierarchical and statist framework
for this crude remake of the capitalist ruling
class was provided by the working-class party,
which was itself modeled on the hierarchical
separations of bourgeois organizations. [104]

The ruling totalitarian-ideological class is the
ruler of a world turned upside down. The more
powerful the class, the more it claims not to
exist, and its power is employed above all to
enforce this claim. It is modest only on this one
point, however, because this officially nonexistent bureaucracy simultaneously attributes
the crowning achievements of history to its
own infallible leadership. Though its existence
is everywhere in evidence, the bureaucracy must

The Stalinists and their allies at
a meeting of the French "United
Left"; speeches by Mitterrand and
Marchais.

be *invisible as a class*. As a result, all social life becomes insane. The social organization of total falsehood stems from this fundamental contradiction. [106]

TEXT FRAME: "The higher we go in this bureaucracy of the mind, the more astonishing pates we meet." (Marx, "Remarks on the Recent Prussian Censorship")

Stalinism was also a reign of terror *within* the bureaucratic class. The terrorism on which this class's power was based inevitably came to strike the class itself, because this class has no juridical legitimacy, no legally recognized status as an owning class which could be extended to each of its members. Its ownership has to be masked because it is based on false consciousness. This false consciousness can maintain its total power only by means of a total reign of terror in which all real motives are ultimately obscured. The members of the ruling bureaucratic class have the right of ownership over society only collectively, as participants in a fundamental lie: they have to play the role of the proletariat governing a socialist society; they have to be actors faithful to a script of ideological betrayal. Yet they cannot actually participate in this counterfeit entity

Brezhnev and other Stalinist rulers receiving flowers. Union bosses in the Renault factory. Renault workers, locked inside their factory by their unions in 1968, look outside at naïve marching leftists flanked and controlled by their own bureaucrats.

Stalin speaks at length.

unless their legitimacy is validated. No bureaucrat can individually assert his right to power,
because to prove himself a socialist proletarian
he would have to demonstrate that he was the
opposite of a bureaucrat, while to prove himself
a bureaucrat is impossible because the bureaucracy's official line is that there is no bureaucracy. Each bureaucrat is thus totally dependent
on the *central seal of legitimacy* provided by the
ruling ideology, which validates the collective
participation in its "socialist regime" of *all the
bureaucrats it does not liquidate*. Although the
bureaucrats are collectively empowered to make
all social decisions, the cohesion of their own
class can be ensured only by the concentration
of their terrorist power in a single person. In
this person resides the only practical truth of
the *ruling lie:* the power to determine an unchal-
lengeable boundary line which is nevertheless
constantly being adjusted. Stalin decides without appeal who is and who is not a member of
the ruling bureaucracy—who should be considered a "proletarian in power" and who branded
"a traitor in the pay of Wall Street and the
Mikado." The atomized bureaucrats can find

their collective legitimacy only in the person of Stalin—the lord of the world who thus comes to see himself as the absolute person, for whom no superior spirit exists. "The lord and master of the world recognizes his own nature—omnipresent power—through the destructive violence he exerts against the contrastingly powerless selfhood of his subjects." He is the power that defines the terrain of domination, and he is also "the power that *ravages* that terrain." [107]

As the Reichstag burns, the Hamburg Communists hold their last meeting. A militant denounces this provocation by the Nazi government. Realizing that the latter intends to ban the Communist Party, he declares (at a time when the chance for civil war has already passed): "Hitler means war!" The police officer in attendance declares the meeting closed. The security police burst into the room and begin beating the Communists, who are singing "The Internationale."

A Nazi officer. General Franco.

German tanks in action; officers of the International Brigades in Spain; the Lincoln Brigade. **SUBTITLE: There's a valley in Spain called Jarama, it's a place that we all know so well. For 'tis there that we wasted our manhood, and most of our old age as well.**

Spanish partisans, pursued by Francoist soldiers, defend themselves on the top of the last hill. Political prisoners lined up in a German concentration camp. At the foot of a Paris housing project a little girl plays alone on a merry-go-round. Place de la Concorde lit up at night. Paris rooftops.

TEXT FRAME: "This social peace, reestablished with so much pain and trouble, had lasted only a few years when those who would enter the history of crime under the name 'situationists' appeared to herald its end."

May 1968 barricades in Paris; fires and street fighting in the night.

When the proletariat discovers that its own externalized power contributes to the constant reinforcement of capitalist society, no longer only in the form of its alienated labor but also in the form of the trade unions, political parties, and state powers that it had created in the effort to liberate itself, it also discovers through concrete historical experience that it is the class that must totally oppose all rigidified externalizations and all forms of specialized power. It bears *a revolution that cannot leave anything outside itself,* a revolution embodying the permanent domination of the present over the past and a total critique of separation; and it must discover the appropriate forms of action to carry out this revolution. No quantitative amelioration of its impoverishment, no illusory participation in a hierarchized system, can provide a lasting cure for its dissatisfaction, because the proletariat cannot truly recognize itself in any particular wrong it has suffered, nor in *the righting of any particular wrong*. It cannot recognize itself even in the righting of many such wrongs, but only in the righting of the *absolute wrong* of being excluded from any real life. [114]

Michel Corrette: Sonata in D Major for Cello and Harpsichord.

More May 1968 footage: Rue Gay-Lussac at dawn; rostrum of the mass assembly in the Sorbonne; tracking shot over members of the Enragés–Situationist International Committee, including Debord.

TEXT FRAME: "Comrades: Considering that the Sud-Aviation factory at Nantes has been occupied for two days by the workers and students of that city and that today the movement is spreading to several factories (NMPP in Paris, Renault in Cléon, etc.), the *Sorbonne Occupation Committee* calls for the immediate occupation of all the factories in France and the formation of Workers' Councils. Comrades: Spread and reproduce this appeal as quickly as possible. Sorbonne, May 16, 3:00 pm."

An October 1917 gathering listens to a speaker. A banner across the west wall of the Sorbonne: "Occupy the factories. Workers' Councils. —Enragés–Situationist International Committee." Ports, train stations, and factories paralyzed by the general strike.

TEXT FRAME: "From this day until the ending of the world of the spectacle, the month of May will never return without evoking memories of us."

Christian Sebastiani; Debord; Patrick Cheval. SUBTITLE: **We few, we happy few, we band of brothers.**

Graffiti on a Puvis de Chavannes fresco in the Sorbonne: "Comrades, humanity won't be happy until the . . ."

The Sorbonne at night, with lights in the windows. The Winter Palace at night. Leaflets being thrown from the windows of the "Jules Bonnot Room," headquarters of the Sorbonne Occupation Committee. In Eisenstein's *Ten Days That Shook the World*, workers pick up packets of leaflets as they come off the presses of revolutionary printers. 1968 wall poster: "Down with the spectacle-commodity society."

TEXT FRAME: "Do not delude yourself that they do not have such a plan. They cannot help but have one; if they did not have one already, circumstances alone would force them to develop one. One conquest leads to another; one victory whets the appetite for more." (Machiavelli, letter to Francesco Vettori)

Shots of occupied Sorbonne.

Graffiti: "Run, comrade, the old world is behind you!"

TEXT FRAME: "From February 25 on, a thousand strange systems burst forth from the impetuous imaginations of innovators and spread through the agitated minds of the crowd. . . . It seemed that the shock of the revolution had reduced the entire society to dust, and that there was an open competition to determine the form of the new structure to be set up in its place. Everyone had their own schemes. Some were printed in the newspapers; others on the posters that soon covered the walls; yet others were proclaimed at open-air meetings. One advocated abolishing the inequality of wealth; another the inequality of education; a third proposed to do away with the oldest of all inequalities, that between man and woman. Remedies were prescribed against poverty and against the curse of labor that has tormented humanity since its earliest days." (Alexis de Tocqueville, *Recollections of the French Revolution of 1848*)

A burning barricade at night.
SUBTITLE: But neither the wood nor the fire find any peace or satisfaction in any warmth, great or small, or in any resemblance between them, until the moment when the fire becomes one with the wood and imparts its own nature to it.

TEXT FRAME: "But then they are accused of vandalism and denounced for disrespecting the machines. There might be grounds for such criticisms if the workers were seeking systematic destruction for its own sake. But that is not the case! If the workers are attacking machines, it is not for the pleasure of it or out of caprice, but because urgent needs oblige them to do so." (Émile Pouget, *Sabotage*)

The music ends.

New signs of negation are proliferating in the most economically advanced countries. Although these signs are misunderstood and falsified by the spectacle, they are sufficient proof that a new period has begun. We have already seen the failure of the first proletarian assault against capitalism; now we are witnessing *the failure of capitalist abundance*. On one hand, anti-union struggles of Western workers are being repressed first of all by the unions; on the other, rebellious youth are raising new protests, protests which are still vague and confused but which clearly imply a rejection of art, of everyday life, and of the old specialized politics. These are two sides of a new spontaneous struggle that is at first taking on a *criminal* appearance. They foreshadow a second proletarian assault against class society. [115]

French riot police around the Flins factory and in the streets of Nantes. Young lumpenproletarians defending Rue Saint-Jacques from the rooftops.

A map of Poland. An armored truck, attacked by rioters, bursts into flame. A crowd of insurgents climbs over the gate of a palace.

In a café in Tangiers a woman walks up to where a gangster is sitting, surrounded by his men, and says: "You must remember me." He replies: "I never remember pretty women, it's too expensive. (*Aside, to one of his men*): So, Van Stratten has a new yacht?" She: "This is not about business, Mr. Tadeusz. We just want you to do us a favor." He: "I never do favors." She: "We only want a little information about Poland." He: "I never give inf—" but stops in mid-sentence and, as the musical background gets louder, says "Poland."

TEXT FRAME: "Once again Poland is covered in a bloody shroud and we remain helpless spectators." (Declaration of French workers at the founding conference of the First International, September 28, 1864)

As capitalism's ever-intensifying imposition of alienation at all levels makes it increasingly hard for workers to recognize and name their own impoverishment, putting them in the position of having to reject that impoverishment *as a whole or not at all,* revolutionary organization has had to learn that *it can no longer combat alienation by means of alienated forms of struggle.* [122]

Street fighting in Italy.

Lenin giving a speech.

The development of class society to the stage of the spectacular organization of nonlife is thus leading the revolutionary project to become *visibly* what it has already been *in essence*. [123]

Italy: riot police leap from their vans and begin beating a crowd of people. West German security forces on foot.

Revolutionary theory is now the enemy of all revolutionary ideology, *and it knows it*. [124]

June 1953: Soviet tanks repel workers in East Berlin.

Long sequence in which American policemen beat Black rioters at night. **SUBTITLE: But if we consider the content of this experience as a whole, this content is seen to be the vanishing work. . . . The vanishing is itself quite real: it is bound up with the work and vanishes with it. The negative perishes along with the positive that it negates.**

TEXT FRAME: " 'It would obviously be easy to make history if we only engaged in struggles when success was guaranteed.' It is just as obvious that to completely destroy this society, we have to be ready to launch a dozen or more assaults as significant as May 1968, and be prepared to accept a certain number of defeats and civil wars as unfortunate but inevitable. The goals that count in history must be carried out with energy and determination."

During an American Civil War battle an officer puts himself at the head of the Seventh Michigan Cavalry and cries: "Seventh Michigan, forward! . . . Trot! . . . Gallop! . . . Charge!"

Mr. Arkadin is holding a masked ball in his Spanish castle. Glass in hand, he says to his guests: "No, not a speech, I'm proposing a toast, in Georgian style. In Georgian toasts a little story always comes first. . . . I had a dream. I found myself in a graveyard where all the tombstones were marked in a curious way—'1822–1826', '1930–1934', always like that, always a very short time between birth and death. In the graveyard was an old man. I asked him how it was that he had lived so long when everyone else in his village had died so young. But no, he told me this: 'It's not that we die early, it is just that here our tombstones do not count the years of a man's life, but rather the length of time he has kept a friend.' Let's drink to friendship."

Ivan Chtcheglov.

Asger Jorn.

The Michigan cavalry continues its charge.

After they are defeated, the same officer who led the charge goes in search of the Fifth and Sixth Michigan regiments. Finding them, he leads them in a new charge.

Arkadin concludes another story: ". . . 'Logic?' cried the dying frog as he started pulling the scorpion down with him, 'Where is the logic in this?' 'I know,' said the scorpion, 'but I can't help it, it's my character!' Let's drink to character!"

After yet another setback, the officer appears in front of the ranks of the First Michigan—the last regiment that remains—and orders yet another charge.

TEXT FRAME: "On the contrary, what constitutes the merit of our theory is not the fact of having had a correct idea, but the fact that we have been naturally led to conceive that idea. To sum up—and this should continually be stressed here, as in the whole domain of practice—the purpose of theory is more to train the practitioner to judge for himself than to serve as an indispensable crutch for each step in the accomplishment of his task." (Clausewitz, *The Campaign of 1814*)

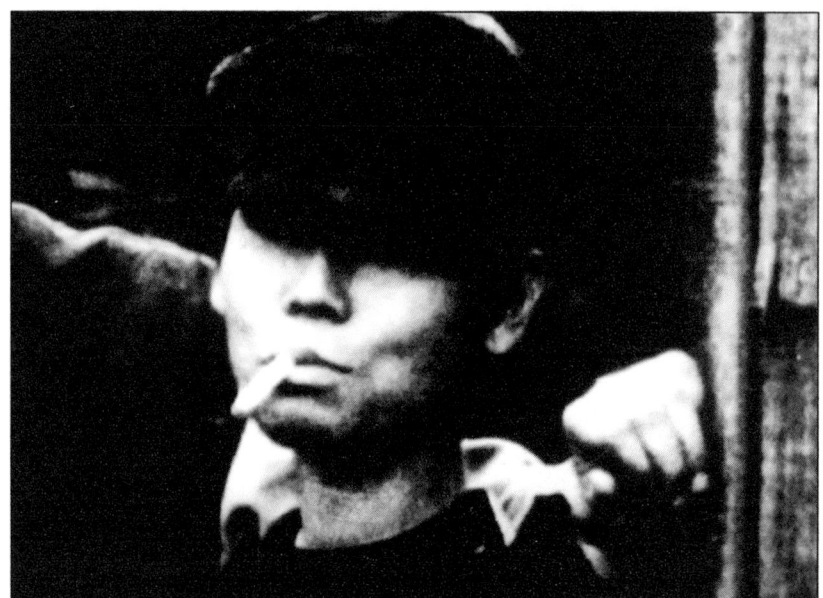

This film is dedicated to Alice Becker-Ho. [p. 43]

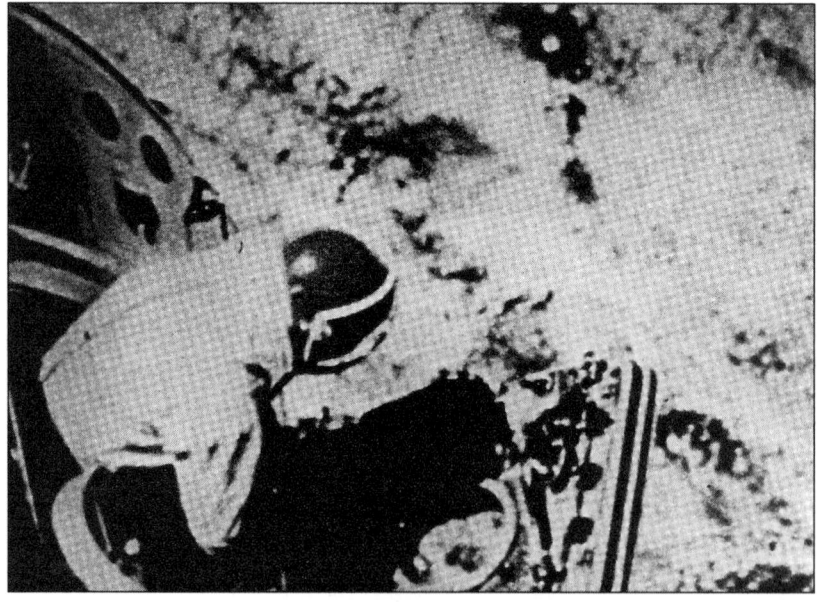

. . . an immense accumulation of spectacles. *Everything that was directly lived has receded . . .* [p. 43]

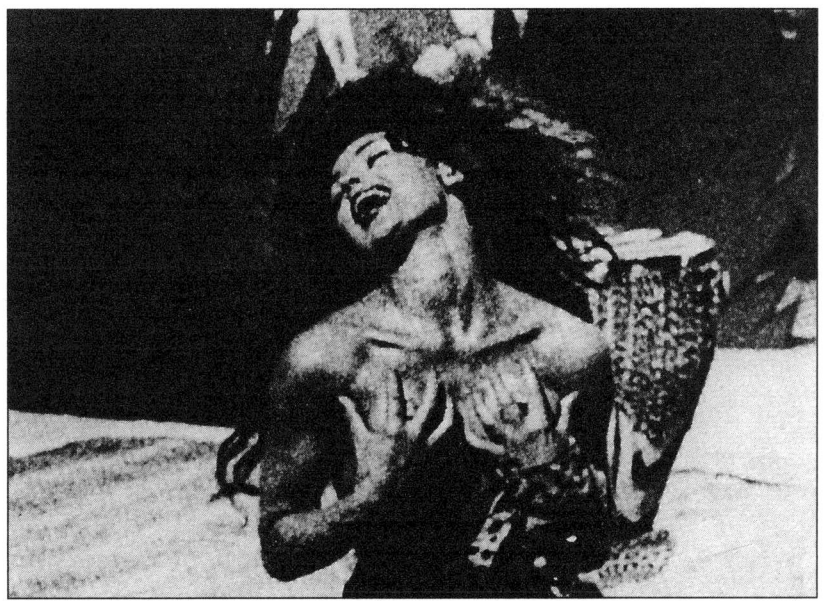

Fragmented *views of reality regroup themselves into a new unity as a* separate pseudoworld *that can only be looked at.* [p. 44]

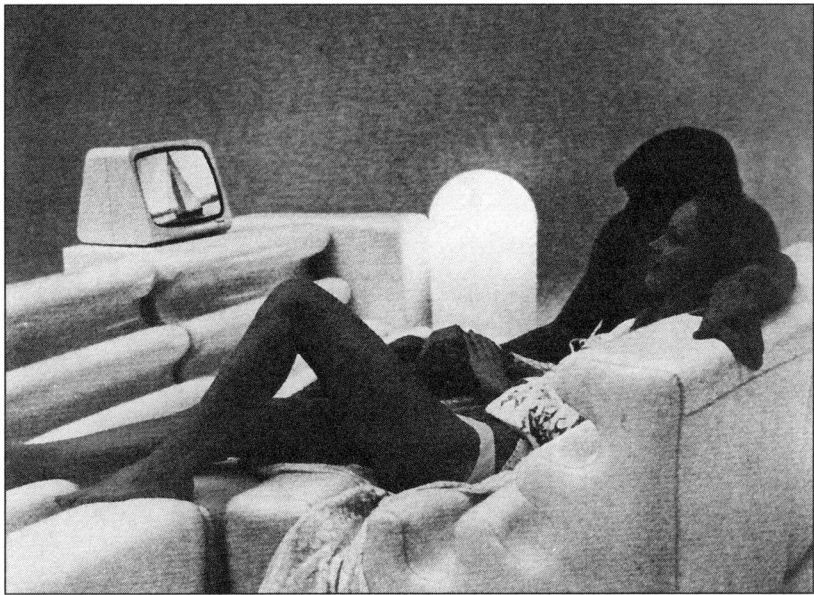

The spectacle thus reunites the separated, but it reunites them only in their separateness. [p. 48]

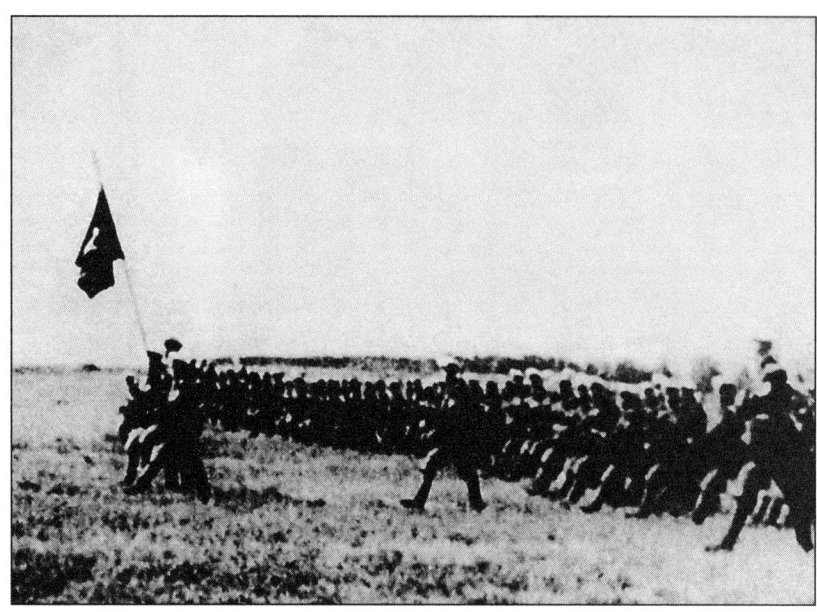

The very style of dialectical theory is a scandal and abomination to the prevailing standards of language . . . [p. 50]

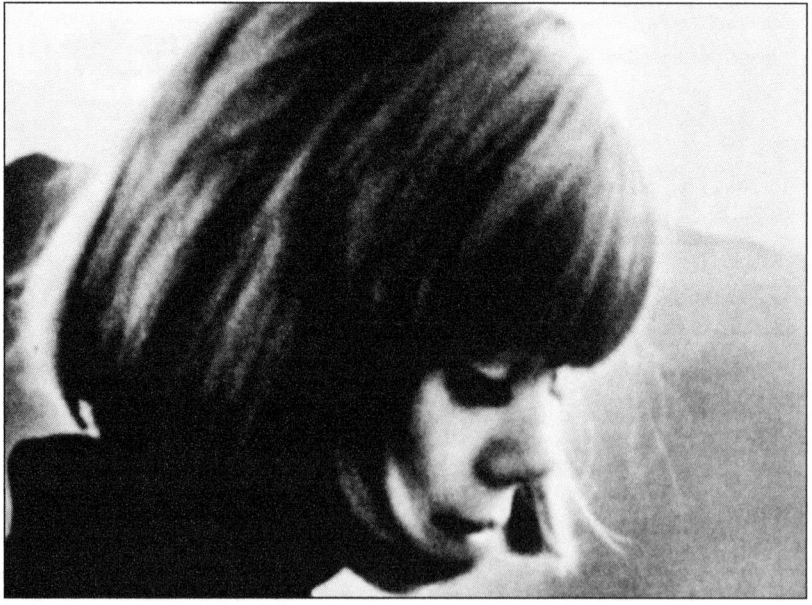

When art becomes independent and paints its world in dazzling colors, a moment of life has grown old. [p. 52]

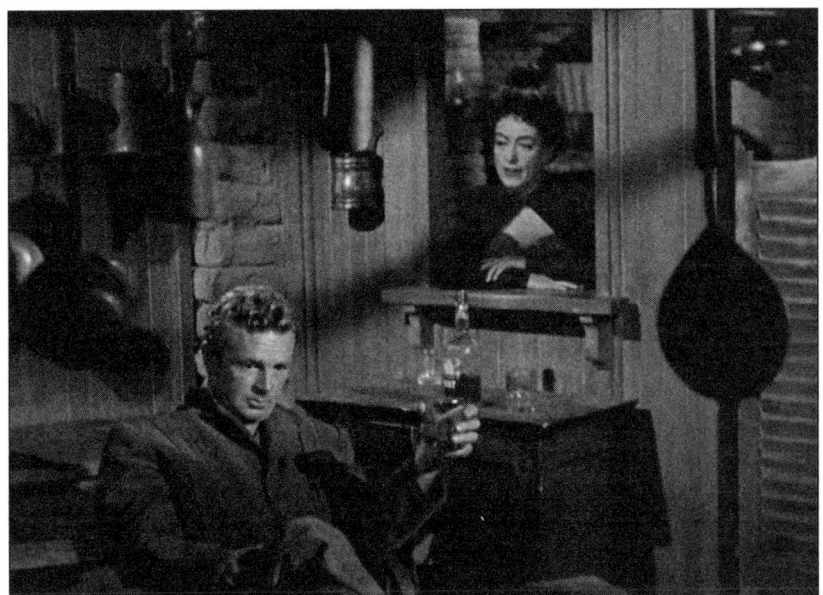

"How many men have you forgotten?" "As many women as you've remembered." [p. 53]

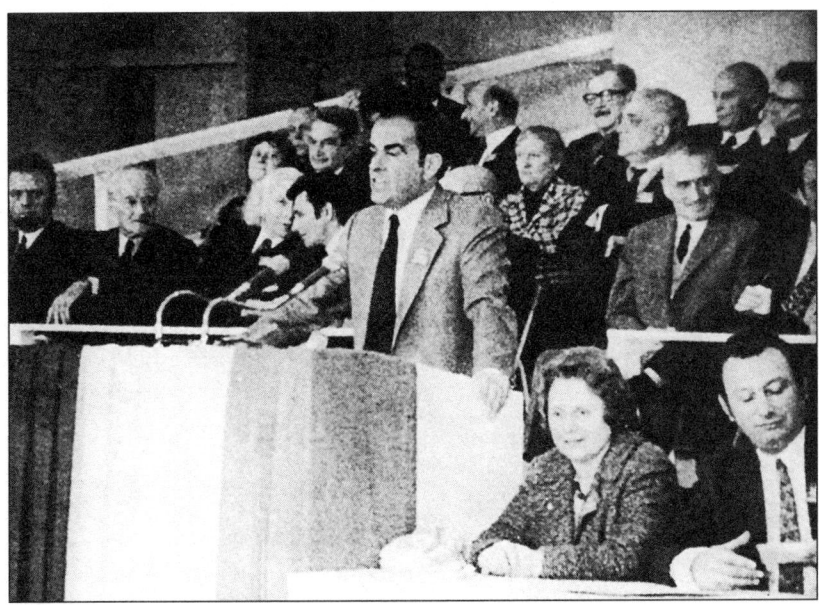

The specialists of spectacular power—a power that is absolute within its realm of one-way communication—are absolutely corrupted by their experience of contempt and by the success of that contempt. [p. 53]

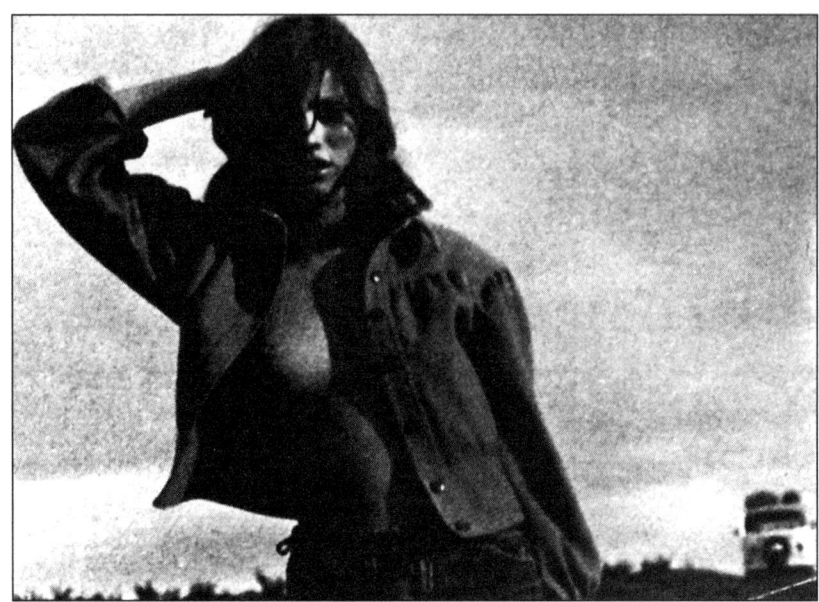

In the spectacle's basic practice of incorporating into itself all the fluid *aspects of human activity so as to possess them in a congealed form* . . . [p. 54]

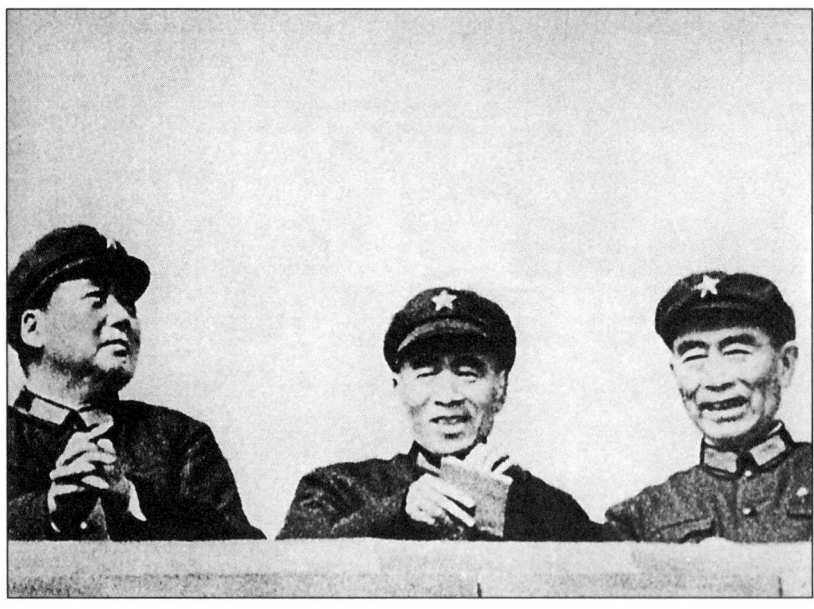

Each new lie *of the advertising industry is an* admission *of its previous lie.* [p. 64]

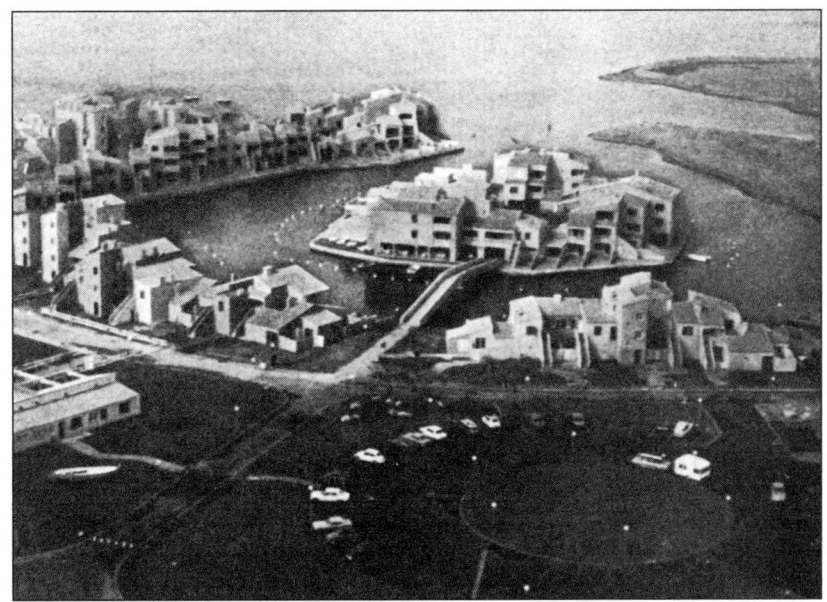

In all previous periods architectural innovations were designed exclusively for the ruling classes. Now for the first time a new architecture has been specifically designed for the poor. [pp. 68–69]

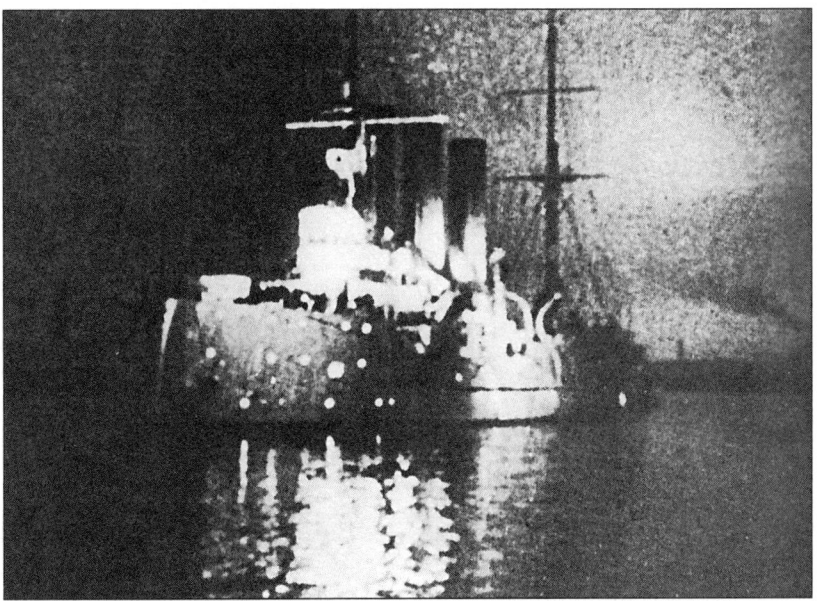

The history that threatens this twilight world could potentially subject space to a directly experienced time. [p. 69]

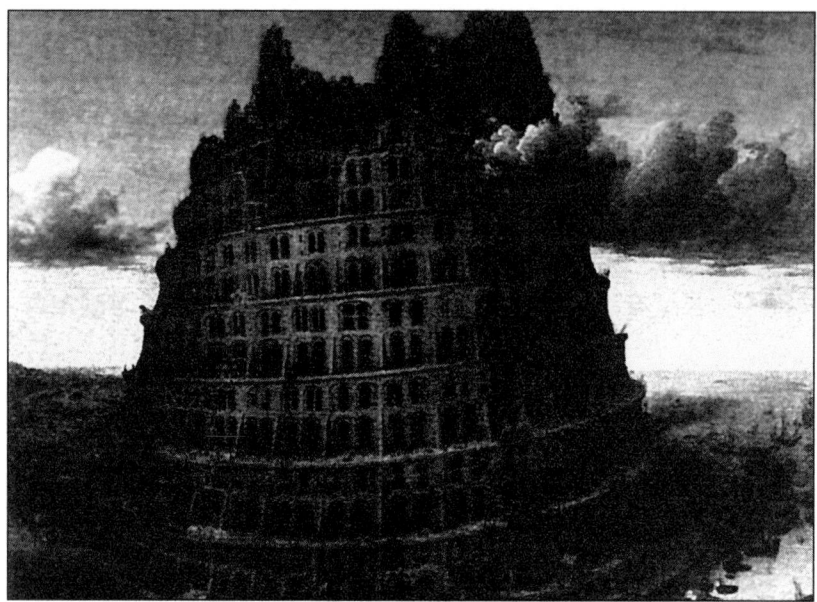

. . . individuals and communities could create places and events commensurate with the appropriation no longer just of their work, but of their entire history. [pp. 69–70]

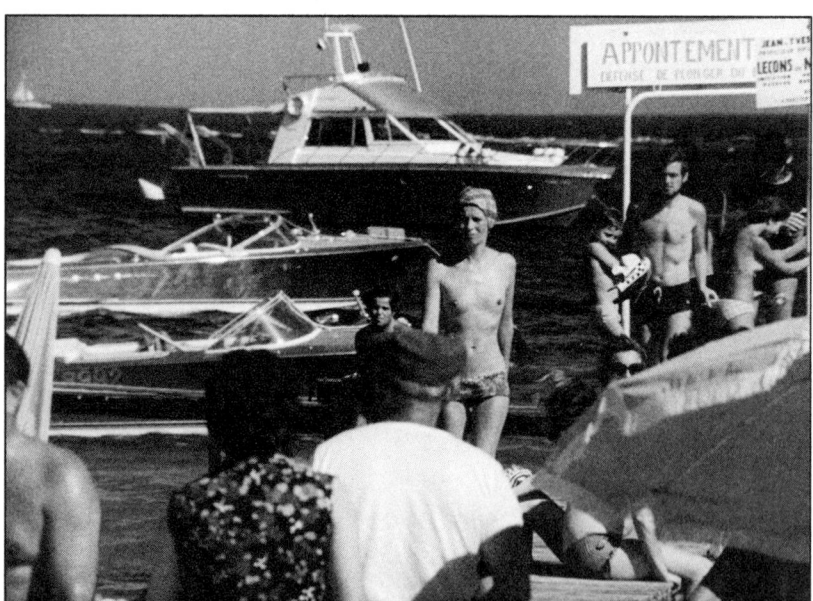

As for the social image of the consumption of time, it is exclusively dominated by leisure time and vacations—moments portrayed, like all spectacular commodities, at a distance *and as desirable by definition.* [p. 72]

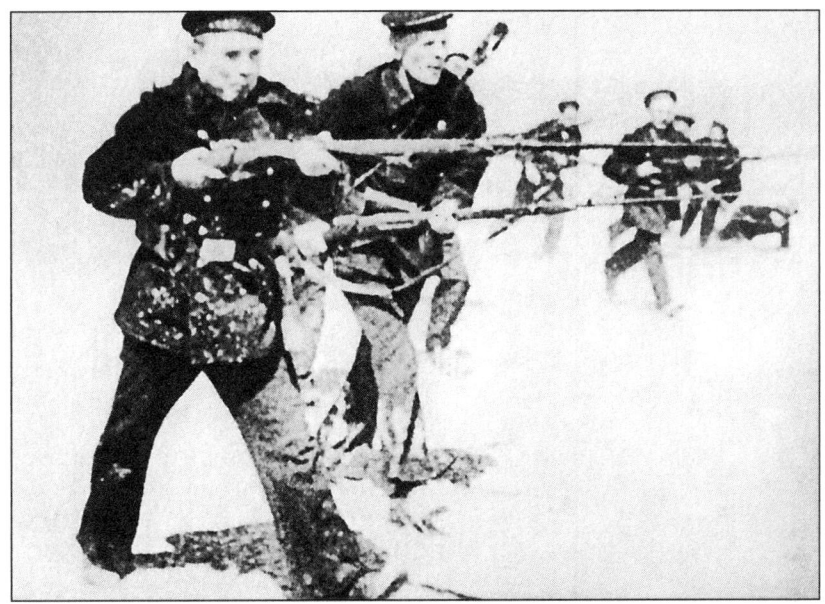

"Arise, downtrodden masses! We'll rebuild the world on new foundations." [p. 82]

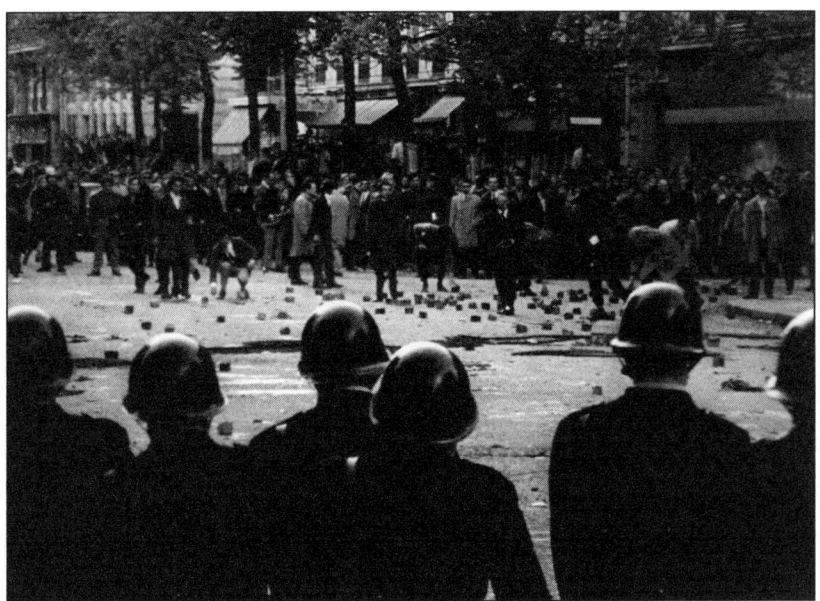

. . . a new period has begun. We have already seen the failure of the first proletarian assault against capitalism; now we are witnessing the failure of capitalist abundance. [p. 95]

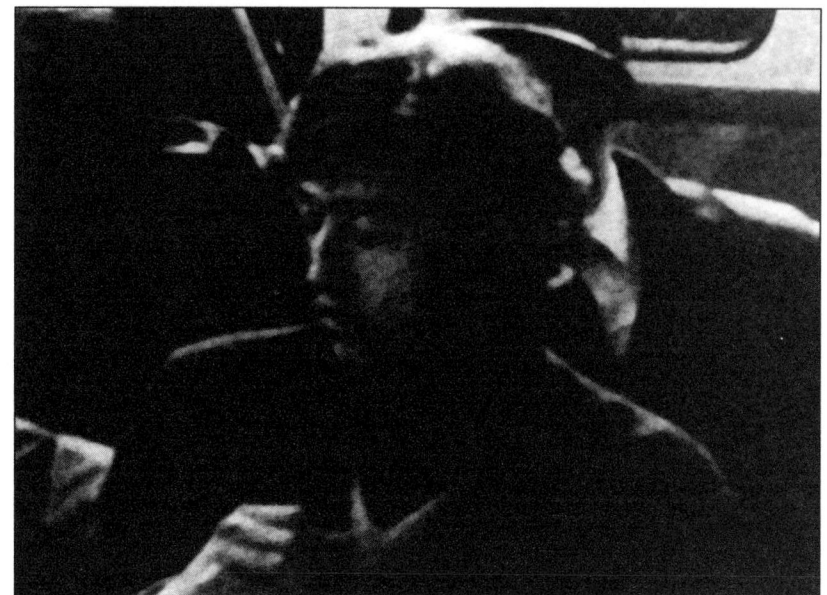

We few, we happy few . . . [p. 93]

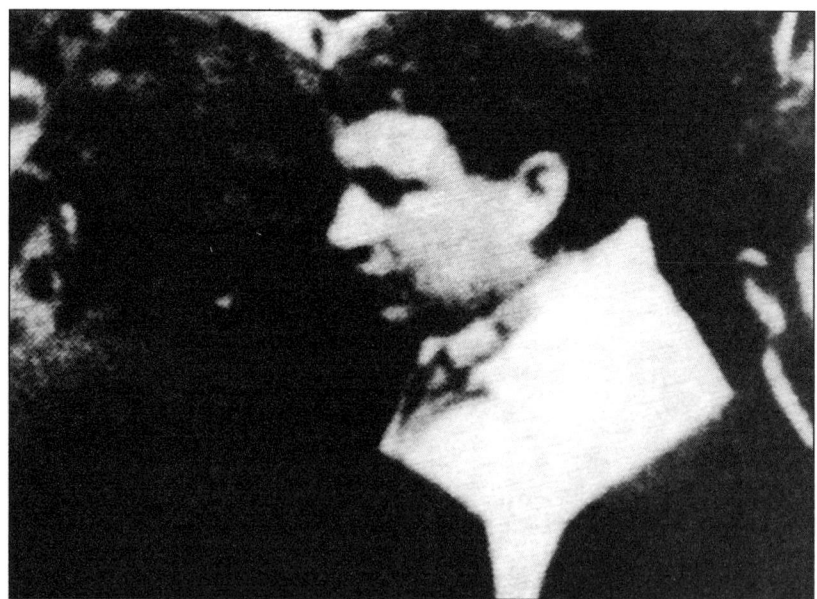

. . . we band of brothers. [p. 93]

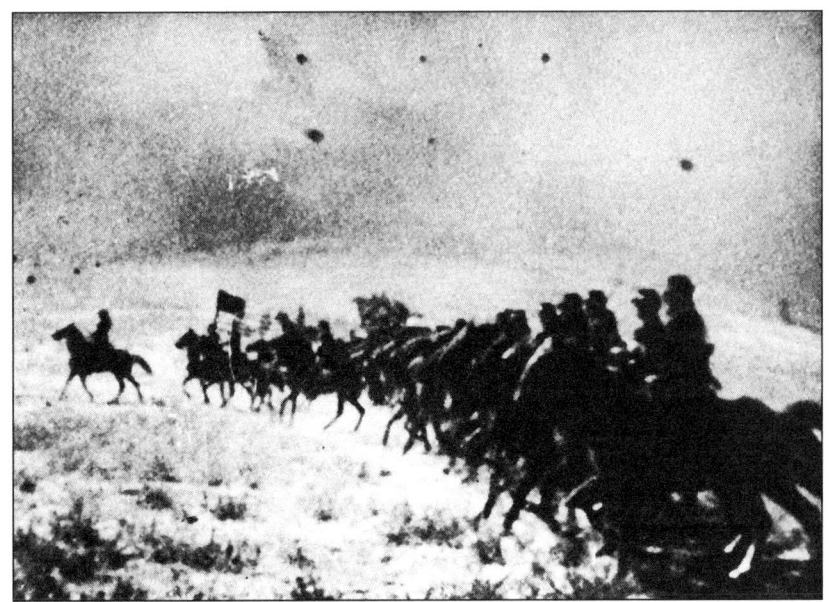

"Seventh Michigan, forward!" [p. 97]

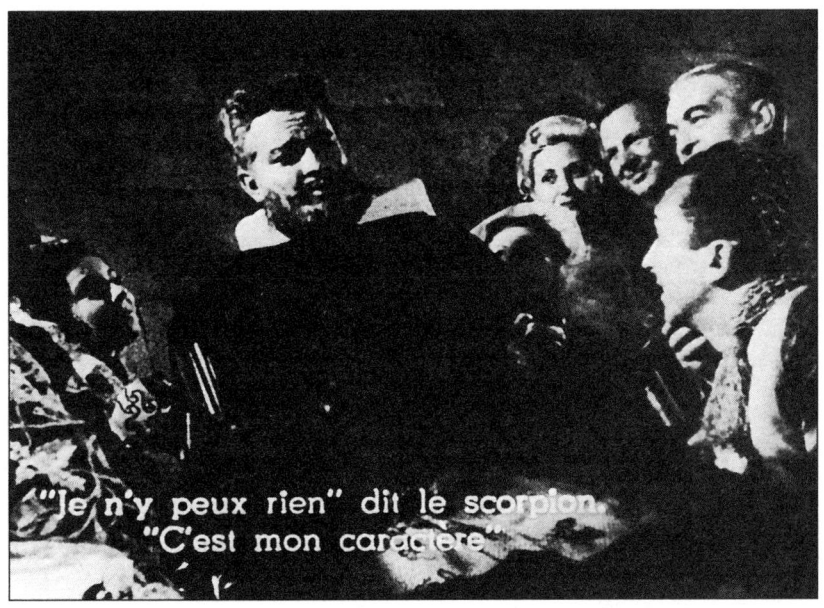

"I know," said the scorpion, "but I can't help it, it's my character!" [p. 98]

Refutation of All the Judgments, Pro or Con, Thus Far Rendered on the Film "The Society of the Spectacle"

The spectacular organization of the present class society has led to two widely evident consequences. The first is a general deterioration in the quality of both products and rationales. The second is the fact that those who claim to find happiness in this society are obliged to maintain a careful distance from the things they pretend to like—because they invariably lack the intellectual or other means that would enable them to attain a direct in-depth knowledge of them, or to incorporate them into a coherent practice, or to develop any genuine taste regarding them.

A commercial extolling some mediocre beverage.

These consequences, which are already so evident when it is a matter of housing conditions,
cultural consumption, sexual liberation, or the
quality of wine, are naturally all the more pro-
nounced when we come to revolutionary theory
and to the formidable language with which that
theory denounces our terminally ill world.

In a German snack bar a model train remote-controlled from the cashier's counter delivers the bill and some mugs of neo-beer to merrily drinking customers, who seem to find the automated delivery of their beverage a satisfactory compensation for its adulterated content.

It is thus hardly surprising that this combination of naïve falsification and ignorant approval,
so characteristic of the modern spectacle, is
reflected in the diversely uncomprehending
responses to the film entitled *The Society of the
Spectacle.*

This particular incomprehension is inevitable,
and will continue to be so for some time to
come. The spectacle is an infirmity more than a
conspiracy. Those who write for the newspapers
and magazines of our time are not concealing
their intelligence: what we see is all they've got.
What could they possibly say of any pertinence
about a film which attacks their habits and ideas
en bloc, and which does so at a time when they

Giscard d'Estaing emerges from the old state palace, where he is met by numerous photographers and reporters. He gets into his car, which he drives himself.

themselves are beginning to sense the collapse of every one of them? The stupidity of their reactions stems from the breakdown of their world.

British troops around a funeral bier.

Those who claim to like my film have liked too many other things to be capable of liking it; and those who say they don't like it have also accepted too many other things for their judgment to have the slightest significance.

A couple enters a roadside restaurant. They respectfully examine the menu, then savor some factory-made ice cream.

The poverty of their discourse reflects the poverty of their lives. You need only look at their surroundings and their occupations, their commodities and their ceremonies, which are on view everywhere. You need only listen to those imbecilic voices giving you contemptuous hourly updates on the current state of your alienation.

Advertising clip: Several automobiles have crashed and almost totally blocked a freeway; but the car with the good brand of tires, arriving at great speed, neatly zigzags its way through and continues down the road.

Advertising clip: A striptease by several young women, hyping some sort of commodity (it's not clear just what). The soundtrack of this commercial has been replaced by a radio announcer reporting in a bland tone, as if it were the most normal thing in the world, the traffic jams and estimated waiting times on all the highways where the mass of listeners are driving to their vacations.

Spectators do not find what they desire; they desire what they find.

Advertising clip: A customer enters a luxurious British store.

The salesman welcomes him with respectful attentiveness. He is given a sample cigarette in order to see if he likes the length. He finds it too long. The salesman cuts it. It's still a little too long. The salesman cuts it even shorter, then holds up a mirror for the customer. He contemplates himself with the cigarette in his mouth and declares himself satisfied.

The spectacle does not debase people to the point of making them love it, but many are paid to pretend that they do. Now that such people can no longer get away with assuring us that this society is completely satisfactory, they hasten to declare themselves dissatisfied with any critique of it. These dissatisfied people all feel they deserved something better. But do they really imagine that anyone is trying to win them over? Do they really believe there is still time for them to rally to such a critique, supposing that they suddenly became convinced of its truth? Do these ill-lodged inhabitants of the land of approbation suppose that they can continue to speak without it being noticed where they're speaking *from*?

The salesman then shows him an ordinary pack of cigarettes, which have been produced in the very size he prefers.
Portugal, April 1974: soldiers with carnations in their rifles march past army trucks; sailors fraternize with civilian demonstrators.

At the podium of the Cannes Film Festival, the best actors, scriptwriters, etc., receive their rewards.

In a freer and more truthful future, people will look back in amazement at the idea that pen pushers hired by the system of spectacular lies could imagine themselves qualified to offer their smug opinions on the merits and defects of a film that is a negation of the spectacle—as if the dissolution of this system was a matter of opinion. Their system is now being attacked in reality and it is defending itself by force. Their counterfeit arguments are no longer accepted, which is why so many of these professional agents of falsification are facing the prospect of unemployment.

Film director Costa-Gavras on this wonderful day.

The most stubborn of these endangered liars still pretend to wonder whether the society of the spectacle actually exists or whether it is perhaps just an imaginary notion that I thought up. But since the woods of history have for the last few years begun to march against their castle of false cards and are continuing at this very moment to close ranks and move in for the kill, most of these commentators are now fawningly praising the excellence of my book, as if they were capable of reading it and as if they

Pan shot over a wall of television screens showing simultaneous live coverage of all the different sporting events taking place at the Olympics in Munich.

A demonstration of Portuguese workers; tanks and soldiers block the roads and hold them back. **Subtitle: Lisbon, February 7, 1975: Thirty-eight federated factories denounce the Stalinists, the labor unions, and the government ministers.**

had already welcomed its publication in 1967 with the same respect. They generally complain, however, that I have abused their indulgence by bringing the book to the screen. This blow is all the more painful because they had never dreamed that such an extravagance was possible. Their anger confirms the fact that the appearance of such a critique in a film upsets them even more than in a book. Here, as elsewhere, they are being forced into a defensive struggle on a second front.

Continuation of the wall of television screens. Long sequence of close-ups of one or another competition. Only human limitations prevent one from seeing everything at once—at least everything involving these particular games.

Many complain that the film is hard to understand. Some say that the images prevent them from understanding the words; others that the words distract from the images. By telling us that they find the film exhausting, and by proudly elevating their individual fatigue into a general criterion of communication, these critics are trying to give the impression that they have no problem understanding—or even perhaps largely agreeing with—the same theory when its exposition is limited to a book. They are attempting to disguise as a mere disagreement between different conceptions of cinema what is actually a conflict between different conceptions of society, and an open war within the existing society.

But if my film is so far beyond them, how can we suppose they are any more capable of understanding everything else that falls to their lot in a society that has so thoroughly conditioned them to mental exhaustion? How could such easily fatigued people find themselves in any better position, amid the incessant cacophony of so many simultaneous commercial and political messages, to see through the crude sophisms designed to make them accept their work and their leisure, or the wisdom of President Giscard, or the taste of food additives? The difficulty is not in my film, but in their servile minds.

No film is more difficult than its era. For example, there are people who understand, and others who do not understand, that when the French were presented with a new ministry called the "Quality-of-Life Department," this was nothing but an age-old ruling-class ploy, designed, as Machiavelli put it, "to allow them to retain at least the name of what they have already lost." There are people who understand, and others who do not understand, that the class struggle in Portugal has from the very beginning been dominated by a direct confrontation between the revolutionary workers organized in autonomous assemblies and the Stalinist bureaucracy allied with a few defeated generals. Those who understand such things will understand my film; and I don't make films for those who don't understand such things, or who make it their business to prevent others from understanding.

During the first days of the Portuguese revolution the Stalinist Cunhal, the socialist Soares, General Spinola, and everyone else with any shred of authority come forward one after another amid the splendors of a national palace to publicly register their commitment to do everything in their power to prevent the revolution from going any further.

Though all the reviews come from the same zone of spectacle-generated pollution, they are as apparently varied as any other present-day commodities. Several of the reviewers claimed that my film filled them with enthusiasm, but none were able to explain why. Whenever I find myself approved of by those who should be my enemies, I ask myself what error they have made in their reasoning. It's usually easy to find. Faced with an unusual number of innovations and an

A series of oil wells with flares.

Brief sequence of a modern cattle farm, showing the chemical and automation technology used to bring the milk and meat of this livestock to a level of quality worthy of the contemporary consumer.

Long tracking shot around an oil exploration platform that is being moved into position by deep-sea tugs.

insolence that is utterly beyond their compre-hension, these avant-garde consumers vainly try to rationalize a ground for approval by attributing these fascinating eccentricities to a nonexistent individual lyricism.

One of them, for example, admires my film for its supposed "lyricism of rage"; another discovered by watching it that the passing of a historical epoch produces a certain melan-choly; others, who greatly overestimate the refinements of present-day social life, attribute to me a certain dandyism. These are nothing but different forms of the perennial tactic of all ruling apologetics: *Deny what exists and explain what does not.* A critical theory that accompanies the dissolution of a society does not concern itself with expressing rage, much less with pre-senting mere images of rage. It seeks to under-stand, to describe, and to precipitate a move-ment that is developing before our very eyes. As for those who present us with their own pseudorage as a sort of newly fashionable artis-tic content, it is obvious that this is merely their way of compensating for the spineless-

Galaxies.

A demonstration of Portuguese workers: "Down with the provisional government!"

ness, compromises, and humiliations of their actual life—which is why spectators so readily identify with them.

Political reactionaries are naturally even more hostile to my film. Thus an apprentice bureaucrat claims to admire my audacity in "making a political film not by telling a story, but by directly filming a theory." Unfortunately, he does not like my theory. He senses that despite my apparent "uncompromising leftism," I am actually shifting toward the right because I systematically attack "the men of the United Left." The cretin's mouth is full of such inflated terminology. What union? What Left? What men?

The "United Left" is, of course, nothing other than the current alliance of the Stalinists with other enemies of the proletariat. Each of the partners knows the others well. They clumsily plot against each other and stridently denounce each other every week. But they have now come together in an effort to sabotage the revolutionary initiatives of the workers, in order—as they themselves admit—to maintain at least the essen-

The Stalinist Cunhal, on a platform with several of his accomplices, firmly chants some lying slogan.
Soares, playing the role of moderate democrat, smiles at everyone, receives flowers, and presides over boring meetings.

tials of capitalism if they can't save all the details. They are the same type of bureaucrats as those who are repressing workers' "counter-revolutionary strikes" in Portugal, just as they did in Budapest not so long ago; the same as those who aspire to take part in a "Historic Compromise" in Italy; the same as those who called themselves "Popular Front governments" when they broke the French strikes of 1936 and sabotaged the Spanish revolution.

A crowd at a meeting, waving red flags. In a newsreel from July 12, 1936, Salengro speaks on a stage at a socialist meeting. (SUBTITLE: **Socialist Roger Salengro, Minister of the Interior of the Popular Front.**) An absurd and repugnant little man, doing his best to imitate Mussolini's oratorical style, he declares: "We will uphold law and order! And we will make the working class understand that its duty and its interest oblige it to listen to our appeals, so that we will not have to resort to more coercive methods. The Popular Front will not be anarchy! The Popular Front will endure and triumph only if it is able to maintain law and order. The working class must understand that its duty and its interest require that it do nothing that might rouse the middle class or the peasant class against it. The day after tomorrow, in a great procession, the tricolor banner of the nation and the red flag of labor will be united. On that day, July 14, the celebration of the

Republic, and of the proletariat, we will call on the people of Paris to continue to uphold their victory of April and May. We will ask the people of France to maintain their confidence in our government—a government that lives only through the people, a government that lives only for the people, and that will triumph only if the people of France help it to triumph."

SUBTITLE (*during the final sentence of the above speech*): **Four months later this man, capable of nothing but scorning the people who had elected him, was driven to suicide by slanders from the extreme right, which failed to appreciate his services to its cause.**

The United Left is only a minor defensive hoax of spectacular society, a temporary expedient that the system only occasionally needs to resort to. I only evoked it in passing in my film, though I naturally attacked it with all the contempt it deserves—just as we have since attacked it in Portugal on a broader and more beautiful terrain.

The Stalinist Cunhal, looking worried.

A cordon of Portuguese soldiers at the top of a monumental stairway, protecting the government at nightfall.

A journalist close to that same Left, who has since achieved a certain notoriety by invoking "freedom of the press" in order to defend his

News agency telex. Technical equipment of a radio station (sound board, etc.).

publication of an implausibly faked document, exhibited a similarly clumsy falsification by insinuating that I failed to attack the bureaucrats of Beijing as sharply as the other ruling classes. He also regrets that a mind of my quality has limited its expression to a "cinema ghetto" where the masses will have little chance to see it. This argument does not convince me. I prefer to remain in obscurity with these masses, rather than to consent to harangue them under the artificial floodlights manipulated by their hypnotizers.

Lisbon: a demonstration of textile workers.

Another sophist of similarly limited mental capacity presents a contrary argument: By publicly denouncing the spectacle, am I not thereby entering the spectacle? This sort of purism, which sounds particularly strange coming from a journalist, is obviously invoked in the hope of convincing people that no one should ever appear in the spectacle as an enemy of it.

Those who do not have even a subordinate post in spectacular society, and who thus have nothing to lose but their ambitious hope of

Students filling their trays in a university cafeteria.

eventually serving in one of its juvenile relief corps, have given more frank and furious expressions of their discontent and even of their jealousy. An anonymous individual of this sort has for some time been expounding the latest trendy ideas in a most appropriate forum: the weekly magazine of the laughable foot soldiers of Mitterrand's electoral constituency.

This anonymous individual concludes that it would have been fine to film my book in 1967, but that in 1973 it was too late. The reason he gives for this conclusion is that it seems crucial to him that from now on everybody should stop talking about everything of which he himself is ignorant—Marx; Hegel; books in general (because they cannot be an adequate means of liberation); any use of film (because it is merely film); theory, above all; and even history itself, which he congratulates himself for having anonymously abandoned.

Such decomposed thought could obviously have oozed forth only from the desolate walls of Vincennes University. Within living memory

Advertising clip: In a desert landscape teenagers in hippie garb gaily follow a bearded young man who walks a little ahead of them. Coming upon an expanse of water, the bearded leader continues on nonchalantly, his "Buggy d'Eram" shoes enabling him to walk on the water. Others with the same brand of shoes follow him and the miracle is repeated. But those of little faith who didn't believe in Buggy d'Eram shoes sink in the water up to their knees and have to remain behind, with no one turning back for them.

Giscard d'Estaing and Chirac welcome the current Portuguese head of state; a squad of troops does the honors.

In a university cafeteria students stand in line waiting for their neo-food.

no Vincennes student has ever come up with a single theory. This is no doubt why we are currently seeing some of them advocate "anti-theory." What else could they parlay into an assistant professorship in that neo-university? Not that they content themselves with that—even the most talentless candidate co-opters are ringing every doorbell, applying for the position of film director or at least of series editor at some publishing house (the anonymous individual of whom I have been speaking does not hide his envy of what he imagines to be the lavish rewards of a cinema career). We can therefore confidently predict that these anti-theories will not easily be reduced to the silence that would seem to be their only logical implication, because in that case their authors would be deprived of the sole "qualification" that elevates them above the ranks of unskilled labor.

Our anonymous imposter gives away his real aim at the end of his review. The reason he wants to dissolve history is so he can elect another, so that he himself can designate the thinkers of the future. And with a straight face

Amphitheaters full of certified neo-thinkers.

Bicycle racers moving at full speed.

The victor, with a garland of flowers.

Tracking shot over the harbor of an industrial zone.

Advertising clip vaunting a brand of trousers: On a music-hall stage several men get dressed in time to music and are applauded by a female audience.

this blockhead nominates for that role Lyotard, Castoriadis, and other crumb-collectors—people who had already shot their bolt more than fifteen years ago without managing to particularly dazzle their century.

Advertising clip for a brand of iced tea. Confederate cavalry set out for war, leaving their homes and festivities behind. Those who have never known those days have never really known the good things of life, etc. The conclusion is of Hegelian brutality: "Their civilization has vanished. All that remains is iced tea."

No loser loves history. Moreover, once they have gone so far as to collectively repudiate history, it is hardly surprising to see these resolutely ultramodern careerists urging us to read co-opted thinkers in their fifties. It's no more contradictory than it is for someone to pride himself on having remained anonymously silent since 1968 while admitting that he has not even reached the point of scorning his professors. Our anonymous critic nevertheless has the merit of having illustrated better than the others the utter ineptitude of the antihistorical perspective he advocates and the real motivations behind these impotent people's pretended disdain for reality.

Confederate officers at a garden party in the same ad; dignified old gentlemen; a loyal Black servant brings them iced tea; couples make idle plans.

Portuguese soldiers break up a demonstration.

In postulating that it was too late to undertake a cinematic adaptation of *The Society of the Spectacle* six years after the appearance of the book, he overlooks the fact that there have not been three books of social critique of such importance published in the last hundred years. He also fails to consider the fact that I myself had written the book. There is no standard of comparison for judging whether I was relatively slow or fast in making the film since it is obvious that the best of my predecessors had no access to the film medium. Everything considered, I must admit that I found it very gratifying to be the first person to carry out this kind of exploit.

Yankee marauders enter a luxurious Southern mansion, loot it, then set it on fire.

The defenders of the spectacle will be as slow to recognize this new use of film as they were in recognizing the fact that a new era of revolutionary opposition was undermining their society; but they will be obliged to recognize it just as inevitably. And they will follow the same sequence: first remaining silent, then speaking beside the point. The reviewers of my film have reached the latter stage.

In Portugal a loudspeaker mounted on a tank urges the crowd to calm down.

Demonstrators chant their demands; in the front line is a little girl more convinced than anyone.

Funeral of the last king of England. Troops march past holding their rifles upside down. Highlanders, sailors, grenadiers, Horse Guards, in ancient uniforms dating from the days of the Empire's power and glory, accompany a coffin surmounted by the globe and scepter.

The specialists of the cinema have said that my film's revolutionary politics were bad; the left-wing political illusionists have said that it was bad cinema. But when one is both a revolutionary and a filmmaker, it is easy to demonstrate that their shared bitterness stems from the fact that the film in question is a precise critique of the society they do not know how to combat; and the first example of a kind of film they do not know how to make.

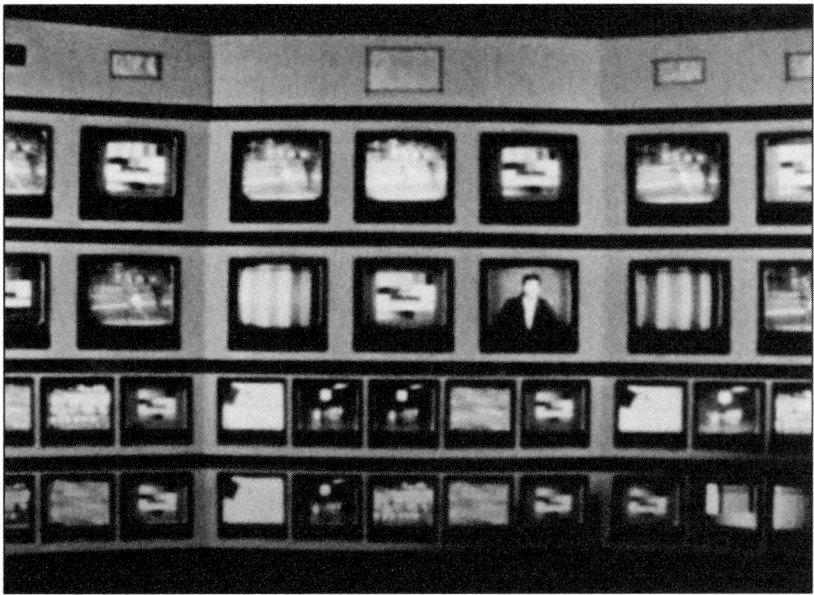

The most stubborn of these endangered liars still pretend to wonder whether the society of the spectacle actually exists or whether it is perhaps just an imaginary notion that I thought up. [p. 115]

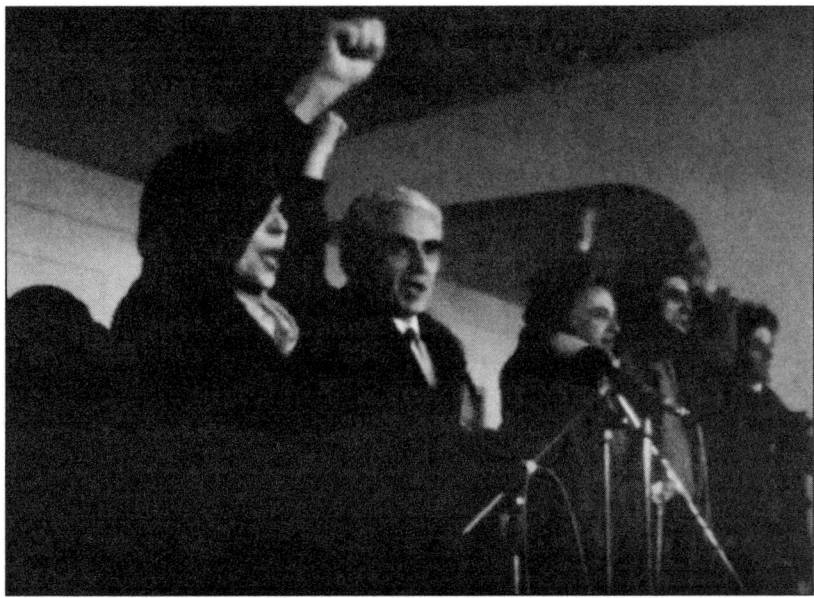

Political reactionaries are naturally even more hostile to my film. [p. 120]

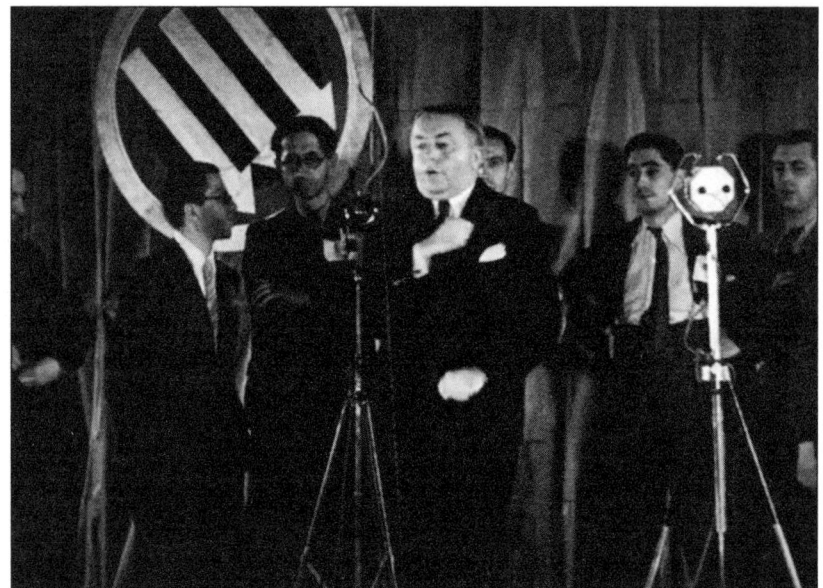

"We will uphold law and order! And we will make the working class understand that its duty and its interest oblige it to listen to our appeals, so that we will not have to resort to more coercive methods. The Popular Front will not be anarchy!"
[p. 121]

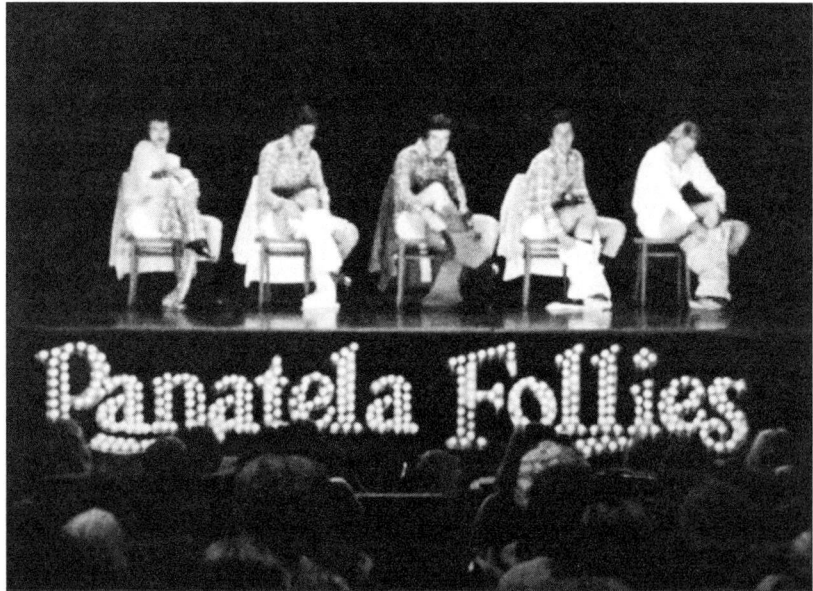

The reason he wants to dissolve history is so he can elect another, so that he himself can designate the thinkers of the future. And with a straight face this blockhead nominates for that role Lyotard, Castoriadis, and other crumb-collectors . . .
[pp. 125–126]

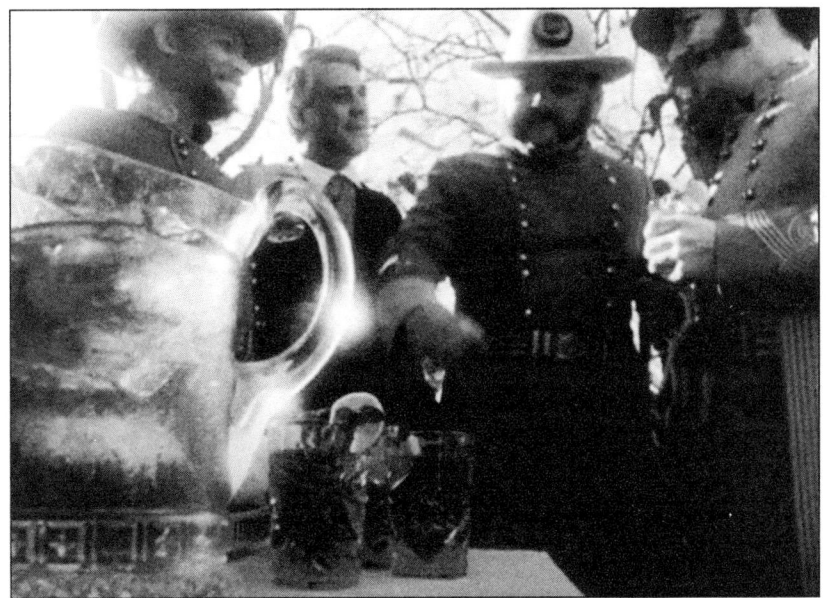

No loser loves history. [p. 126]

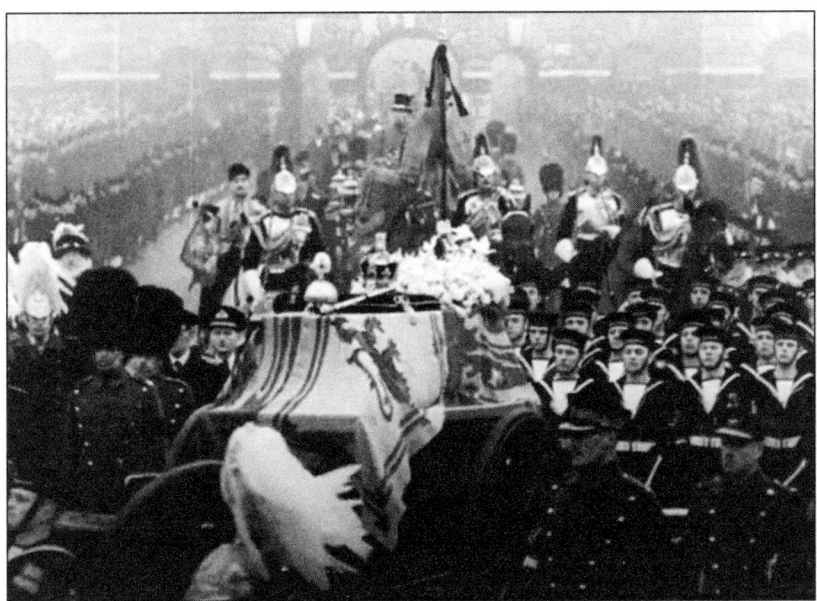

The specialists of the cinema have said that my film's revolutionary politics were bad; the left-wing political illusionists have said that it was bad cinema. [p. 128]

In girum imus nocte et consumimur igni

I will make no concessions to the public in this film. I believe there are several good reasons for this decision, and I am going to state them.

In the first place, it is well known that I have never made any concessions to the dominant ideas or ruling powers of my era.

Moreover, nothing of importance has ever been communicated by pampering a public, not even one like that of the age of Pericles; and in the frozen mirror of the screen the spectators are not looking at anything that might suggest the respectable citizens of a democracy.

But most importantly: this particular public, which has been so totally deprived of freedom

A contemporary movie audience, photographed from the screen at which they are staring fixedly, so that the spectators find themselves face to face with nothing but themselves.

and which has tolerated every sort of abuse, deserves less than any other to be treated gently. The advertising manipulators, with the usual impudence of those who know that people tend to justify whatever affronts they don't avenge, calmly declare that "People who love life go to the cinema." But this life and this cinema are equally paltry, which is why it hardly matters if one is substituted for the other.

A large complex of neo-dwellings.

A modern employee taking a bath with her young son. Tracking shot toward a bed adorning the same room.

The movie-going public, which has never been very bourgeois and which is scarcely any longer working-class, is now recruited almost entirely from a single social stratum, though one that has been considerably enlarged—the stratum of low-level skilled employees in the various "service" occupations that are so necessary to the present production system: management, control, maintenance, research, teaching, propaganda, entertainment, and pseudocritique. Which suffices to give an idea of what they are. This public that still goes to the movies also, of course, includes the young of the same breed who are merely at the apprenticeship stage for one or another of these functions.

People waiting patiently outside a movie theater.

Panoramas of present-day factories and their wastes.

A clothing store with two young customers.

From the realism and the achievements of this splendid system one could already infer the personal capacities of the underlings it has produced. Misled about everything, they can only spout absurdities based on lies—these poor wage earners who see themselves as property owners, these mystified ignoramuses who think they're educated, these zombies with the delusion that their votes mean something.

How harshly the mode of production has treated them! With all their "upward mobility" they have lost the little they had and gained what no one wanted. They share poverties and humiliations from all the past systems of exploitation without sharing in the revolts against those systems. In many ways they resemble slaves, because they are herded into cramped habitations that are gloomy, ugly, and unhealthy; ill-nourished with tasteless and adulterated food; poorly treated for their constantly recurring illnesses; under constant petty surveillance; and maintained in the modernized illiteracy and spectacular superstitions that reinforce the power of their masters. For

Advertising photo of a modern employee couple in their main room, where their two children are playing.

the convenience of present-day industry they are transplanted far from their own neighborhoods or regions and concentrated into new and hostile environments. They are nothing but numbers on charts drawn up by idiots.

They die in droves on the freeways, and in each flu epidemic and each heat wave, and with each mistake of those who adulterate their food, and with each technical innovation profitable to the numerous entrepreneurs for whose environmental developments they serve as guinea pigs. Their nerve-racking conditions of existence produce physical, intellectual, and psychological degeneration. They are always spoken to like obedient children—always willing to do what they're told as long as they're told that they "must" do it. But above all they are treated like retarded children, forced to accept the delirious gibberish of dozens of recently concocted paternalistic specializations, which one day tell them one absurdity and the next day perhaps the very opposite.

View from above of the furnishings of the same dwelling, without its inhabitants.

Tahitian natives dancing on a beach.

Separated from each other by the general loss of any language capable of describing reality (a loss

Close-up of the same couple.

which prevents any real dialogue), separated by their relentless competition in the conspicuous consumption of nothingness and thus by the most groundless and eternally frustrated envy, they are even separated from their own children, who in previous eras were the only property of those possessing nothing. Control of these children is taken from them at an early age—these children who are already their rivals, who laugh at their parents' blatant failure and pay no attention to their simple-minded opinions. Understandably despising their origin, these children feel more like offspring of the reigning spectacle than of the particular servants of the spectacle who happen to have begotten them, and think of themselves as only half-castes of such slaves. Behind the façade of simulated rapture among these couples and their progeny there is nothing but looks of hatred.

But these privileged workers of a totally commodified society differ from slaves in that they themselves must provide for their own upkeep. In this regard their condition is more akin to

Close-up of the few books in the dwelling.

A huge bed, with room enough for a man to host two orgasm-faking women at the same time.

Close-up of the two previously seen children.

A consumer in a supermarket with her child, who is pushing a still partially empty shopping cart.

An employee couple on a foam couch with a telephone.

Close-up of the child with the shopping cart.

Close-up of the child's smiling mother.

One employee couple welcomes another, their spiteful glances avoiding each other.

serfdom, because they are exclusively attached to some particular company and dependent on its successful functioning, without receiving anything in return; and especially because they are compelled to reside within a single space: the same circuit of ever-identical dwelling units, offices, freeways, vacation spots, and airports.

Employees on a business trip in an express train.

But they also resemble modern proletarians because of the precariousness of their means of support, which conflicts with the continual spending to which they have been conditioned; and because they have to hire themselves out on an open market without owning the instruments of their labor. They need money to buy commodities, because things have been so arranged that they have no enduring access to anything that has not been commodified.

Pan shot down the façade of a tower of neo-dwellings to a kiosk marked "Idea Box," designed to elicit compliments.

Pan shot down another similar façade to a car emerging from an underground parking lot.

But in their economic situation they are more like peons, in that they are no longer left even the momentary handling of the money around which their entire activity revolves. They have to spend it immediately because they don't receive enough to save. But even so, sooner or later they

Informal gathering at the home of some modern employees, eating and playing Monopoly at the same table.

find themselves obliged to consume on credit; and the credit they are granted is docked from their pay, forcing them to work even more to free themselves from debt. Since the distribution of goods is totally interlinked with the organization of production and the state, their rations of food and of space are sharply reduced in both quantity and quality. Though nominally remaining free workers and consumers, they are scorned everywhere and have no real possibility of redress.

Another gathering of the same sort, with four guests and two bottles.

I am not going to fall into the simplistic error of equating the condition of these high-ranking wage slaves with previous forms of socioeconomic oppression. First of all because, if one leaves aside their surplus of false consciousness and their purchases of two or three times as much of the miserable junk that constitutes virtually the entire market, it is clear that they share the same sad life as all the other wage earners of today. It is, in fact, with the naïve hope of distracting attention from this annoying awareness that so many of them jabber so much about how uneasy they feel about living

A display of factory-produced neo-foods decorated with a "quality" label.

A table of employees turned toward a television, which they all watch with equal interest.

in the lap of luxury while people in distant lands are crushed by destitution.

Another reason not to confuse them with the unfortunates of the past is that their social position has certain unmistakably modern traits. For the first time in history we are seeing highly specialized economic professionals who, outside their work, have to do everything for themselves. They drive their own cars and are beginning to have to personally fill them with gasoline; they do their own shopping and their own so-called cooking; they serve themselves in the supermarkets and in the entities that have replaced railroad dining cars. It may not have taken them very long to obtain their flimsy "professional qualifications," but after they have put in their allotted hours of specialized work they still have to do everything else with their own hands. Our era has not yet managed to supersede the family, or money, or the division of labor; yet one could say that these people have already been almost totally deprived of their practical reality through sheer dispossession. Those who had never had any substance have lost it for the shadow.

Several employees serving themselves and consuming various neo-foods while standing.

A fashionably dressed employee in a correspondingly fashionable setting.

The illusory nature of the riches that the present society claims to distribute would have been amply demonstrated—had it not already been evident in so many other respects—by the simple fact that never before has a system of tyranny maintained its lackeys, its experts, and its court jesters so shabbily. They work overtime in the service of emptiness, and emptiness rewards them with coinage in its own image. This is the first time that poor people have imagined themselves to be part of an economic elite, despite all the glaring evidence to the contrary. Not only do these miserable spectators work, nobody else works for them, least of all the people they pay. Even their retailers regard themselves rather as their overseers, judging whether or not they are sufficiently fervent in snapping up the ersatz goods they have the duty to buy. Nothing can hide the built-in obsolescence of all their possessions—the rapid deterioration not only of their material goods, but even of their legal rights to the few properties they may own. They have received no inheritance, and they will leave none.

An employee couple with two children in a bathroom.

An aging employee couple standing in front of their automobile.

An employee trying to cross a congested thoroughfare.

Two cars wrecked in the middle of a freeway.

Destruction of a car and its human appendage in a crash test by the manufacturer's research department.

Since the cinema public needs more than anything to face these bitter truths, which concern it so intimately but which are so widely repressed, it cannot be denied that a film that for once renders it the harsh service of revealing that its problems are not so mysterious as it imagines, nor even perhaps so incurable if we ever manage to abolish classes and the state—it cannot be denied that such a film has at least that one virtue. It will have no other.

This public, which likes to pretend that it is a connoisseur of everything while it in fact does nothing but justify everything it has been forced to undergo, passively accepting the constantly increasing repugnance of the food it eats, the air it breathes, and the dwellings it inhabits—this public grumbles about change only when it affects the cinema to which it has become accustomed. And in fact this is the only one of its habits that seems to have been respected. For a long time I have been perhaps the only person to offend it in this domain. All the other filmmakers, even those who are up-to-date enough to echo a few issues already made fashionable by

Repeat of the previously seen advertising photo of the family of modern employees in their main room, with a slow tracking shot toward the center.

Beginning of a run-of-the-mill preview: "Coming soon to this theater," followed by the title: The Most Wonderful Day of My Life.

Another preview: "Coming soon to this theater" and "You'll rediscover the thrills of your youth." Title: The Black Arrow of Robin Hood. Cavalcades, arrow shots, sword thrusts, gatherings in castles and forests.

the press, continue to presume the innocence of this public, continue to use the same old cinematic conventions to show it the same sort of distant adventures enacted by stars who have lived in its place—stars whose most intimate affairs it can ogle through the media keyhole.

A rider falls, struck by an arrow. Voice-over: "Meet again the man who became a legend with his daring exploits on behalf of the oppressed. . . . *The Black Arrow of Robin Hood* is the story of a man without fear, who never hesitated to fight single-handedly against a tyrant." An enraged nobleman shouts: "Go away! Get out, all of you! Robin Hood is dead and gone!" An army advances, singing, toward hostile ramparts. With appropriate background music, the voice-over resumes: "No! Robin Hood is more alive than ever, and he will thrill you with his amazing daring."

The cinema I am talking about is a deranged imitation of a deranged life, a production skillfully designed to communicate nothing. It serves no purpose but to while away an hour of boredom with a reflection of that same boredom. This craven imitation is the dupe of the present and the false witness of the future, feeding on itself through a mass of fictions and grandiose spectacles that amount to nothing

Complete preview for a completely mediocre Western.

but a useless accumulation of images that time sweeps away. What childish respect for images! This Vanity Fair is well suited to these plebeian spectators, constantly oscillating between enthusiasm and disappointment; lacking in taste because they have had no happy experience of anything, and refusing to admit their unhappy experiences because they lack courage as well as taste. Which is why they never cease being taken in by every sort of fraud, general or particular, that appeals to their self-interested credulity.

Amazingly enough, despite all the obvious evidence to the contrary, there are still some cretins, among the specialized spectators hired to edify their fellow viewers, who claim that it is "dogmatic" to state some truth in a film unless it is also *proved* by images. The latest fashion in intellectual lackeydom enviously refers to whatever describes its servitude as "the master discourse." As for the ludicrous dogmas of its actual bosses, it identifies with them so completely that it doesn't even recognize their existence. What needs to be proved by images? Nothing is ever proved except by the real movement that

dissolves existing conditions—that is, the existing production relations and the forms of false
consciousness that have developed on the basis
of those relations.

No error has ever collapsed for lack of a good
image. For those who believe that the capital-
ists are well equipped to manage with continually increasing rationality our continually
increasing happiness and the ever more diverse
pleasures of our purchasing power, these figures will appear to be capable statesmen; and
those who believe that Stalinist bureaucrats
constitute the party of the proletariat will see
these as fine working-class mugs. The existing
images only reinforce the existing lies.

Dramatized anecdotes have been the building
blocks of the cinema. Its perennial characters
have been inherited from the theater and the
novel, though they act on a more spacious and
mobile stage with more directly visible cos-
tumes and settings. It is a particular society,
not a particular technology, that has made
the cinema like that. It could have consisted of

Pan shot of the government
ministers of the Fifth Republic.

French Stalinist leaders.

Mao Zedong toward the end of
his reign.

Close-up of a long kiss.

historical analyses, theories, essays, memoirs. It could have consisted of films like the one I am making at this moment.

In the present film, for example, I am simply stating a few truths over a background of images that are all trivial or false. This film disdains the image-scraps of which it is composed. I do not wish to preserve any of the language of this outdated art, except perhaps the reverse shot of the only world it has observed and a tracking shot across the fleeting ideas of an era. I pride myself on having made a film out of whatever rubbish was at hand; and I find it amusing that people will complain about it who have allowed their entire lives to be dominated by every kind of rubbish.

Zorro punches someone on a railroad track. His foot is caught between two rails. A train approaches. The villain leaves. Zorro gestures in vain, then sees that his whip is within reach. He grabs it, uses it to flick the rail switch, and jumps free just before the train goes by.

Long tracking shot of troops landing on a beach, June 6, 1944.

I have merited the universal hatred of the society of my time, and I would have been annoyed to have any other merits in the eyes of such a society. But I have noticed that it is in the cinema that I have aroused the most extreme and unanimous outrage. This distaste has been so intense that I have even been plagiarized much less in

Tracking shot from a boat, moving from Giudecca Island toward Venice.

this domain than elsewhere—up until now at least. My very existence as a filmmaker remains a generally refuted hypothesis. I thus see myself placed beyond all the laws of the genre. But as Swift remarked, "It is no small satisfaction to present a work that is beyond all criticism."

What this era has written and filmed is so utterly contemptible that the only way anyone in the future will be able to offer even the slightest justification for it will be to claim that there was literally *no alternative*—that for some obscure reason absolutely nothing else was possible. Unfortunately for those who are reduced to such a clumsy excuse, my example alone will suffice to demolish it. And since this gratifying accomplishment has required relatively little time and trouble, I have seen no reason to forgo it.

Despite what some would like to believe, we can hardly expect revolutionary innovations from those whose profession is to monopolize the stage under the present social conditions. It is obvious that such innovations can come only

A Venetian lady.

Zorro, guns in hand, holds his enemy at bay. Then he gallops away, pursued by the bad guys, shooting back at them from time to time like a Parthian, without even bothering to turn around.

from people who have received universal hostility and persecution, not from those who receive government funding. More generally, despite the conspiracy of silence on this matter, it can be confidently affirmed that no real opposition can be carried out by individuals who become even slightly more socially elevated through manifesting such opposition than they would have been through refraining. We already have the well-known example of those flourishing political and labor-union functionaries, always ready to prolong the grievances of the proletariat for another thousand years in order to preserve their own role as its defender.

Tracking shot from a boat along a windowless wall of San Giorgio Island.

For my part, if I have succeeded in being so deplorable in the cinema, it is because I have been much more criminal elsewhere. From the very beginning I have devoted myself to overthrowing this society, and I have acted accordingly. I took this position at a time when almost everybody believed that this despicable society (in its bourgeois or bureaucratic version) had the most promising future. And since then I have not, like so many others, changed my views one or several times with the changing of the times. It is rather the times that have changed in accordance with my views. This is one of the main reasons I have aroused such animosity on the part of my contemporaries.

An Afghan hound shows an extreme reluctance to get into an automobile.

Thus, instead of adding one more film to the thousands of commonplace films, I prefer to explain why I shall do nothing of the sort. I am going to replace the frivolous adventures typically recounted by the cinema with the examination of an important subject: myself.

Zorro rides on horseback alongside a moving train, then jumps onto the last car. He climbs a wall, grabs a machine gun, and points it at some bad guys, who surrender.

An old intellectual, the victim of an assassination, asks Zorro: "But before I die, may I know who you are?" Zorro sends everyone else away and lifts his mask.

I have sometimes been reproached—wrongly, I believe—for making difficult films. Now I am actually going to make one. To those who are annoyed that they can't understand all the allusions, or who even admit that they have no idea of what I'm really getting at, I will merely reply that they should blame their own sterility and lack of education rather than my methods;

Establishing shots and close-ups of a Kriegspiel board game on which two armies are deployed.

they have wasted their time at college, bargain shopping for worn-out fragments of second-hand knowledge.

Considering the story of my life, it is obvious to me that I cannot produce a cinematic "work" in the usual sense of the term. I think the substance and form of the present communication will convince anyone that this is so.

I must first of all repudiate the most false of legends, according to which I am some sort of theoretician of revolutions. The petty people of the present age seem to believe that I have approached things by way of theory, that I am a builder of theory—a sort of intellectual architecture which they imagine they need only move in to as soon as they know its address, and which, ten years later, they might even slightly remodel by rearranging a few sheets of paper, so as to attain the definitive theoretical perfection that will assure their salvation.

But theories are only made to die in the war of time. Like military units, they must be sent into battle at the right moment; and whatever their

Colonel Custer leads the last charge of the Seventh Cavalry Regiment at Little Big Horn.

merits or insufficiencies, they can only be used
if they are on hand when they're needed. They
have to be replaced because they are constantly
being rendered obsolete—by their decisive victories even more than by their partial defeats.
Moreover, no vital eras were ever engendered by
a theory; they began with a game, or a conflict,
or a journey. What Jomini said of war can also
be said of revolution: "Far from being an exact
or dogmatic science, it is an art subject to a few
general principles, and even more than that, an
impassioned drama."

What passions do we have, and where have they
led us? Most people, most of the time, have
such a tendency to follow ingrained routines
that even when they propose to revolutionize
life from top to bottom, to make a clean slate
and change everything, they nevertheless see no
contradiction in following the course of studies
accessible to them and then taking up one or
another paid position at their level of competence (or even a little above it). This is why
those who impart to us their thoughts about
revolutions usually refrain from letting us
know how they have actually lived.

The regiment, completely
surrounded by Indians on
horseback, halts and dismounts.

Tracking shot from a boat,
beginning in the Giudecca Canal
and moving toward Giudecca
Island.

But I, not being that type of person, can only tell of "the knights and ladies, the arms and loves, the gallant conversations and bold adventures" of a unique era.

Others may define and measure the course of their past in relation to their advancement in some career, or their acquisition of various kinds of goods, or in some cases their accumulation of socially recognized scientific or aesthetic works. Not having known any such frame of reference, I merely see, when I look back on the passage of this disorderly time, the elements that consti-tuted it for me, or the words and faces that evoke them—days and nights, cities and persons, and underlying it all, an incessant war.

I have passed my life in a few countries in Europe, and it was in the middle of the century, when I was nineteen, that I began to lead a fully inde-pendent life; and immediately found myself at home with the most ill-famed of companions.

A map of Europe.

Debord at nineteen.

It was in Paris, a city that was then so beautiful that many people preferred to be poor there rather than rich anywhere else.

A map of Paris at the end of the nineteenth century.

Who, now that nothing of it remains, will be able to understand this, apart from those who remember its glory? Who else could know the pleasures and exhaustions we experienced in these neighborhoods where everything has now become so dismal?

Various aerial photos of Paris, viewed as stills or traversed in tracking shots.

"Here was the abode of the ancient king of Wu. Grass now grows peacefully on its ruins. There, the vast palace of the Tsin, once so splendid and so dreaded. All this is gone forever—events, people, everything constantly slips away, like the ceaseless waves of the Yangtze that vanish into the sea."

Couperin: Royal Concerto #4 (Prelude).

The music ends.

The Paris of that time, within the confines of its twenty districts, was never entirely asleep; on any night a bacchanal might shift from one neighborhood to another, then to another and yet another. Its inhabitants had not yet been driven out and dispersed. A people remained who had barricaded their streets and routed their kings a dozen times. They were not con-

Crowd shots on the Boulevard du Crime, reconstructed for *The Children of Paradise*.

tent to subsist on images. When they lived in their own city, no one would have dared to make them eat or drink the sort of products that the chemistry of adulteration had not yet dared to invent.

The houses in the center were not yet deserted, or resold to cinema spectators born elsewhere, under other exposed-beam roofs. The modern commodity system had not yet fully demon-strated what can be done to a street. The city planners had not yet forced anyone to travel far away to sleep.

Governmental corruption had not yet darkened the clear sky with the artificial fog of pollution which now permanently blankets the mechani-cal circulation of things in this vale of desola-   More aerial photos of Paris.
tion. The trees were not yet dead from suffoca-tion; the stars were not yet extinguished by the progress of alienation.

Liars were in power, as always; but economic development had not yet given them the means to lie about everything, or to confirm their lies by falsifying the actual content of all production. One would have been as astonished then to find printed or built in Paris all the books that have since been composed of cement and asbestos, and all the buildings that have since been built out of dull sophisms, as one would be today to see the sudden reappearance of a Donatello or a Thucydides.

Morning in the Les Halles district.

Musil, in *The Man Without Qualities,* notes that "there are intellectual pursuits in which a man may take more pride in writing a brief article than a thick volume. If, for example, someone were to discover that under certain hitherto unobserved circumstances stones were able to speak, it would require only a few pages to describe and explain such a revolutionary phenomenon." I shall thus limit myself to a few words to announce that, whatever others may say about it, Paris no longer exists. The destruction of Paris is only one striking example of the fatal illness that is currently wiping out all the major cities, and that illness is in turn only one of the numerous symptoms of the material decay of this society. But Paris had more to lose

Tracking shot of Paris while moving up the Seine.

than any other. Bliss it was to be young in that city when for the last time it glowed with so intense a flame.

There was at that time on the left bank of the river—you cannot enter the same river twice, nor twice touch the same perishable substance—a neighborhood where the negative held court.

The 6th Arrondissement seen from above, with the Seine in the foreground.

It is a commonplace that in periods shaken by momentous changes, even the most innovative people have a hard time freeing themselves from many outdated ideas and tend to retain at least a few of them, because they find it impossible to totally reject as false and worthless assertions that are universally accepted.

Teenagers dancing.

Comic strip: Prince Valiant at a table in the "Cave of Time." A young woman says to him: "This cave is the trophy room of Time, which none dare enter."

It must be added, however, when one has practical experience of this type of situation, that such difficulties cease to matter the moment a group of people begins to base its real existence on a deliberate rejection of what is universally accepted, and on total indifference to the possible consequences.

Graffiti on a wall: "Never work!"

A group at a café counter at the end of the night.

Prince Valiant replies to the young woman: "I do not understand the meaning of your words, but your wine is potent: already my head swims."

Those who had gathered in this neighborhood seemed to have publicly and from the very beginning adopted as their sole principle of action the secret that the Old Man of the Mountain was said to divulge only on his deathbed to the most loyal lieutenant among his fanatical followers: "Nothing is true, everything is permitted." They accorded no importance whatsoever to those of their contemporaries who were not among them, and I think they were right in this; and if they related to anyone from the past, it was Arthur Cravan, deserter of seventeen nations, or perhaps also the cultivated bandit Lacenaire.

Saint-Germain-des-Prés people at a café terrace. Then inside the same café—a guitar tune, encounters, conversations.

Lacenaire says to some members of the owning class: "It takes all kinds to make a world—or to unmake it." They reply: "Very clever. Only a little play on words, but amusing." "Most amusing." "Indeed."

In this setting extremism had declared itself independent of any particular cause and disdained to entangle itself in any particular project. A society which was already tottering, but which was not yet aware of this because the old rules were still respected everywhere else, had momentarily left the field open for that

A Kotoko city on the bank of the Niger.
Another one.

The previously seen group of drinkers at dawn.

ever-present but usually repressed sector of society: the incorrigible underworld; the salt of the
earth; people quite sincerely ready to set the
world on fire just to make it shine.

Continuation of teenagers
dancing.

"Article 488. The age of adulthood is 21 years; a
person of that age is capable of all acts of civil
life."

THE SCREEN BECOMES BLANK
WHITE.

"A science of situations needs to be created,
which will borrow elements from psychology,
statistics, urbanism, and ethics. These elements
must be focused toward a totally new goal: the
conscious creation of situations."

"But no one talks about Sade in this film."

"Order reigns but doesn't govern."

"*Gun Crazy*. You remember. That's how it was.
No one was good enough for us. And yet . . .
Hailstones striking banners of glass. We won't
forget this cursed planet."

"Article 489. An adult who is usually in a state of imbecility or dementia, or who has frequent fits of rage, must be maintained in custody even if he has intervals of lucidity."

"Once again, after all the untimely answers and the aging of youth, night falls from on high."

"Like lost children we live our unfinished adventures."

In the balconies of a theater an indignant crowd chants: "Curtain!"

A film I made at that time, which naturally outraged the most advanced aesthetes, was like that from start to finish; and those piti-ful sentences were spoken over a completely blank white screen, interspersed with extreme-ly long passages of silence during which the screen remained completely dark. Some, no doubt, would like to believe that subsequent experience led to a more mature development of my talents or intentions. Experience of what—of some *improvement* in what I had already rejected? Don't make me laugh. Why should someone who strove to be so intolerable

A modern factory, through various openings, spews thick clouds of white fumes that cover virtually the entire screen.

in the cinema when he was young turn out to be more acceptable once he's older? What has been so bad can never really improve. People may say, "As he has aged, he has changed"; but he has also remained the same.

Debord at forty-five.

Lacenaire says to Garance: "I'm not cruel, I'm logical. I declared war on society long ago." Garance asks: "And have you killed many people lately, Pierre-François?" Lacenaire: "No, my angel. Look, no trace of blood, only a few ink stains! But rest assured, Garance, I'm preparing something extraordinary. . . . Even as a child, I was more lucid and more intelligent than the others. They never forgave me for it.. . . . What idiocy! But what a prodigious destiny!. . . I have no vanity, I have only pride. And I am sure of myself, absolutely sure. Petty thief by necessity, murderer by vocation, my path is already set, and I shall walk it with my head held high—until it falls under the guillotine, of course! . . . My father was always telling me: 'Pierre-François, you'll end up on the scaffold'." Garance: "He was right, Pierre-François, one should always listen to one's parents."

Although the select population of this momentary capital of disturbances included a certain number of thieves and occasionally a murderer or two, their life was primarily characterized by a prodigious inactivity; and of all the crimes and

Shady-looking characters enter the Redbreast Tavern.

offenses denounced there by the authorities, it was this that was sensed as the most threatening.

A thief approaches a table to ask an expert to evaluate some jewelry for him: "Is this real or fake?" . . . The expert turns to his neighbor, a newcomer: "What do you think of that, actor? Nothing to say? You're a wise man! Never say anything." An informer, who is also a peddler, enters, reciting his spiel: "Have you dreamed of cats? Or dogs? Have you seen troubled waters? Here's the explanation of all your dreams —a real book, with illustrations!" He greets the owner and warns him: "Lacenaire and his pals aren't far away. You've been warned." Lacenaire and his companions enter, including Garance.

It was the best possible labyrinth for ensnaring visitors. Those who lingered there for two or three days never left again, at least not until it had ceased to exist; but by then the majority had already seen the end of their none too numerous years. No one left those few streets and tables where the "highest of time" had been discovered.

Drinks are served at Lacenaire's table.

Garance asks: "So if I understand rightly, you are all some sort of philosophers?" Lacenaire: "Why not?" Garance exclaims: "I'm glad to hear it! Philosophy is so gay and pretty and decent!" One of Lacenaire's henchmen suggests throwing out someone who doesn't belong there. Lacenaire consents. The henchman gets up and makes his way through the dancers to the person concerned.

He grabs the intruder and shoves him through the front window.

Everyone took pride in having sustained such a magnificently disastrous challenge; and in fact I don't believe that any of those who passed that way ever acquired the slightest honest reputation in the world.

The owner protests: "What about my windows?" Lacenaire answers from his seat: "Why, can't we have fun anymore at the Redbreast?" while making a throat-cutting gesture. The owner, in a conciliatory tone: "Oh, Monsieur Lacenaire, I only meant . . ."

Each of us had more drinks every day than the number of lies told by a labor union during an entire wildcat strike. Gangs of police, guided by numerous informers, were constantly launching raids under every sort of pretext—most often searching for drugs or for girls under eighteen. I couldn't help remembering the charming hooligans and proud young women I hung out with in those shady dives when much later—the years having passed like our nights back then, without the slightest renunciation—I heard a song sung

Two police vans pull up in front of the Café des Poètes. Policemen rush in, blocking all the exits and demanding to see everyone's IDs.

A young woman goes by in a street at night.

by prisoners in Italy: "It's there you find those young girls who give you everything; first hello, and then their hand . . . . There's a bell in Via Filangieri; each time it rings, someone has been condemned. . . . The flower of youth dies in prison."

A corrupted minor.

Exterior view of the prison where the Baader–Meinhof Group were assassinated.

Andreas Baader and Gudrun Enslin.

Though they despised all ideological illusions and were quite indifferent to what might later prove them right, these reprobates had not disdained to openly declare what was to come. Putting an end to art, announcing in the middle of a cathedral that God was dead, plotting to blow up the Eiffel Tower—such were the little scandals sporadically indulged in by those whose ongoing way of life was itself such a big scandal. They asked themselves why certain revolutions had failed; and whether the proletariat actually existed; and if so, what it might be.

A man with a hat enters a Saint-Germain-des-Prés dive and talks for a long time with the owner.

Some drinkers philosophizing in another seedy bar.

An actress in another film sums up a discussion: "Some believe he thinks of us, others that he thinks us; yet others believe that he is asleep and that we are his dream—his bad dream."

When I talk about these people, I may seem to be making fun of them; but that is not so. I

Tracking shot over other tables occupied by the same sort of riffraff.

drank their wine and I remain faithful to them. And I don't believe that anything I have done since then has made me better in any way than they were back then.

Considering the overpowering forces of habit and the law, which continually pressured us to disperse, none of us could be sure we would still be there at the end of the week. Yet everything we would ever love was there. Time burned more intensely than elsewhere, and would soon run out. We felt the earth shake.

A schoolgirl flees through the streets at night.

The entrance of a dingy café.

A Venetian conspirator says to his companion: "Soon we'll reach the mainland. Then we'll be able to meet more often."

Suicide carried off many. "Drink and the devil had done for the rest," as a song says.

People in a cellar bar.

Midway on the journey of real life we found ourselves surrounded by a somber melancholy, reflected by so much sad banter in the cafés of lost youth.

A young woman slowly goes through a revolving door in the same neighborhood.

The decor and the company together.

" 'Tis all a checkerboard of nights and days, where Destiny with men for pieces plays: hither

An encounter in the previously seen cellar bar.

and thither moves and checks and slays, and one by one back in the closet lays."

Chess players.

"How many ages hence shall this our lofty scene be acted over, in states unborn and accents yet unknown!"

Ivan Chtcheglov.

"What is writing? The guardian of history. . . . What is man? A slave of death, a passing traveler, a guest on earth. . . . What is friendship? The equality of friends."

Gil J Wolman.

Robert Fonta.

Ghislain de Marbaix.

"Bernard, what do you want from the world? Do you see there anything that can satisfy you? . . . She vanishes, fleeing like a ghost which, having given us some sort of contentment while it remained with us, leaves nothing but disquietude in its wake. . . . Bernard, Bernard, he used to say, this green youth will not last forever."

Debord at twenty.

She who was the most beautiful that year.

Art Blakey: "Whisper Not."

The music ends.

But nothing expresses this restless and exitless present better than this ancient sentence that turns completely back on itself, being

Tracking shot in a deserted Parisian square at night.

constructed letter by letter like an inescapable labyrinth, thus perfectly uniting the form and content of perdition: *In girum imus nocte et consumimur igni.* We turn in the night, consumed by fire.

Pan shot across a Les Halles intersection at night.

Pan shot across a square and some houses at night, ending at the lights of a still-open café.

The same woman reappears.

"A generation goes and another generation comes, but the earth remains forever. The sun rises and the sun goes down, and hastens to the place where it rises. . . . All the rivers run to the sea, yet the sea is not full; they return to the place where they started and flow again. . . . For every thing there is a season, and a time for every purpose under heaven: . . . a time to kill and a time to heal; a time to break down and a time to build up; . . . a time to rend and a time to sew; a time to keep silent and a time to speak. . . . Better is the sight of the eyes than the wandering of desire, for that too is vanity and a striving after wind. . . . For who knows what is good for man while he lives the few days of his vain life, which pass like a shadow?"

Long tracking shot following a troop of soldiers emerging from an adjacent street and running along a canal; losing many men under enemy fire; and finally crossing a bridge.

"No, let us cross over the river and rest under the shade of those trees."

The Seine and the western tip of the Île de la Cité.

It was there that we acquired the toughness that has stayed with us all the days of our life, and that has enabled several of us to remain so lightheartedly at war with the whole world. And as for myself in particular, I suspect that the circumstances of that time were the apprenticeship that enabled me to make my way so instinctively through the subsequent chain of events, which included so much violence and so many breaks, and where so many people were treated so badly—passing through all those years as if with a knife in my hand.

Perhaps we might not have been quite so ruthless if we had found some already-initiated project that seemed to merit our support. But there was no such project. The only cause we supported we had to define and launch ourselves. There was nothing above us that we could respect.

For someone who thinks and acts in this manner, there is no point in listening a moment too long to those who find something good, or

Tracking shot from a boat, along the walls of the Venice Arsenal.

even merely something worth tolerating, within the present conditions; nor to those who stray from the path they seemed to have intended to follow; nor even, in some cases, to those who simply don't catch on in time. Other people, years later, began advocating the revolution of everyday life with their timid voices or prostituted pens—but from a distance and with the calm assurance of astronomical observation. But someone who has actually taken part in an endeavor of this kind, and who has escaped the dazzling catastrophes that accompany it or follow in its wake, is not in such an easy position. The heats and chills of such a time never leave you. You have to discover how to live the days ahead in a manner worthy of such a fine beginning. You want to prolong that first experience of illegality.

This is how, little by little, a new era of conflagrations was set ablaze, of which none of us alive at this moment will see the end. Obedience is dead. It is wonderful to note that disturbances originating in a lowly and ephemeral little neighborhood have ended up shaking the entire world order. (Such methods would obviously never shake up anything in a harmonious society that was capable of controlling all its forces; but it is now evident that our society was quite the contrary.)

As for myself, I have never regretted anything I have done; and being as I am, I must confess that I remain completely incapable of imagining how I could have done anything any differently.

Despite the harshness of the first phase of the conflict, our side tended toward a static, purely defensive position. Our spontaneous experimentation was not sufficiently conscious of itself; and since it was confined primarily to its particular locale, we had also tended to neglect the significant possibilities for subversion in the seemingly hostile world all around us. When we saw our defenses being overwhelmed and some of our comrades beginning to falter, a few of us felt that we should take the offensive: that instead of entrenching ourselves in the thrilling fortress of a moment, we should

Custer's regiment, in circle formation, is shot at during successive charges from the Indians who surround it. His soldiers fall one after another. The Indians finally overrun the position and kill all the defenders.

break out into the open, make a sortie, then hold our ground and devote ourselves quite simply to totally destroying this hostile world—in order to rebuild it, if possible, on other bases. There had been precedents to this, but they had been forgotten. We had to discover where the course of things was leading, and to refute that course so thoroughly that it would eventually be compelled to change directions in line with our own tastes. As Clausewitz amusingly remarks, "Whoever has genius must use it—that's one of the rules of the game." And Baltasar Gracián: "You must traverse the paths of time to reach the point of opportunity."

Custer alone remains standing. Throwing away his empty revolvers, he grabs his sword, which had been stuck in the ground in front of him, and awaits the onslaught of the victors.

But can I ever forget the one whom I see everywhere in the greatest moment of our adventures —he who in those uncertain days opened up a new path and forged ahead so rapidly, choosing those who would accompany him? No one else was his equal that year. It might almost have been said that he transformed cities and life merely by looking at them. In a single year he discovered enough material for a century of

Ivan Chtcheglov.

Comic strip: Riding in search of adventure, Prince Valiant "approaches the mysterious beam of light which shone where no human should be."

Pan shot over a palace at night. The shadow of an off-camera person at a crossroad.

demands; the depths and mysteries of urban space were his conquest.

"The Third Man" appears for a moment on a doorstep.

Comic strip: Prince Valiant and a companion, both in disguise. "Within the citadel hangs the heavy silence of an unhappy people. As the two friends make their way toward the palace, there is a sudden blast of trumpets."

The powers that be, with their pitiful falsified information which misleads them almost as much as it bewilders those under their administration, have not yet realized just how much the rapid passage of this man has cost them. But what does it matter? The names of ship-wreckers are only writ in water.

An ancient castle.

Prince Valiant passes some buildings in flames.

Ivan Chtcheglov.

Couperin: New Concerto #11 (1st movement).
Comic strip sequence: Prince Valiant, wrapped in a cloak: "After a long ride he comes to the sea, over which a great storm is brewing." He approaches a coastal village: "Lights shining faintly through the storm suggest a possible shelter." He enters a tavern: "He finds a tavern frequented by sailors and travelers from distant and mysterious lands." Travelers are conversing at every table: "As the storm rages outside, strange tales are told of fabulous isles and wondrous walled cities." A man traveling on foot: "Meanwhile a haggard wanderer approaches the tavern, bearing astounding news. (Next week: 'Rome Has Fallen!')"

We did not seek the formula for overturning the world in books, but in wandering. Ceaselessly drifting for days on end, none resembling the one before. Astonishing encounters, remarkable obstacles, grandiose betrayals, perilous enchantments—nothing was lacking in this quest for a different, more sinister Grail, which no one else had ever sought. And then one ill-fated day the finest player of us all got lost in the forests of madness. But there is no greater madness than the present organization of life.

Did we eventually find the object of our quest? There is reason to believe that we obtained at least a fleeting glimpse of it; because it is undeniable that from that point on we found ourselves capable of understanding false life in the light of true life, and possessed with a very strange power of seduction: for no one since then has ever come near us without wishing to follow us. We had rediscovered the secret of dividing what was united. We did not go on television to announce our discoveries. We did not seek grants from academic foundations or

The music fades out.

Dawn, Rue des Innocents.

Comic strip: "Dawn reveals a majestic castle, hidden in a valley in the heart of the mountains."
Another castle.

Castle of Ludwig II of Bavaria.

Tracking shot from a boat: entrance to the harbor of San Giorgio Island.

Lookouts and smugglers in a working-class district of Venice.

praise from the newspaper intellectuals. We brought fuel to the fire. In this manner we enlisted irrevocably in the Devil's party—the "historical evil" that leads existing conditions to their destruction, the "bad side" that makes history by undermining all established satisfaction.

Tracking shot from a boat in a very narrow canal of Venice.

The Devil in *Les Visiteurs du Soir*, who has just entered the main hall of the castle: "Oh, what a splendid fire! I dearly love fire! And it loves me. Look, see how affectionate its flames are, licking my fingers like a puppy would. It's so delectable! . . . But excuse me, I haven't introduced myself. Though it's true that my name and titles will not mean much to you—I come from so far away. Forgotten in his own country, unknown elsewhere, such is the fate of the traveler."

Those who have not yet begun to live but who are saving themselves for a better time, and who therefore have such a horror of growing old, are waiting for nothing less than a permanent paradise. Some of them locate this paradise in a total revolution, others in a career promotion, some even in both at once. In either case they are waiting to access what they have gazed upon in the inverted imagery of the spectacle: a happy, eternally present unity. But those who

Film preview: A crooner sings in a modern decor of the 1930s.

TEXT FRAME: "Coming soon to this theater."

Pan shot over the night lights of present-day Boulevard Saint-Germain.

have chosen to strike with the time know that
the time that is their weapon is also their master.
And they can hardly complain about this, because
it's an even harsher master to those who have no
weapons. If you don't fall in line with the decep-
tive clarity of this upside-down world, you are
seen, at least by those who believe in that world,
as a controversial legend, an invisible and mal-
evolent ghost, a perverse Prince of Darkness.
Which is in fact a fine title—more honorable
than any which the present system of floodlit
enlightenment is capable of bestowing.

We thus became emissaries of the Prince of
Division—"he who has been wronged"—and
undertook to drive to despair those who identi-
fied with humanity.

In the years that followed, people from twenty
countries entered into this obscure conspiracy of

Façades on Île Saint-Louis at
night.

The Devil asks some chess
players: "Have I interrupted your
game?" One of them responds:
"It doesn't matter, I was beaten
from the start." The Devil moves
one of the pieces: "You think so?
Checkmate. See, you've won.
Chess is such a simple game!"

Gilles and Dominique approach
the castle to which they will
bring so much trouble. In the
background is the music of their
song: "Sad lost children."

At night in the castle Dominique
says to Gilles: "Other people love
us, and they suffer for us. We
watch them and then we go
away. A fine journey, with the
Devil paying the expenses."

Asger Jorn.
Giuseppe Pinot-Gallizio.
Attila Kotányi.
Donald Nicholson-Smith.

limitless demands. How many hurried journeys! How many long disputes! How many
clandestine meetings in all the ports of Europe!

A train passes.

Thus was mapped out a program calculated to
undermine the credibility of the entire organization of social life. Classes and specializations,
work and entertainment, commodities and
urbanism, ideology and the state—we showed
that it all needed to be scrapped. And this program promised nothing more than an autonomy without rules or restrictions. These perspectives have now been widely adopted, and
people everywhere are fighting for or against
them. But back then they would certainly have
seemed delirious, if the behavior of modern
capitalism had not been even more delirious.

Pan shot over the participants
of the 8th Conference of the
Situationist International in
Venice.

Troops in echelon formation on
a battlefield. Slow movements
filmed from above.

There were indeed a few individuals who were
in more or less practical agreement with one or
another of our critiques; but there was no one
who recognized them all, let alone who was capable of articulating them and developing them in
practice. Which is why no other revolutionary
endeavor of this period has had the slightest influence on the transformation of the world.

Our agitators disseminated ideas that a class society *cannot stomach*. The intellectuals in the service of the system—themselves even more obviously in decline than the system itself—are now cautiously investigating these poisons in the hope of discovering some antidotes; but they won't succeed. They used to try just as hard to ignore them—but just as vainly, so great is the power of a truth spoken in its time.

A naval battle sequence during World War II.

A salute from all the cannons of a battleship.

While our seditious intrigues spread across Europe and even began to reach other continents, Paris, where one could so easily pass unnoticed, was still at the heart of all our journeys, the most frequented of our meeting places. But its landscapes had been ruined and everything was deteriorating and falling apart.

The Seine, in the center of Paris.

The Impasse de Clairvaux.

Aerial views of Paris: toward Place de la Contrescarpe, then up the Seine past the Quai de Bercy.

And yet the setting sun of this city left, in places, a few glimmers of light as we watched the fading of its final days, finding ourselves within surroundings that would soon be swept away, enraptured with beauties that will never return. We would soon have to leave it—this city which for us was so free but which was going to fall

Art Blakey: "Whisper Not."

Another woman wandering the streets.
More views of Paris.

completely into the hands of our enemies. *The music ends.*
Their blind law was already being relentlessly
applied, reconstructing everything in their own
image like a graveyard: "O wretchedness! O
grief! Paris is trembling."

We would have to leave it, but not without
having made an attempt to seize it by brute
force; we would finally have to abandon it, after
having abandoned so many other things, in
order to follow the road determined by the   Tracking shot of two armies
                                                confronting each other on a
necessities of our strange war, which has led us   Kriegspiel board.
so far.

For our aim had been none other than to
provoke a practical and public division between
those who still want the existing world and
those who will decide to reject it.

Other eras have had their own great conflicts,   Pan shot over a map of the ancient
                                                   world, from the Roman Empire to
conflicts which they did not choose but which   the Chinese Empire.
nevertheless forced people to choose one side
or the other. Such conflicts dominate whole
generations, founding or destroying empires
and their cultures. The mission is to take Troy

—or to defend it. There's a certain resemblance among these moments when people are on the verge of separating into opposing camps, never to see each other again.

At the beginning of the American Civil War, West Point cadets are at the point of going their separate ways. An oath of loyalty to the Union is read to them.

The colonel in charge of the Academy says: "Any officer or cadet who does not feel that he can in good conscience comply with the terms of this oath should line up to the right of this battalion." A mounted officer comes forward: "Gentlemen of the South, step forward from the ranks!" The Southerners do so and line up behind him. The colonel orders the remaining cadets to close ranks, then has the band play "Dixie" as the others march off.

It's a beautiful moment when an assault against the world order is set in motion.

The Light Brigade, in battle formation behind its flag-bearers, begins its famous charge into the "Valley of Death" at Balaklava.

From its almost imperceptible beginning you already know that, whatever happens, very soon nothing will ever again be the same as it was.

The charge begins slowly, picks up speed, passes the point of no return, and irrevocably collides with what seemed unassailable: the bulwark which was so solid and well defended, but which is also destined to be shaken and thrown into disorder.

That's what we did, emerging from the night, raising once again the banner of the "good old cause" and marching forth under the cannon-fire of time.

Along the way many of us died or were taken prisoner; many others were wounded and permanently put out of action; and certain elements even let themselves slip to the rear out of lack of courage; but I believe I can say that our formation as a whole never swerved from its line until it plunged into the very core of destruction.

The Russian commander is astonished at the strange foolhardiness of this frontal attack. Cannons open fire. The cavalry, heading right into them, fall by the dozens. The Light Brigade breaks into a gallop and continues its charge in extended formation. It is almost totally annihilated.

I have never quite understood those who have so often reproached me for having squandered this fine troop in a senseless assault, perhaps even out of some sort of Neronian self-indulgence. I admit that I was the one who chose the moment and direction of the attack, and I therefore take full responsibility for everything that happened. But what did these critics expect? Were we supposed to refrain from fighting an enemy that was already on the move against us? And didn't I always put myself

several steps ahead of the front line? Those who
never take action would like to believe that you
can freely determine the quality of your fellow
combatants and the time and place where you
can strike an unstoppable and definitive blow.
But in reality you have to act with what is at
hand, launching an attack on one or another
realistically attackable position the moment you
see a favorable opportunity; otherwise you fade
away without having done a thing. The strategist
Sun Tzu recognized long ago that "advantage
and danger are both inherent in maneuver." And
Clausewitz notes that "in war neither side is ever
certain about the situation of the other. One
must become accustomed to acting in accordance with general probabilities; it is an illusion
to wait for a time when one will be completely
aware of everything." Despite the fantasies of the
spectators of history who try to set up shop as
strategists and who see everything from the van-
tage point of Sirius, the most sublime theory can
never guarantee an event. On the contrary, it is
the unfolding of an event that may or may not
verify a theory. Risks must be taken, and you
have to pay up front to see what comes next.

Other equally distant but less lofty spectators, having seen the end of this attack but not its beginning, have failed to take into account the differences between the two stages, and have detected some faults in the alignment of our ranks and concluded that by that point our uniforms were no longer impeccably egalitarian. I think this can be attributed to the enemy fire that had pounded us for so long. As a struggle approaches its culmination, it becomes more important to judge the result than the deportment. To listen to those who seem to be complaining that the battle was begun without waiting for them, the main result was the fact that an avant-garde was sacrificed and completely pulverized in the collision. In my opinion that was precisely its purpose.

Avant-gardes have only one time; and the best thing that can happen to them is to have enlivened their time without outliving it. After them, operations move onto a vaster terrain. Too often have we seen such elite troops, after they have accomplished some valiant exploit, remain on hand to parade with their medals and then turn against the cause they previously supported. Nothing of this sort need be feared from those whose attack has carried them to the point of dissolution.

I wonder what more some people had hoped for. The particular wears itself out fighting. A historical project can hardly expect to preserve an eternal youth, sheltered from every blow.

Sentimental objections are as vain as pseudo-strategical quibbles. "Yet your bones will waste away, buried in the fields of Troy, your mission unfulfilled."

On a battlefield King Frederick II of Prussia rebuked a hesitant young officer: "Dog! Were you hoping to live forever?" And Sarpedon says to Glaukos in the Twelfth Book of *The Iliad:* "My friend, if you and I could escape this battle and live forever, ageless and immortal, I myself would never fight again. . . . But a thousand deaths surround us and no man can escape them. So let us move in for the attack."

When the smoke clears, many things appear changed. An age has passed. Don't ask now what good our weapons were: they remain in the throat of the reigning system of lies. Its air of innocence will never return.

The few survivors of the 17th Lancers who have managed to reach the enemy battery thrust their lances into the traitor they had sought.

After this splendid dispersal, I realized that I had to quickly conceal myself from a fame that threatened to become far too conspicuous. It is well known that this society signs a sort of peace treaty with its most outspoken enemies by granting them a place in its spectacle. I am, in fact, the only present-day individual with any negative or underground notoriety whom it has not managed to get to appear on that stage of renunciation.

Warships change course and move into the distance, leaving a smoke screen behind them.

A man passes a deserted crossroad in Venice.

Leading his squadron's engagement, an admiral asks: "How much fuel do we have left?" His flag captain replies: "We'll have to stop fighting in two hours, sir." The admiral raises his binoculars to his eyes. The musical accompaniment crescendos.

TEXT FRAME: "At this point the spectators, who have already been deprived of everything else, will also be deprived of images."

THE SCREEN BECOMES TOTALLY DARK.

The difficulties do not end there. I would find it just as repugnant to become an authority within the opposition to this society as to be one within this society itself; which is not putting it too mildly. I have thus refused to take the lead of all sorts of subversive ventures in several different regions, each more antihierarchical than the others but whose command I was nevertheless offered on the basis of my talent and experience in these matters. I wanted to show that it is possible for someone to achieve some historical successes and yet remain as poor in power and prestige as before (what I have had on a purely personal level from the beginning has always been enough for me).

I have also refused to polemicize about a thousand details with the numerous interpreters and co-opters of what has already been done. I had no interest in awarding diplomas in some sort of fantasized orthodoxy, nor in judging among diverse naïve ambitions that would collapse soon enough on their own. These people were unaware that time does not wait; that good intentions are not enough; and that nothing can be acquired or held on to from a past that can no longer be rectified. The underlying movement that will carry our historical struggles as far as they may go remains the sole judge of the past—insofar as that movement continues to act in its own time. I have managed things in such a way as to prevent any pseudocontinuation from falsifying the history of our operations. Those who eventually do better will be qualified to comment on their predecessors, and their comments will not go unnoticed.

I have found ways of intervening from farther away, while being aware that, as always, the majority of observers would have much preferred that I remain silent. I have long striven to maintain an obscure and elusive existence, and this has enabled me to further develop my strategical experiments, which had already begun so well. As someone not without abilities once put it, this is a field which no one can ever master. The results of these investigations—and this is the only good news in the present communication—will not be presented in cinematic form.

Close-ups of Kriegspiel battles.

But all ideas are inevitably vain when greatness can no longer be found in each day's existence—the complete works of the kennel-bred thinkers marketed at this stage of commodity decomposition cannot disguise the taste of the fodder they've been raised on. This is why I spent those years living in a country where I was little known. The spatial arrangement of one of the best cities that ever was, and the company of certain persons, and what we did with our time—all this formed a scene much like the happiest revels of my youth.

Crude reenactment of an officer's ball of the old British India Army, advertising some neo-beverage.

In the midst of a rich wood-paneled decor, a bottle of one of the miserable neo-beers produced by the latest chemical-industrial processes.

Bird's-eye view of Florence when it was a free city.

Alice and Celeste.

Celeste nude.

Nowhere did I seek a peaceable society—which is fortunate, because I never found one. I'm widely slandered in Italy, where I am rumored to be a terrorist. But I am quite indifferent to the most diverse accusations because it has been my lot to provoke them wherever I've roamed, and because I know why. The only thing of importance to me is what captivated me in that country and what could not have been found elsewhere.

Tracking shot over an aerial photo of Florence, from the Oltrarno to the Signoria.

I see her again, she who was like a stranger in her own town. ("Each of us is a citizen of the one

A Florentine woman.

true city; but in your meaning, I am one who passed my earthly exile in Italy.") I see again "the banks of the Arno, full of farewells."

And I too, like so many others, have been banished from Florence.

Tracking shot across an aerial photo of Florence, slowly moving down the Arno River.

Art Blakey: "Whisper Not."

Celeste's face; then other nude young women.

The music ends.

In any case, one traverses an era like one passes the Dogana promontory—that is to say, rather quickly.

Tracking shot from a boat, passing the Dogana promontory.

At first, as it's approaching, you don't notice it. Then you discover it as you come abreast of it, and you cannot fail to recognize that it was designed to be seen in this particular way and no other. But already we are rounding the cape, and leaving it behind us, and heading into unknown waters.

"When we were young we to a master went, and took great pride in learned argument. But what did all this lead to in the end? We came forth like water and are gone like the wind."

Group photo of dadaists.
Cardinal de Retz.
General von Clausewitz.

Tracking shot from an airplane machine-gunning troops that have just landed on a beach; the troops scatter.

Years have gone by and the characters in *Children of Paradise* have all become famous in one way or another. Lacenaire and Garance meet again. She asks him: "But tell me, what has happened with you?" He replies: "I've become famous. I've pulled off a few little crimes that created quite a sensation—the name of Lacenaire has more than once filled the pages of the judicial chronicles." Garance smiles: "Why, that's glory, Pierre-François." Lacenaire: "Yes, it's a beginning. All the same, I would have preferred a dazzling literary success."

In a space of twenty years you can really live in only a small number of homes. These of mine have all been poor, but they have always been well situated. Those were admitted who deserved to be; the rest were turned away at the door. Freedom then had few other such havens.

A house on the Impasse de Clairvaux.

Another on Rue Saint-Jacques.

Another on Rue Saint-Martin.

Another in the hills of Chianti.

Another in Florence.

Another in the mountains of Auvergne.

"Where are those merry companions of times gone by?" These are dead; another lived even more quickly, until the iron gates of insanity snapped shut.

Ghislain de Marbaix.

Robert Fonta. Asger Jorn.

Comic strip: Prince Valiant overpowered by guards.

Enchained in prison in *Les Visiteurs du Soir,* Gilles sings: "Sad lost children, we wander in the night. Where are the flowers of day, the pleasures of love, the lights of life? Sad lost children, we wander in the night. The devil cunningly carries us away, far from our beloved ones. Our joyful youth is gone, and so are our loves." After the first two sentences, the soundtrack of the song continues over the following images: an unknown woman; the Light Brigade (in a remake of the old film) rides to battle; a young former love; another current one; others from the past.

The sensation of the passing of time has always been vivid for me, and I have been attracted by it just as others are allured by dizzying heights or by water. In this sense I have loved my era, which has seen the end of all existing security and the dissolution of everything that was socially ordained. These are pleasures that the practice of the greatest art would not have given me.

Debord at nineteen.
At twenty-five.
At twenty-seven.

At thirty-one.

At forty-five.

Rembrandt's last self-portrait.

As for what we have done, how could the present outcome be assessed? The landscape we are now traversing has been devastated by a war this society is waging against itself, against its own potentialities. The uglification of everything was probably an inevitable price of the conflict. If we have begun to win, it is because the enemy has pushed its mistakes so far.

A row of giant towers besieges the old Paris.

Views of the current neo-Paris and of other landscapes ravaged for the sake of commodity abundance.

The most fundamental issue in this war, for which so many fallacious explanations have been given, is that it is no longer a struggle between conservatism and change; it is a struggle over which *kind* of change it will be. We, more than anyone else, were the people of change in a changing time. The owners of society, in order to maintain their position, were obliged to strive for a change that was the opposite of ours. We wanted to rebuild everything and so did they, but in diametrically opposed directions. What they have done is a sufficient negative demonstration of the nature of our own project. Their immense works have led them to nothing but this corruption. Their hatred of the dialectic has brought them to this cesspit.

A dump for modern industrial wastes.

We had to destroy (and we had good weapons for doing this) any illusion of dialogue between these antagonistic perspectives. The facts would then speak for themselves. They have.

Scottish troops disembarking to the sound of bagpipes.

It has become ungovernable, this wasteland where new sufferings are disguised with the

Destruction and fires aboard a warship; evacuation of the wounded.

name of former pleasures, and where people are so afraid. They turn in the night, consumed by fire. They wake up in alarm and gropingly search for life. And word is getting around that those who have been expropriating that life have ended up losing it themselves.

A huge complex of neo-dwellings.

This civilization is on fire; the whole thing is capsizing and sinking. What splendid torpedoing!

A battleship keels over and sinks.

And what has become of me amid this appalling collapse—this shipwreck which I believe was necessary, and which it could even be said that I have worked for, since it is certainly true that I have avoided working at anything else?

Debord.

Could I apply what a poet of the T'ang Dynasty wrote, "On Parting from a Traveling Companion," to this point in my own history?

A Mexican goes by on a horse, leading a second horse that is carrying his baggage, and descends toward a river.

"Dismounting from my horse, I offered him the wine of farewell and asked him the goal of his journey. He replied: 'I have not succeeded in worldly affairs, so I am returning to the southern mountains to seek repose.' "

But no, I can see quite clearly that for me there will be no repose; first of all because nobody does me the honor of thinking that I have not succeeded in worldly affairs. But fortunately no one could say that I have been successful in such affairs, either. It thus must be admitted that there has been neither success nor failure for Guy Debord and his extravagant pretensions.

It was already the dawn of this exhausting day that we are now seeing draw to a close when the young Marx wrote to Ruge: "You can hardly claim that I think too highly of the present time. If I nevertheless do not despair of it, it is because its own desperate situation fills me with hope."

Preparing an era for a voyage through the cold waters of history has in no way dampened these passions of which I have presented such fine and sad examples.

A relief map of the mountains of Auvergne.

The previously seen Auvergne house, this time covered with snow.

Tracking shot from a boat, from one end to the other of a Venice canal.

As these final reflections on violence continue to demonstrate, for me there will be no turning back and no reconciliation.

No wising up and no settling down.

Having passed the last houses on the canal, the view opens onto a vast expanse of empty water.

Subtitle: To be gone through again from the beginning.

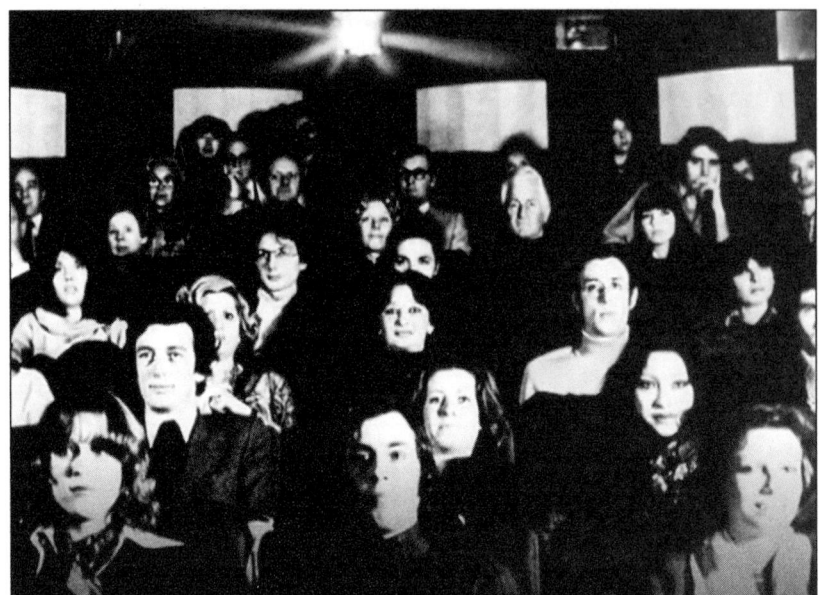

Nothing of importance has ever been communicated by pampering a public, not even one like that of the age of Pericles; and in the frozen mirror of the screen the spectators are not looking at anything that might suggest the respectable citizens of a democracy. [p. 133]

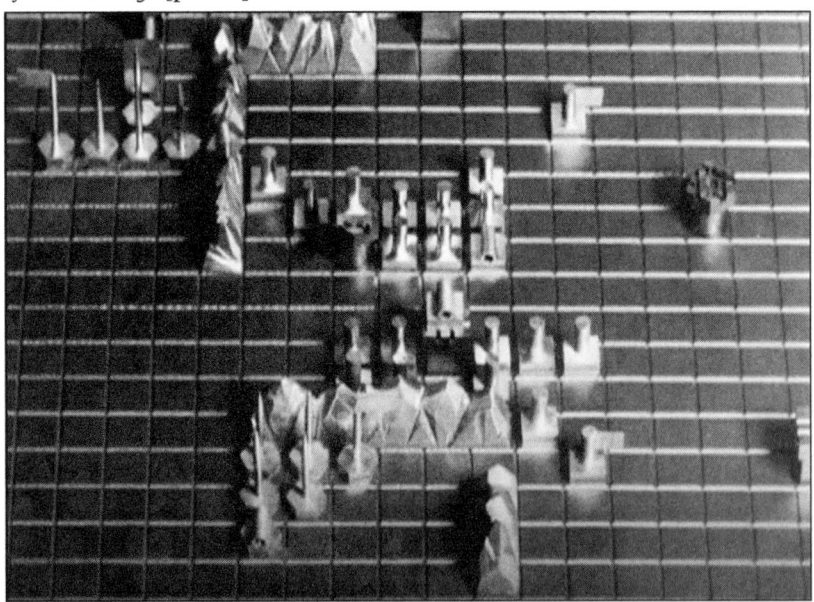

I have sometimes been reproached—wrongly, I believe—for making difficult films. Now I am actually going to make one. [p. 149]

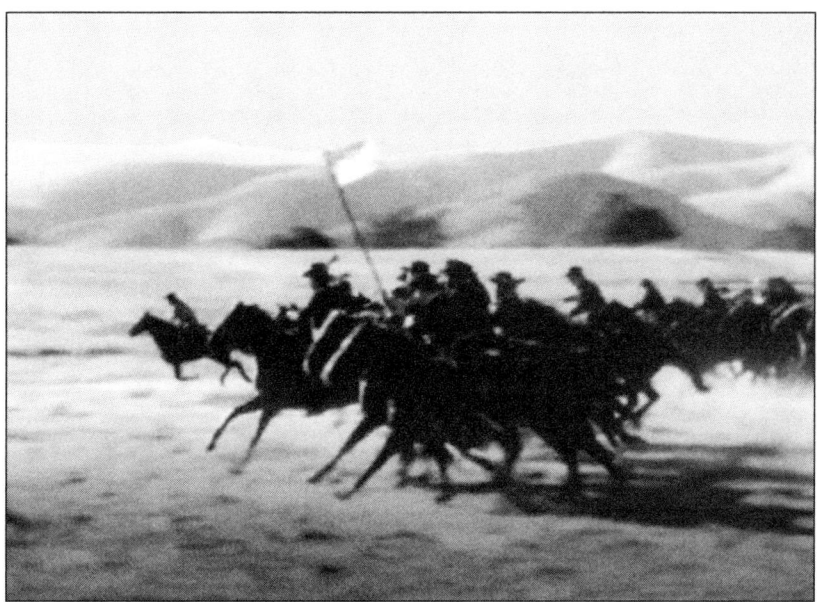

But theories are only made to die in the war of time. Like military units, they must be sent into battle at the right moment . . . [p. 150]

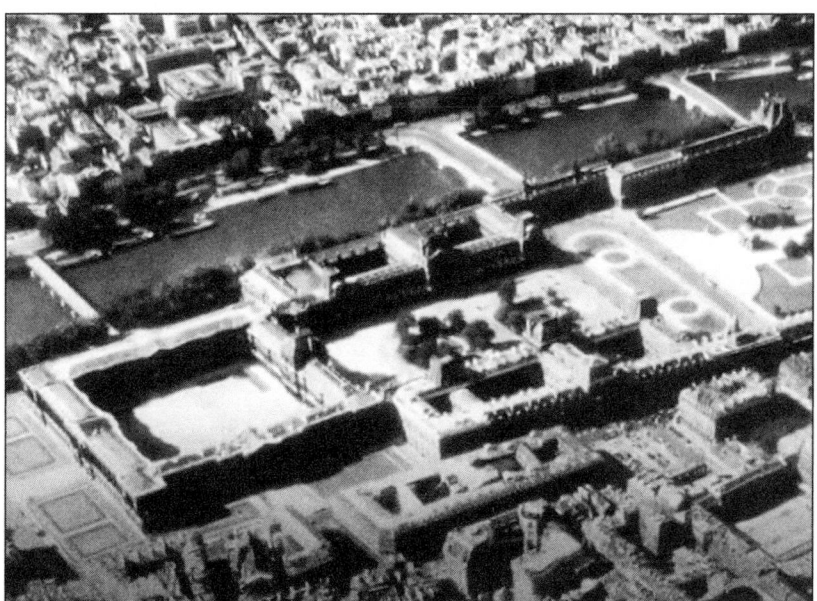

"Here was the abode of the ancient king of Wu. Grass now grows peacefully on its ruins. There, the vast palace of the Tsin, once so splendid and so dreaded. All this is gone forever—events, people, everything constantly slips away . . ." [p. 153]

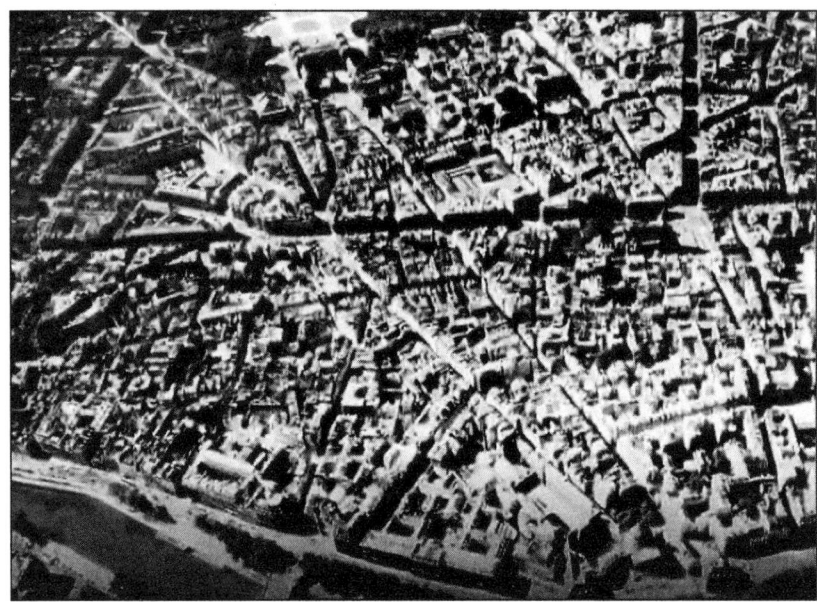

There was at that time on the left bank of the river—you cannot enter the same river twice, nor twice touch the same perishable substance—a neighborhood where the negative held court. [p. 156]

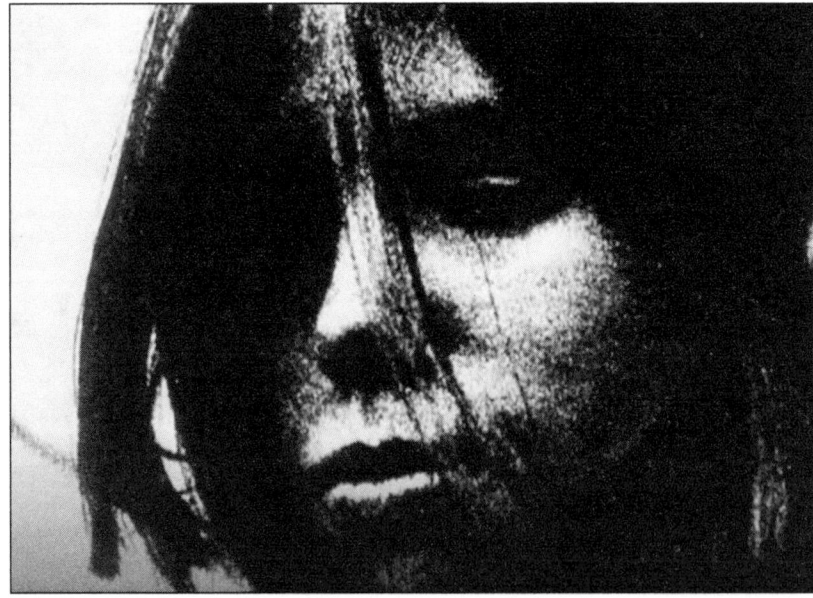

"It's there you find those young girls who give you everything; first hello, and then their hand . . ." [p. 163]

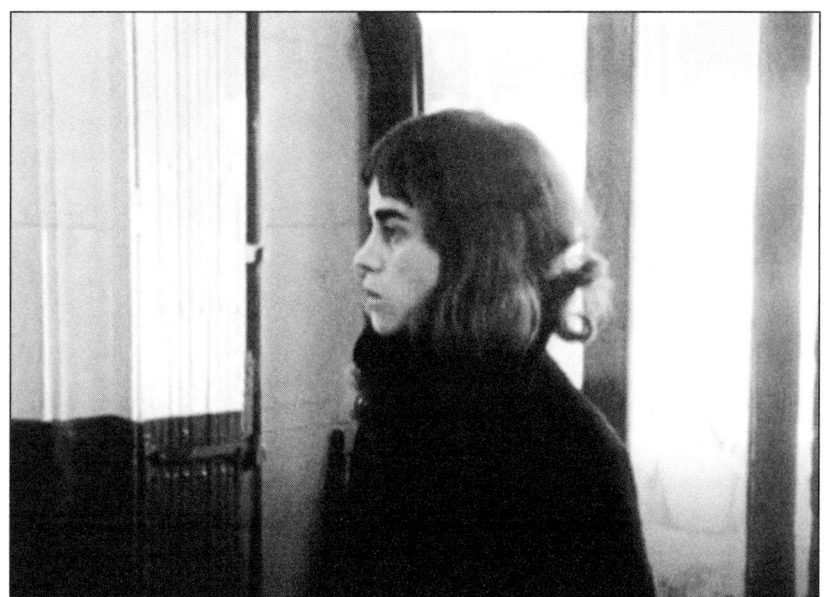

Midway on the journey of real life we found ourselves surrounded by a somber melancholy . . . [p. 164]

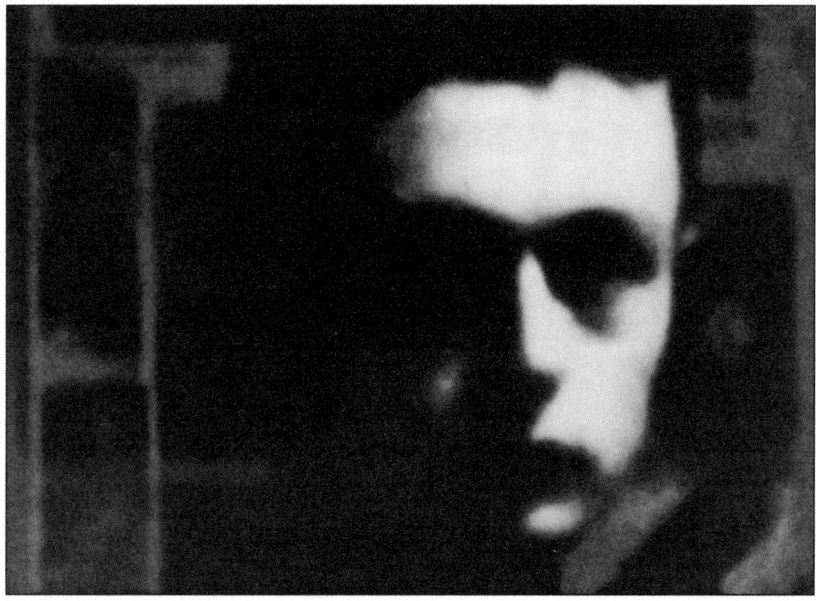

"How many ages hence shall this our lofty scene be acted over, in states unborn and accents yet unknown!" [p. 165]

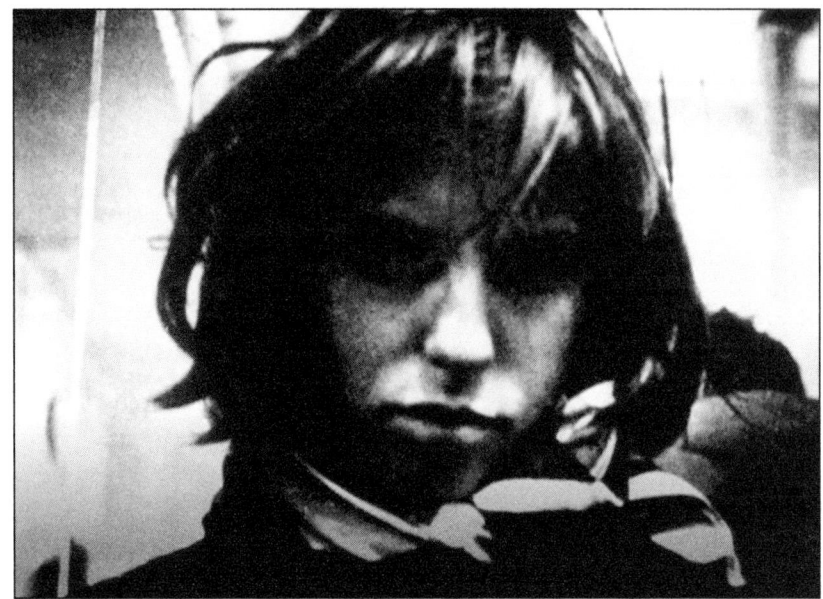

"She vanishes, fleeing like a ghost which, having given us some sort of contentment while it remained with us, leaves nothing but disquietude in its wake."
[p. 165]

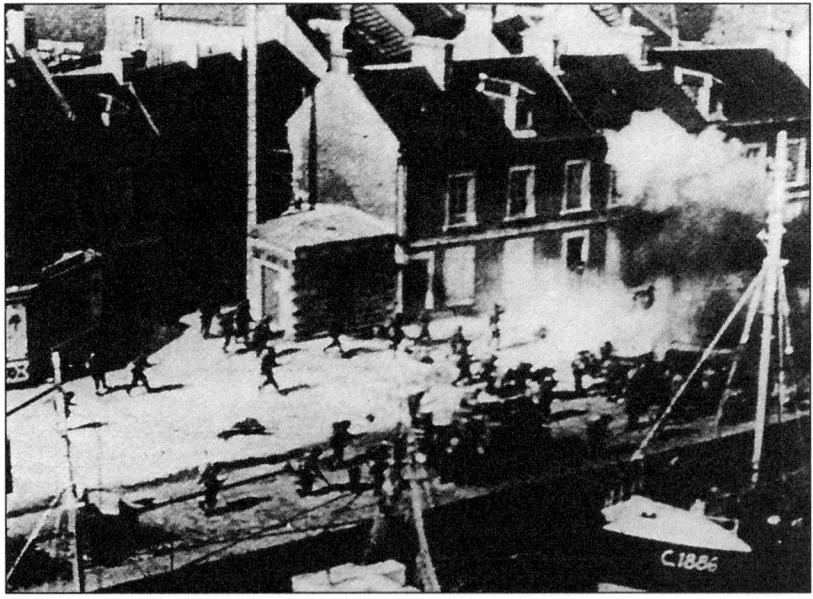

"A generation goes and another generation comes, but the earth remains forever. The sun rises and the sun goes down, and hastens to the place where it rises. . . ."
[p. 166]

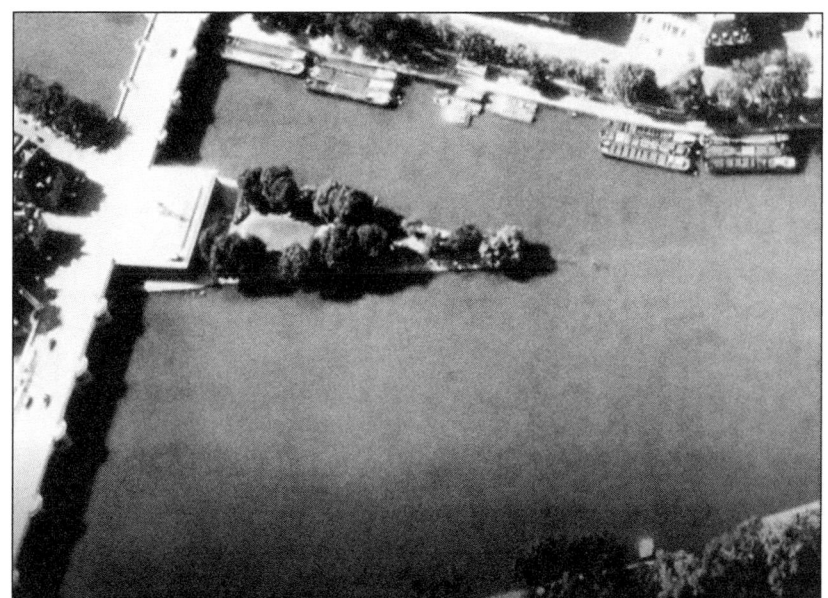

"No, let us cross over the river and rest under the shade of those trees." [p. 166]

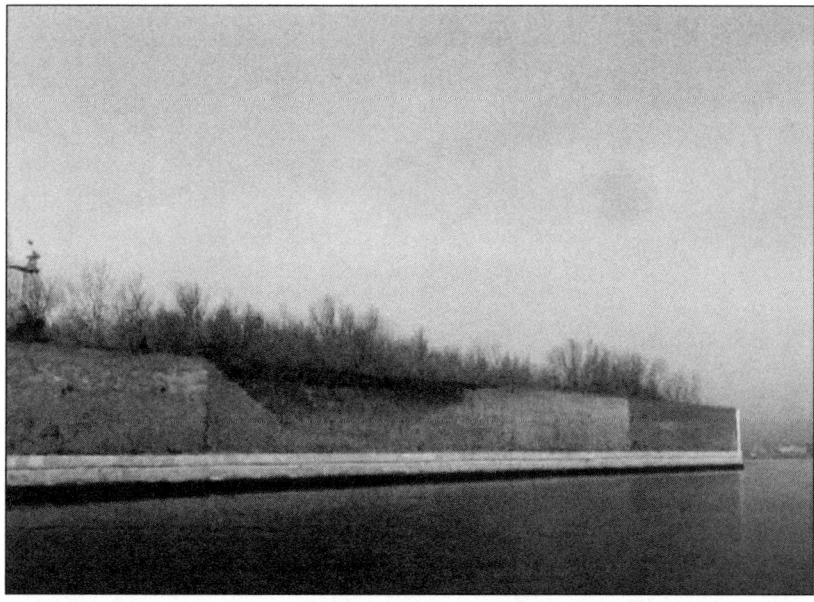

As for myself, I have never regretted anything I've done; and being as I am, I must confess that I remain completely incapable of imagining how I could have done anything any differently. [p. 169]

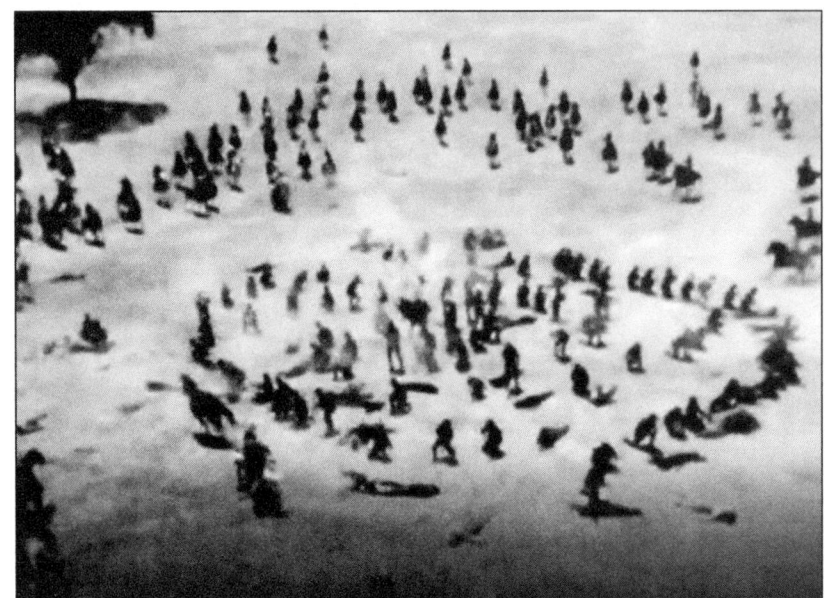

When we saw our defenses being overwhelmed and some of our comrades beginning to falter, a few of us felt that we should take the offensive. [p. 169]

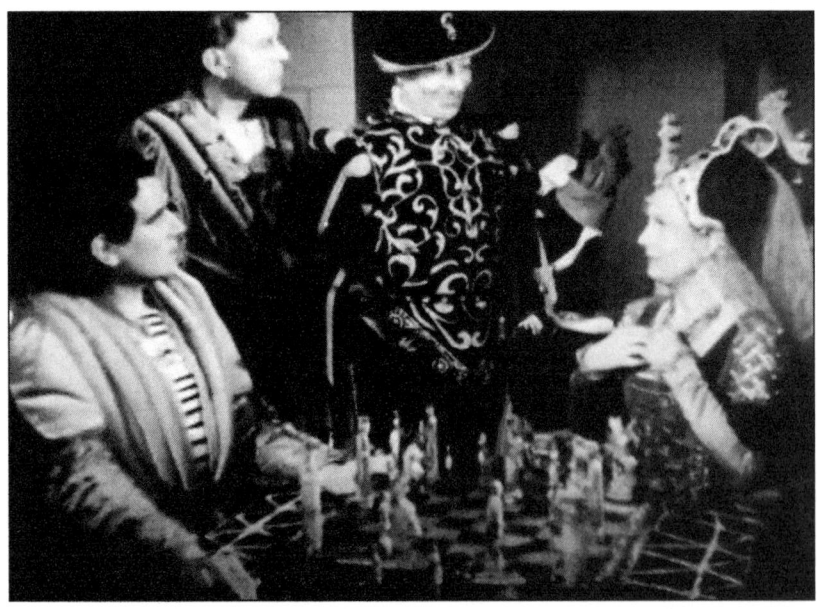

"Chess is such a simple game!" [p. 174]

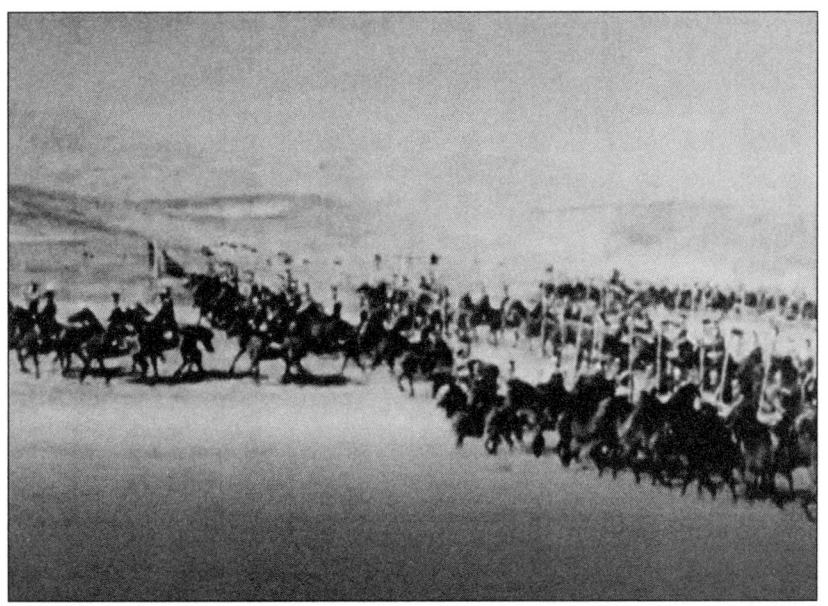

It's a beautiful moment when an assault against the world order is set in motion.
[p. 178]

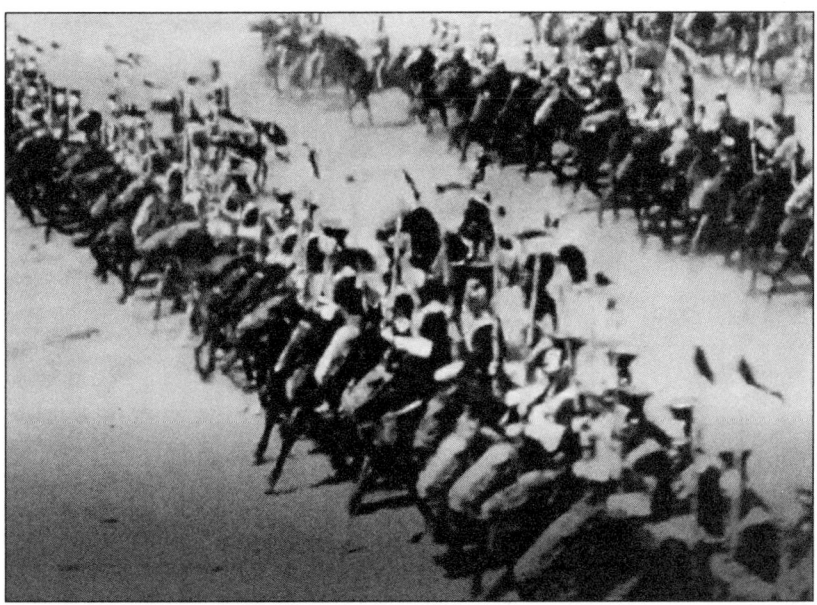

The charge begins slowly, picks up speed, passes the point of no return . . . [p. 178]

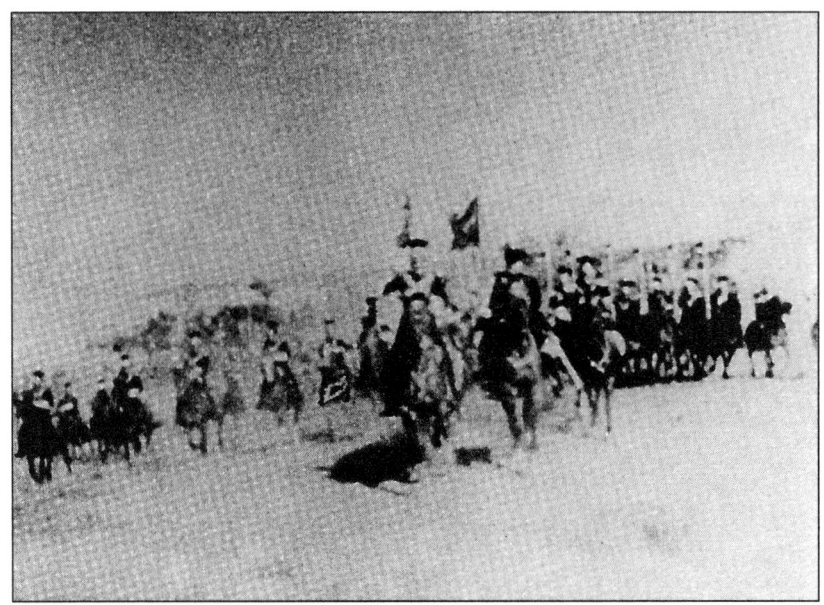

That is what we did, emerging from the night, raising once again the banner of the "good old cause" and marching forward under the cannon fire of time. [p. 179]

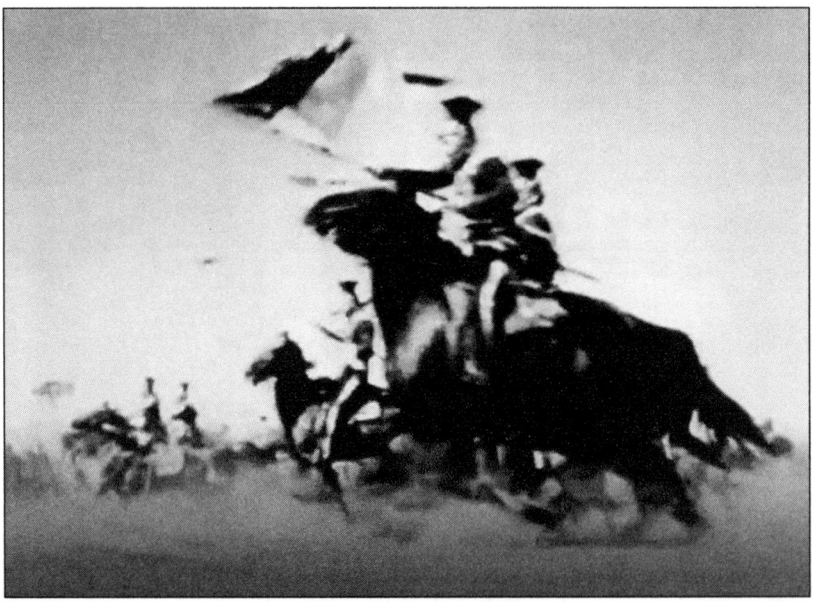

I have never quite understood those who have so often reproached me for having squandered this fine troop in a senseless assault, perhaps even out of some sort of Neronian self-indulgence. [p. 179]

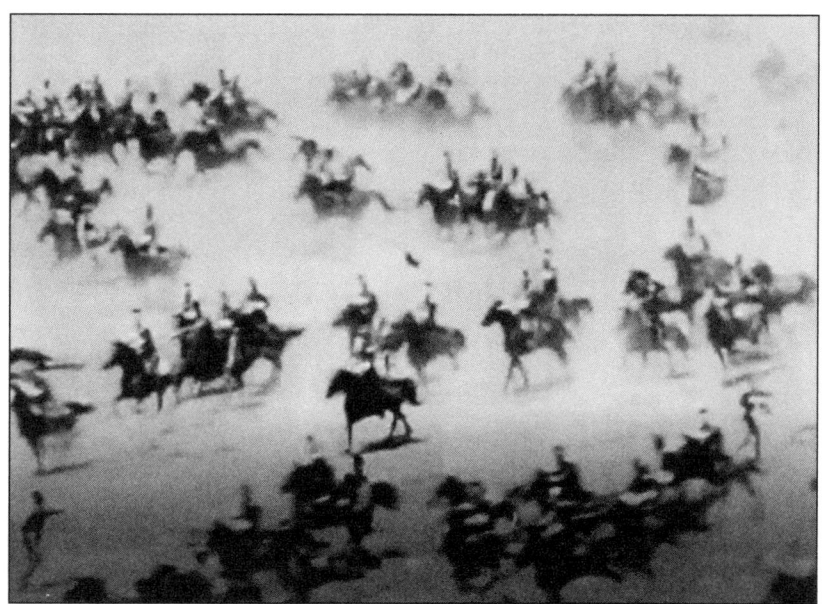

Sentimental objections are as vain as pseudostrategical quibbles. "Yet your bones will waste away, buried in the fields of Troy, your mission unfulfilled." [p. 182]

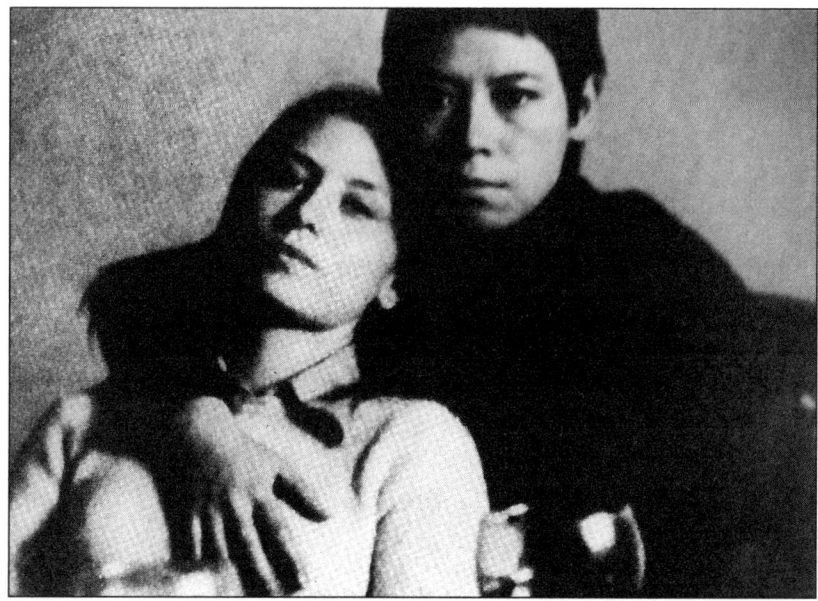

The spatial arrangement of one of the best cities that ever was, and the company of certain persons, and what we did with our time—all this formed a scene . . . [p. 186]

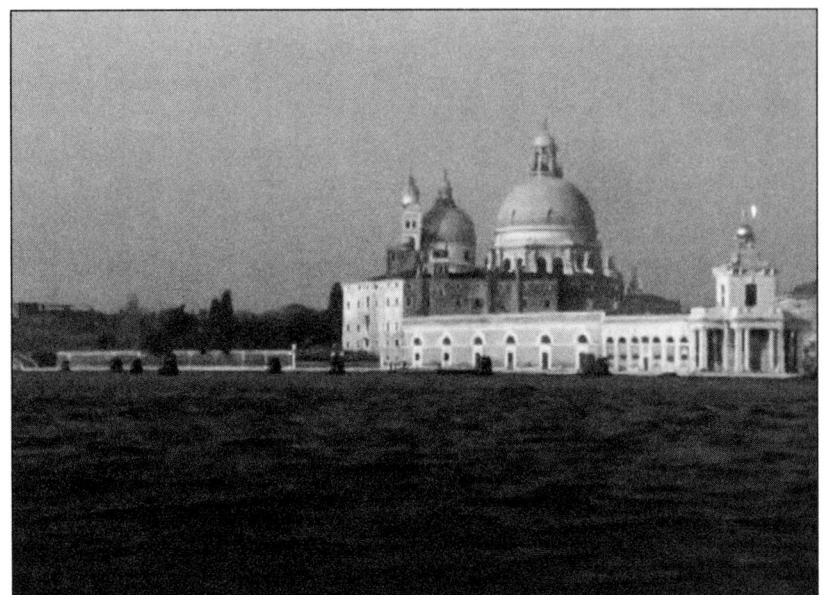

In any case, one traverses an era like one passes the Dogana promontory—that is to say, rather quickly. [p. 187]

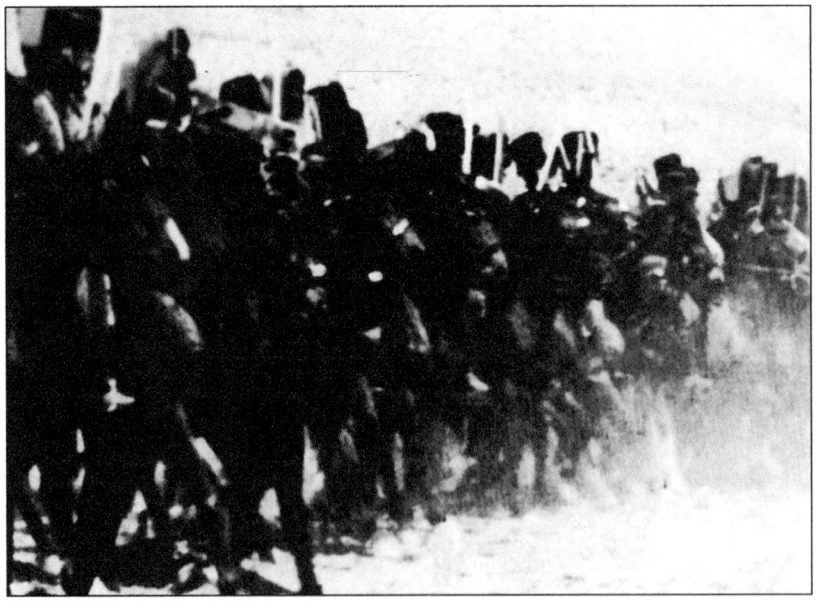

"We wander in the night. The devil cunningly carries us away." [pp. 188–189]

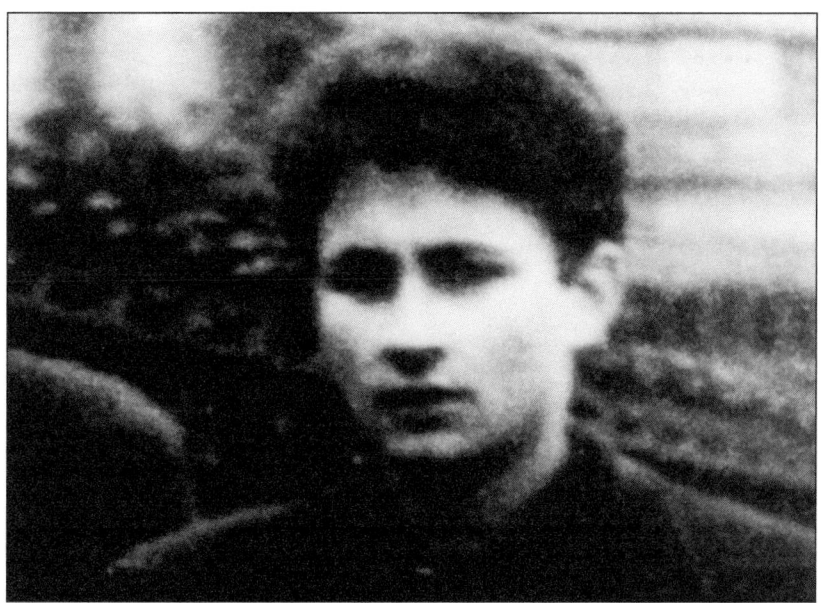

The sensation of the passing of time has always been vivid for me . . . [p. 189]

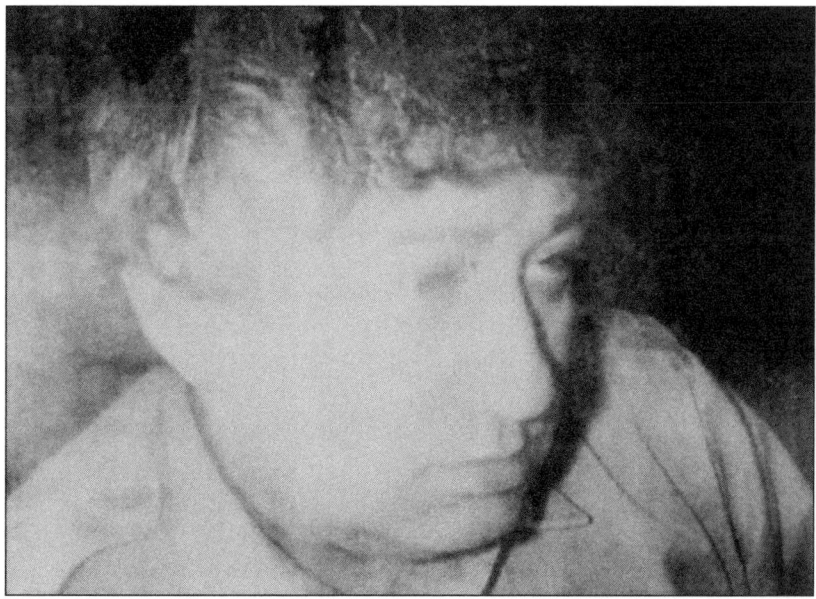

In this sense I have loved my era, which has seen the end of all existing security and the dissolution of everything that was socially ordained. [p. 189]

Guy Debord:
His Art and His Time

Upon the publication of *Comments on the Society of the Spectacle* in 1988, Franz-Olivier Giesbert expresses his strong disapproval of Guy Debord.

Lino Léonardi plays accordion to Aristide Bruant's song "Lézard."

"I'll never work,
Even if I'm hard up.
Never!"

Lino Léonardi's music for François Villon's poems.

GUY DEBORD: HIS ART AND HIS TIME

I. HIS ART

View of Pont Neuf.

The Paris of old is there no more (alas, the form of a city changes more rapidly than the heart of a mortal).

Views of Pont Neuf recreated in a film by Leos Carax.

Guy Debord did very little art, but he did it to the extreme.

Photo of Guy Debord.

In 1952 he showed that the cinema could be reduced to this blank white screen.

The screen remains white for ten seconds.

And to this blank black screen.

The screen remains black for one minute and twenty seconds.

Since that time Debord has maintained the same indifference to the tastes and judgments of public opinion. He has also been accused of many other immoralities; notably for not having been very disinterested when it was a matter of easy money, having regularly obeyed the principle: "Don't look a gift horse in the mouth."

Page from *Mémoires*.
Graffiti: "Never work."
Manuscript of the first page of *The Society of the Spectacle*.
Directive 1: "Supersession of art."
Directive 2: "Realization of philosophy."

The fine bunch of hoodlums whom he constantly hung out with, and who greatly influenced his extravagances.

Photos of Alice Becker-Ho, Ghislain de Marbaix, Jacques Herbute, Ivan Chtcheglov, Gil J Wolman, Asger Jorn, and Toñí López-Pintor.

The music stops.

II. HIS TIME

Pont Neuf wrapped up by Christo.

I am now going to be antitelevisual in form as I have been in content.

The little that remains of the Aral Sea.
Forest fires.

I shall write my thoughts in order, in a plan without confusion. If they are correct, any of them will follow from the others. That is the true order.

Music by Lino Léonardi.
A trapped Colombian girl.

This Andean girl, trapped in a mudslide following a volcanic eruption, provided media operators around the whole world an opportunity to speak in ethical terms about the ethical code they might need to decide on in certain extreme circumstances: Should such images be shown? Or why should the world be deprived of them?

These professionals have all firmly concluded that nothing of the world's misfortunes should be hidden. No false squeamishness of the public should prevent them from showing what someone had the merit of filming—especially in such rare cases as this when what was filmed actually happened to be true.

In this way, the media want to demonstrate that they are everywhere, and always dedicated to truth at any cost. And they are convinced that a closely examined detail is usually an exact and unambiguous model of the truth.

The music stops.
Women wrestling in Japan.
Prospecting for oil under the Paris Basin.

Sometimes, on Sunday . . .

Implosion of housing projects.

What was so poorly constructed must be demolished even more quickly.

Forests withered by acid rain.

Economics was thought to be a science. That was obviously not the case. We now know that it was neither the first nor the last of the enemy's sciences to reveal its fallaciousness.

Storm Troopers marching before 1934.

1933 was one of the most sinister dates in the history of this century —a century that has scarcely known any good ones.

Assassination of Kennedy in Dallas.

The "democratic" state has become increasingly alien.

Repression of Tienanmen in Beijing, 1989.

The warlord who ruled in Beijing at that time accurately recognized that "the fate of the Party and of the State was at stake in Tienanmen Square." He acted accordingly; and he's still in power, utterly indifferent to all the ideologies of recent media fashions.

Tanks in the streets of Moscow.

Tonton Macoute in Haiti.

Gunshots during a demonstration in Algiers.

The unverifiable world.

A Somali woman lynched before the impassive eyes of United Nations forces sent to "restore hope."

Students in a professional high school. Schools being ransacked. Attacks on teachers. Young people justifying all that.

Music by Lino Léonardi.

The most modern historical developments have accurately illustrated what Thomas Hobbes thought the life of mankind must have been like before it arrived at civilization and the state: "solitary, poor, nasty, brutish, and short."

The music stops.

"Radio Paris lies, Radio Paris is German."

Paris under the Occupation.

Paris today.

Today, Nazi Time encompasses all Europe.

Shift to winter time.

Film of the American Atomic Energy Commission about a radioactive alert.

Chernobyl, probably never-ending.

Launching of a 24/7 news channel.

Anne Sinclair interviews Georgina Dufoix: responsible but not guilty.

Wage earners have the right to vote.
And you'd evaluate how much each of you would stand to gain?
Wage earners have the right to vote.

Film of Arthur Cravan training for a boxing match. Photo of Cravan.

Music by Lino Léonardi.

At the origin of dadaism we find the poet-boxer Arthur Cravan, who during the First World War was a "deserter from seventeen nations."

The music stops.

The Buren Columns at the Palais Royal.

Bar codes.

Neo-dadaism is state dadaism, which can produce a small shock effect only by manifesting itself in national palaces.

Nuclear artwork: a flock of fake sheep graze at the foot of the Cattenom nuclear power plant.

Nuclear power likes to be surrounded by images of its totem animal. Magritte might have written: "This is not a sheep."

Silvio Berlusconi interrupts his vacation in Sardinia.

Funeral of Pierre Bérégovoy.

Long line waiting to get into the Louvre.

Music by Lino Léonardi.

The culture of the entire past is the object of a universal consensus and an egalitarian admiration. But in each of its concrete manifestations, it often ends up being as inauthentic as today's reconstituted Pont Neuf.

Long line waiting to get into the Musée d'Orsay.

Odor of cancer at Rue Daguerre.
Odor of cancer at Rue de Buci.
Cancer is covered by Social Security.

The music stops.

Chinese protesters sing "The Internationale" at Tienanmen Square in 1989.

The dialectic is still very much alive. Everything is being brought back into play.

Claire Chazal interviews Bernard Tapie.

Whenever Bernard Tapie talks about himself, you wonder what dishonesty the poor victim could possibly have been accused of.

Speech by Yasser Arafat at UNESCO.

Philippe Alexandre, Serge July, and Christine Ockrent on Channel 9's *Front Page* program.

Three media barons discuss the news of the world and share it with us in intimate detail.

The new politico-literary salons of Paris.

The excellence of each talking head is confirmed by the admiring looks of the other two.

Cough it up! We'll see what comes out.

ACT UP demonstration, with a statement by an ACT UP spokesman on World AIDS Day, December 1991.

With the pill, no drinking, no smoking. Are you kidding?

Immunological prevention is a thing of the past.

Live reunion of the Boutboul family.

Same clip with soundtrack from *Fantastic Lottery Nights*.

Catastrophic floods at Vaison-la-Romaine.

A virtual landscape.

Video ad for the Alsace-Lorraine DRSP (Regional Department of Penitentiary Services).

But where is this leading?

What are they trying to sell us?

You guessed it: prison labor.

This DRSP reveals itself as the most legitimate heir of the factory labor of old.

Mass of corpses during an epidemic in Rwanda.

Music by Lino Léonardi.

Portraits:

Alice Becker-Ho, author of *L'Essence du Jargon*

Ghislain-Gontran de Saint-Ghislain des Noyers de Marbaix,
     author of *Monsieur Gontran*

Jacques Herbute, a.k.a. Barate

Ivan Vladimirovitch Chtcheglov,
     author of *Formulary for a New Urbanism*

Gil J Wolman, author of *L'Anticoncept*

Asger Jorn, author of *Pour la Forme*

Toñí López-Pintor, a.k.a. l'Andalouse

The music stops.
Mitterrand at the Pantheon after his election in 1981.
Torches lit and waved at a concert.
Opening of a G-7 summit at Naples. Clinton jogs with his entourage.

In summer 1994 the leading democratic powers, who under the label "G-7" are going to collectively decide on all the most important administrative aspects of the new global society, arrive triumphantly at Naples.

Documents

A User's Guide to Détournement

(excerpts)

Every reasonably aware person of our time is aware of the obvious fact that art can no longer be justified as a superior activity, or even as a compensatory activity to which one might honorably devote oneself. The reason for this deterioration is clearly the emergence of productive forces that necessitate other production relations and a new practice of life. In the civil-war phase we are engaged in, and in close connection with the orientation we are discovering for certain superior activities to come, we believe that all known means of expression are going to converge in a general movement of propaganda that must encompass all the perpetually interacting aspects of social reality.

There are several conflicting opinions about the forms and even the very nature of educative propaganda, opinions that generally reflect one or another currently fashionable variety of reformist politics. Suffice it to say that in our view the premises for revolution, on the cultural as well as the strictly political level, are not only ripe, they have begun to rot. It is not just returning to the past which is reactionary; even "modern" cultural objectives are ultimately reactionary since they depend on ideological formulations of a past society that has prolonged its death agony to the present. The only historically justified tactic is extremist innovation.

The literary and artistic heritage of humanity should be used for partisan propaganda purposes. It is, of course, necessary to go beyond any idea of mere scandal. Since opposition to the bourgeois notion of art and artistic genius has become pretty much old hat, Marcel Duchamp's drawing a mustache on the *Mona Lisa* is no more interesting than the original version of that painting. We must now push this process to the point of negating the negation. Bertolt Brecht, revealing in a recent interview in *France-Observateur* that he makes cuts in the classics of the theater in order to make the performances more educative, is much closer than Duchamp to the revolutionary orientation we are calling for. We must note, however, that in Brecht's case these salutary alterations are narrowly limited by his unfortunate respect for culture as defined by the ruling class—that same respect, taught in the newspapers of the worker parties as well as in the primary schools of the bourgeoisie, which leads even the reddest working-class districts of Paris always to prefer *The Cid* over *Mother Courage*.

It is in fact necessary to eliminate all remnants of the notion of personal property in this area. The appearance of new necessities outmodes previous "inspired" works. They become obstacles, dangerous habits. The point is not whether we like them or not. We have to go beyond them.

Any elements, no matter where they are taken from, can be used to make new combinations. The discoveries of modern poetry regarding the analogical structure of images demonstrate that when two objects are brought together, no matter how far apart their original contexts may be, a relationship is always formed. Restricting oneself to a personal arrangement of words is mere convention. The mutual interference of two worlds of feeling, or the bringing together of two independent expressions, supersedes the original elements and produces a synthetic organization of greater efficacy. Anything can be used.

It goes without saying that one is not limited to correcting a work or to integrating diverse fragments of out-of-date works into a new one; one can also alter the meaning of those fragments in any appropriate way, leaving the imbeciles to their slavish reference to "citations."

Such parodistic methods have often been used to obtain comical effects. But such humor is the result of contradictions within a condition whose existence is taken for granted. Since the world of literature seems to us almost as distant as the Stone Age, such contradictions don't make us laugh. It is thus necessary to envisage a parodic-serious stage where the accumulation of detourned elements, far from aiming to arouse indignation or laughter by

alluding to some original work, will express our indifference toward a meaningless and forgotten original, and concern itself with rendering a certain
sublimity. . . .

Détournement not only leads to the discovery of new forms of talent; in
addition, clashing head-on with all social and legal conventions, it cannot fail
to be a powerful cultural weapon in the service of a real class struggle. The
cheapness of its products is the heavy artillery that breaks through all the
Chinese walls of understanding. It is a real means of proletarian artistic education, the first step toward a *literary communism*.

Ideas and creations in the realm of détournement can be multiplied at
will. For the moment we will limit ourselves to showing a few concrete possibilities in various current sectors of communication—it being understood that
these separate sectors are significant only in relation to present-day technologies, and are all tending to merge into superior syntheses with the advance of
these technologies. . . .

It is obviously in the realm of the cinema that détournement can attain
its greatest effectiveness and, for those concerned with this aspect, its greatest
beauty.

The powers of film are so extensive, and the absence of coordination of
those powers is so glaring, that virtually any film that is above the miserable
average can provide matter for endless polemics among spectators or professional critics. Only the conformism of those people prevents them from discovering equally appealing charms and equally glaring faults even in the worst
films. To cut through this absurd confusion of values, we can observe that
Griffith's *Birth of a Nation* is one of the most important films in the history of
the cinema because of its wealth of innovations. On the other hand, it is a
racist film and therefore absolutely does not merit being shown in its present
form. But its total prohibition could be seen as regrettable from the point
of view of the secondary, but potentially worthier, domain of the cinema. It
would be better to detourn it as a whole, without necessarily even altering the
montage, by adding a soundtrack that made a powerful denunciation of the
horrors of imperialist war and of the activities of the Ku Klux Klan, which are
continuing in the United States even now.

Such a détournement—a very moderate one—is in the final analysis nothing more than the moral equivalent of the restoration of old paintings in
museums. But most films only merit being cut up to compose other works.
This reconversion of preexisting sequences will obviously be accompanied by
other elements, musical or pictorial as well as historical. While the cinematic

rewriting of history has until now been largely along the lines of Sacha Guitry's burlesque re-creations, one could have Robespierre say, before his execution: "In spite of so many trials, my experience and the grandeur of my task convinces me that all is well." If in this case an appropriate reuse of a Greek tragedy enables us to exalt Robespierre, we can conversely imagine a neorealist-type sequence, at the counter of a truck stop bar, for example, with one of the truck drivers saying seriously to another: "Ethics was formerly confined to the books of philosophers; we have introduced it into the governing of nations." One can see that this juxtaposition illuminates Maximilien's idea, the idea of a dictatorship of the proletariat. . . .

Finally, when we have got to the stage of constructing situations—the ultimate goal of all our activity—everyone will be free to detourn entire situations by deliberately changing this or that determinant condition of them.

The methods that we have briefly examined here are presented not as our own invention, but as a generally widespread practice which we propose to systematize.

In itself, the theory of détournement scarcely interests us. But we find it linked to almost all the constructive aspects of the presituationist period of transition. Thus its enrichment, through practice, seems necessary.

This article, by Guy Debord and Gil J Wolman, appeared in the Belgian surrealist journal Les Lèvres Nues *#8 (May 1956). The translation is from the* Situationist International Anthology: Revised and Expanded Edition *(PM Press, 2026), pp. 14–21.*

Technical Notes on the First Three Films

Howls for Sade, a feature-length film created in June 1952, contains no images whatsoever. The soundtrack is accompanied by a completely blank white screen during the spoken dialogues. These dialogues, which altogether total no more than twenty minutes, are broken up into short fragments amid passages of total silence totaling one hour (the final portion of the film consisting of an uninterrupted 24-minute period of silence). During the silences the screen, and thus the theater, remain totally dark.

The voices—all monotone—are Gil J Wolman (Voice 1), Guy Debord (Voice 2), Serge Berna (Voice 3), Barbara Rosenthal (Voice 4), Isidore Isou (Voice 5).

The film contains no other sound or accompaniment, with the exception of a solo lettrist improvisation by Wolman during the first white screen passage, immediately before the beginning of the dialogue. The first two statements comprise the only credits.

The content of this film should be considered in the context of the lettrist avant-garde of the period, both on the most general level, where it represents a negation and supersession of Isou's conception of "discrepant cinema," and on the anecdotal level, from the mode of using double first names (Jean-Isidore, Guy-Ernest, Albert-Jules, etc.) or the reference to Berna, the organizer of the Easter 1950 scandal at Notre Dame, to the dedication to Wolman, creator of the preceding lettrist film, the admirable *L'Anticoncept*. Other aspects should be considered in the light of positions since developed by the situationists, particularly the use of *detourned passages*. Among all the passages drawn from various external sources (newspapers, Joyce, the Civil Code, etc.) mixed into the dialogue of this film (with its equally indiscriminate use of different styles of writing), the present Scandinavian Institute for Comparative Vandalism edition has retained the use of quotation marks only for four of them, which are treated as conventional quotations since they would probably otherwise not be recognizable. The first three are by Isou (respectively, from his *Esthétique du cinéma*, from a letter to Debord, and from *Précisions sur ma poésie et moi*); the fourth is a line from a John Ford Western (*Rio Grande*).

The first showing of *Howls for Sade*—in Paris, June 30, 1952, at the Ciné-club d'Avant-Garde, then directed by A.-J. Cauliez, in the Musée de l'Homme building—was violently disrupted almost from the beginning by the audience and the film club managers. Several lettrists then dissociated themselves from such a crudely extremist film. The first complete showing took place October 13 of the same year at the Ciné-club du Quartier Latin in the Sociétés Savantes room, defended by a group of "left-lettrists" and a couple dozen additional supporters from Saint-Germain-des-Prés. A few months later the presence of these same people prevented the same film club from presenting a *Sadistic Skeleton* which had been announced and attributed to a certain "René-Guy Babord," a joke which was seemingly intended to consist merely of turning out all the theater lights for a quarter of an hour.

* * *

On the Passage of a Few Persons Through a Rather Brief Unity of Time is a 600-meter short (20 minutes), 35 mm, black and white. Produced by the Dansk-Fransk Experimentalfilmskompagni, it was shot in April 1959 and edited in September 1959.

Cameraman: André Mrugalski. Editing: Chantal Delattre. Assistant Director: Ghislain de Marbaix. Assistant Cameraman: Jean Harnois. Continuity: Michèle Vallon. Grip: Bernard Largemain. Laboratory GTC.

The spoken commentary is read in somewhat apathetic and tired-sounding voices by Jean Harnois (Voice 1, tone of a radio announcer), Guy Debord (Voice 2, more sad and subdued), and Claude Brabant (Voice 3, a little girl).

The sound track during the opening credits is from a recording of a discussion during the Third Conference of the Situationist International in Munich, primarily in French and German. The Handel theme is from the ballet suite *The Origin of Design;* the two themes by Michel-Richard Delalande are from *Caprice* #2 (a.k.a. *Grande Pièce*).

The spoken commentary includes a large portion of detourned phrases, drawn indiscriminately from classic thinkers, a science-fiction novel, and the worst pop sociologists. In order to go against the usual documentary practice regarding spectacular scenery, each time that the camera is on the verge of coming upon a monument this has been avoided by shooting in the opposite direction, *from the viewpoint of the monument* (just as the young Abel Gance shot a passage from the *viewpoint of a snowball*). The initial plan for this documentary envisaged more détournements from other films, particularly recent ones (for example, during the passage on the failure of revolutionary efforts of the 1950s, this sequence of two different scenes: a worried young woman, in the luxurious decor of a detective film, telephones someone to urge him to wait; the Russian general in *For Whom the Bell Tolls,* seeing planes pass overhead, replies to a telephone that it is unfortunately too late, that the offensive is already launched and that it will fail like so many others). These extensive film-quotations were ultimately prevented because several distributors refused to sell reproduction rights for at least half of the scenes selected, which refusal destroyed the montage envisaged. Instead, more extensive use was made of the Monsavon soap ad, whose star was to have a brighter future.

André Mrugalski is responsible for the sequence of detail photos detourning the style of "art documentaries."

This short film can be considered as notes on the origins of the situationist movement; notes which thus naturally include a reflection on their own language.

* * *

Critique of Separation was shot September–October 1960 and edited January–February 1961. Production: Dansk-Fransk Experimentalfilmskompagni. 20-minute short, 35 mm, black and white. GTC Laboratory; sound recorded at Studio Marignan.

Cameraman: André Mrugalski. Editing: Chantal Delattre. Assistant Cameraman: Bernard Davidson. Continuity: Claude Brabant. Grip: Bernard Largemain.

Before the credits, a hodgepodge of meaningless images is punctuated by a series of text frames—"Coming soon to this screen . . . One of the greatest antifilms of all time! . . . Real people! A true story! . . . On a theme the cinema has never dared to confront!"—while Caroline Rittener reads the following passage from André Martinet's *Elements of General Linguistics:* "When one considers how natural and beneficial it is for man to identify his language with reality, one realizes the level of sophistication he had to attain in order to be able to dissociate them and make each an object of study." All the rest of the film's commentary is spoken by Guy Debord. Caroline Rittener also plays the young woman in the film. The music is by François Couperin and Bodin de Boismortier.

The images in *Critique of Separation* are often taken from comics, ID photos, and newspapers, or from other films. In many cases subtitles are added, which may be rather difficult to follow at the same time as the spoken commentary. The people who have been directly filmed are almost always none other than members of the film crew.

The relation between the images, the spoken commentary, and the subtitles is neither complementary nor indifferent, but is intended to itself be critical.

From Contre le Cinéma *(Institut Scandinave de Vandalisme Comparé, 1964), a collection of the scripts of Debord's first three films.*

Letter about *On the Passage*

You have rightly noticed the difference in the text-image relation between the first and second parts of *Passage*. Detourned phrases can be found throughout the film, but the majority are in the first part. My plan was as follows: The film begins like a typical, technically ordinary documentary. Gradually it becomes less clear and more disappointing, which might at first seem to be the result of a pretentious "ideological" interpretation of an otherwise clear subject, because the text appears increasingly inadequate and pompously inflated in relation to the images (the tone of Lefebvre = Marx-Goldman-Huizinga!). The question then arises: What is the subject of this film?—which I think represents an irritating and upsetting break with the habitual spectacle.

With the appearance of the first blank screen, the film begins to contradict itself in every way—and thus becomes *more clear* as its creator *takes sides against it*. It is both a rather explicitly anti-art-film about the unaccomplished work of this era and an ultimately realistic description of a way of life deprived of coherence and significance. The form corresponds to the content. It does not describe this or that particular activity (merchant marine, oil exploration, some historic monument to admire—or even to demolish, as in Franju's magnificent *Hôtel des Invalides*), but the very core of present-day activity in general, which is empty. It is a portrayal of the absence of "real life." This slow movement of exposure and negation is what I was trying to embody in *Passage*. But very summarily and arbitrarily, I must admit. Despite the prevalent fixation on the economic obstacles, the main problem is actually that short films are quite unsuitable for truly experimental cinema. Their very brevity tends to encourage a moderate, neatly edited form of expression. But it does seem interesting to *detourn* the fixed form of the traditional documentary, and this tends to tie us to the inviolable 20-minute limit.

Letter from Debord to André Frankin (an early SI member), January 26, 1960. From Debord's Correspondance, *vol. 1, pp. 302–303.*

For a Revolutionary Judgment of Art

(excerpts)

Chatel's article on Godard's film [*Breathless*] in *Socialisme ou Barbarie* #31 [February 1961] can be characterized as film criticism dominated by revolutionary concerns. The analysis of the film assumes a revolutionary perspective on society, confirms that perspective, and concludes that certain tendencies of cinematic expression should be considered preferable to others in relation to the revolutionary project. It is obviously because Chatel's critique thus sets out the question in all its fullness, instead of merely debating various questions of taste, that it is interesting and calls for discussion. Specifically, Chatel finds *Breathless* a "valuable example" supporting his thesis that an alteration of "the present forms of culture" depends on the production of works that offer people "a representation of their own existence."

A revolutionary alteration of the present forms of culture can be nothing less than the supersession of all aspects of the aesthetic and technological apparatus that constitutes an aggregation of spectacles separated from life. It is not in its surface meanings that we should look for a spectacle's relation to the problems of the society, but at the deepest level, at the level of *its function as a spectacle*. "The relation between authors and spectators is only a transposition of the fundamental relation between directors and executants. . . . The spectacle-spectator relation is in itself a staunch bearer of the capitalist order" (*Preliminaries Toward Defining a Unitary Revolutionary Program* [*SI Anthology*, p. 390].

One must not introduce reformist illusions about the spectacle, as if it could be eventually improved from within, ameliorated by its own specialists under the supposed control of a better-informed public opinion. To do so would be tantamount to giving revolutionaries' approval to a tendency, or an appearance of a tendency, in a game that we absolutely must not play; a game that we must reject in its entirety in the name of the fundamental requirements of the revolutionary project, which can in no case produce an aesthetics because it is already entirely beyond the domain of aesthetics. The point is not to engage in some sort of revolutionary art-criticism, but to make a revolutionary critique of all art. . . .

Art criticism is a second-degree spectacle. The critic is someone who makes a spectacle out of his very condition as a spectator—a specialized and therefore ideal spectator, expressing his ideas and feelings *about* a work in which he does not really participate. He re-presents, restages, his own non-intervention in the spectacle. The weakness of random and largely arbitrary fragmentary judgments concerning spectacles that do not really concern us is imposed on all of us in many banal discussions in private life. But the art critic makes a show of this kind of weakness, presenting it as *exemplary*.

Chatel thinks that if a portion of the population recognizes itself in a film, it will be able to "look at itself, admire itself, criticize itself, or reject itself—in any case, to use the images that pass on the screen for its own needs." Let us first of all note that there is a certain mystery in this notion of using such a flow of images to satisfy authentic needs. Just how they are to be used is not clear. It would first of all seem to be necessary to specify which needs are in question in order to determine whether those images can really serve as means to satisfy them. Furthermore, everything we know about the mechanism of the spectacle, even at the simplest cinematic level, absolutely contradicts this idyllic vision of people equally free to admire or criticize themselves by recognizing themselves in the characters of a film. But most fundamentally, it is impossible to accept this division of labor between uncontrollable specialists presenting a vision of people's lives to them and audiences having to recognize themselves more or less clearly in those images. Attaining a certain accuracy in describing people's behavior is not necessarily positive. Even if Godard presents people with an image of themselves in which they can undeniably recognize themselves more than in the films of Fernandel, he nevertheless presents them with a false image in which they recognize themselves falsely.

Revolution is not "showing" life to people, but bringing them to life. A revolutionary organization must always remember that its aim is not getting its adherents to listen to convincing talks by expert leaders, but getting them to speak for themselves, in order to achieve, or at least strive toward, an equal degree of participation. The cinematic spectacle is one of the forms of pseudo-communication (developed, in lieu of other possibilities, by the present *class* technology) in which this aim is radically unfeasible. Much more so, for example, than in a cultural form such as a university-style lecture with questions at the end, in which dialogue and audience participation, though subjected to rather unfavorable conditions, are not absolutely excluded. . . .

The revolutionary movement must accord a central place to criticism of culture and everyday life. But any examination of these phenomena must first of all be disabused, not respectful toward the given modes of communication. The very foundations of existing cultural relations must be contested by the critique that the revolutionary movement needs to really bring to bear on all aspects of life and human relationships.

From a 1961 article, published the following year in Notes Critiques: Bulletin de recherche et d'orientation révolutionnaire #3 *(Bordeaux). The translation is from the* SI Anthology *(pp. 393–397).*

Cinema and Revolution

Berlin Film Festival correspondent J.P. Picaper is awestruck by the fact that "in *The Gay Science* (an ORTF–Radio Stuttgart production, banned in France) Godard has pushed his admirable self-critique to the point of projecting sequences shot in the dark or even of leaving the spectator for an almost unbearable length of time facing a blank screen" (*Le Monde*, 8 July 1969). Without seeking more precisely what constitutes "an almost unbearable length of time" for this critic, we can see that Godard, following the latest fashions as always, is adopting a destructive style just as belatedly plagiarized and pointless as all the rest of his work, this negation having been expressed in the cinema before he had ever begun the long series of pretentious pseudoinnovations that aroused such enthusiasm among student audiences during the previous period. The same journalist reports that Godard, through one of the characters in his short film *L'Amour*, confesses that "revolution cannot be put into images" because "the cinema is the art of lying." The cinema has no more been an "art of lying" than has any of the rest of art, which was dead in its totality long before Godard, who has not *even* been a modern artist, that is, who has not even been capable of the slightest personal originality. This Maoist liar is thus winding up his bluff by trying to arouse admiration for his brilliant discovery of a noncinema cinema, while denouncing a sort of inevitable falsehood in which he has participated, but no more so than have many others. Godard was in fact immediately *outmoded* by the May 1968 revolt, which caused him to be recognized as a spectacular manufacturer of a superficial, pseudocritical, *co-optive* art rummaged out of the trashcans of the past (see "The Role of Godard" in *Internationale Situationniste* #10 [*SI Anthology*, pp. 228–230]). At that point Godard's career as a filmmaker was essentially over, and he was personally insulted and ridiculed on several occasions by revolutionaries who happened to cross his path.

The cinema as a means of revolutionary communication is not inherently mendacious just because Godard or Jacopetti has touched it, any more than all political analysis is doomed to duplicity just because Stalinists have written. Several new filmmakers in various countries are currently attempting to utilize films as means of revolutionary critique, and some of them will partially succeed in this. However, the limitations both in their aesthetic conceptions and even in their grasp of the nature of the present revolution will in our opinion prevent them for some time still from going as far as is necessary. We believe that at the moment only the situationists' positions and methods, as formulated by René Viénet in our previous issue ["The Situationists and the New Forms of Action Against Politics and Art," *SI Anthology*, pp. 273–277], are adequate for a directly revolutionary use of cinema—though political and economic conditions still present obvious obstacles to the realization of such films.

It is known that Eisenstein wanted to make a film of *Capital*. Considering his formal conceptions and political submissiveness, it can be doubted if his film would have been faithful to Marx's text. But for our part, we are confident that we can do better. For example, as soon as it becomes possible Guy Debord will himself make a cinematic adaptation of *The Society of the Spectacle* that will certainly not fall short of his book.

Article in Internationale Situationniste *#12 (1969). The translation is from the* SI Anthology *(pp. 378–379).*

_____

On *The Society of the Spectacle*
(reply to a critic of the book)

During the early 1950s Claude Lefort was a revolutionary and one of the main theorists of the journal *Socialisme ou Barbarie*—regarding which we stated in *Internationale Situationniste* #10 that it had sunk to run-of-the-mill academic speculation on the level of *Arguments* and that it was bound to disappear (which it confirmed by folding a month or two later). By that time Lefort had already been separated from it for years, having been in the forefront of the opposition to any form of revolutionary organization, which he denounced as inevitably doomed to bureaucratization. Since this distressing discovery he has consoled himself by taking up an ordinary academic career and writing in *La Quinzaine Littéraire*. In the February 1, 1968 issue of that periodical this very knowledgeable but domesticated man makes a critique of *The Society of the Spectacle*. He begins by acknowledging that the book has some merits. Its use of Marxian methodology, and even of détournement, has not escaped him, though he fails to notice its debt to Hegel. But the book nevertheless seems academically unacceptable to him for the following reason: "Debord adds thesis upon thesis, but he does not advance; he endlessly repeats the same idea: that the real is inverted in ideology, that ideology, changed in its essence in the spectacle, passes itself off for the real, and that it is necessary to overthrow ideology in order to bring the real back into its own. It makes little difference what particular topic he treats, this idea is reflected in all the others. It is only due to his exhaustion that he has stopped at the 221st thesis." Debord readily admits that he found, at the 221st thesis, that he had said quite enough and had accomplished exactly what he had set out to do: to make an "endless" description of what the *spectacle* is and how it can be overthrown. The fact that "this idea is reflected in all the others" is precisely what we consider the characteristic of a *dialectical book*. Such a book does not have to "advance," like some doctoral dissertation on Machiavelli, toward the approval of a board of examiners and the attainment of a diploma. (And as Marx put it in the Afterword to the second German edition of *Capital,* regarding the way the dialectical "method of presentation" may he viewed, "This reflecting may make it seem as if we had before us a mere *a priori* construction.") *The Society of the Spectacle* does not hide its *a priori* engagement, nor does it attempt to derive its conclusions from academic argumentation. It is written only to show the *concrete* coherent field of application of a thesis that already exists at the outset, a thesis deriving from the investigations that revolutionary criticism has made of modern capitalism. In our opinion, it is basically *a book that lacked nothing but one or more revolutions*. Which were not long in coming. But Lefort, having lost all interest in this kind of theory and practice, finds that the book is an ivory tower world closed in on itself: "One would have expected this book to be a violent attack against its adversaries, but in fact this ostentatious discourse has no other aim than showing off. Admittedly it has a certain beauty. The style is flawless. Since any question that does not have an automatic response has been banished from the very first lines, one would search in vain for any fault." The misinterpretation is total: Lefort sees a sort of Mallarméan purity in a book which, as a *negative* of spectacular society (in which also, but in an inverse manner, any question that does not have an automatic response is banished at every moment), ultimately seeks nothing other than to *overthrow* the existing *relation of forces* in the factories and the streets.

After this general rejection of the book, Lefort still wants to play the Marxist regarding a few details in order to remind us that this is his specialty, the reason he gets assignments from intellectual periodicals. Here he begins to falsify in order to give himself the opportunity of introducing pedantic reminders of things that are obvious. He solemnly announces that Debord has changed "the commodity into the spectacle," a transformation that is "full of consequences." He ponderously summarizes what Marx says on the commodity, then falsely charges Debord with having said that "the production of the phantasmagoria governs that of commodities," whereas in fact the *exact opposite* is clearly stated in *The Society of the Spectacle*, notably in the second chapter, where the spectacle is defined as simply a *moment* of the development of commodity production. Lefort can thus arrive at the absurd conclusion that "according to Debord, all history is futile"! He also refers to Debord as "a strange offspring of Marx, intoxicated by the famous analysis of the fetishism of the commodity." We won't go into a debate about the best ways to become intoxicated—a matter that academics know little about—but we will note that Lefort was more surprised than we were when history suddenly returned in May 1968, that "bacchanalia of truth where no one remains sober" (Hegel) in which one could already see *crowds* of people intoxicated by the discovery of the possibility of *destroying* the commodity and the spectacle at the heart of pseudolife. . . .

From "How Not To Understand Situationist Books," Internationale Situationniste #12 *(1969). The translation is from the* SI Anthology *(pp. 339– 341).*

On *The Society of the Spectacle*
(*announcement of the film*)

Until now it has generally been assumed that film is a completely unsuitable medium for presenting revolutionary theory. This view was mistaken. The lack of any serious attempts in this direction stemmed simply from the historical lack of a modern revolutionary theory during virtually the entire period of the cinema's development; as well as from the fact that the potentials of cinematic composition, despite so many declarations of intent on the part of filmmakers and so much feigned satisfaction on the part of a miserable public, have as yet scarcely been liberated.

Published in 1967, *The Society of the Spectacle* is a book whose theoretical insights have profoundly influenced the new current of social critique that is now more and more openly undermining the established world order. Its present cinematic adaptation, like the book itself, does not offer a few partial political critiques, but a total critique of the existing world; that is, a critique of all aspects of modern capitalism and of its general system of illusions.

The cinema is itself an integral part of this world, serving as one of the instruments of the separate *representation* that opposes and dominates the actual proletarianized society. As revolutionary critique engages in battle on the very terrain of the cinematic spectacle, it must thus *turn the language of that medium against itself* and give itself a form that is itself revolutionary.

The text and images of this film form a coherent whole; but the images are never mere direct *illustrations* of the text, much less demonstrations of it (cinematic "demonstrations" are in any case never reliable due to the unlimited possibilities of manipulation offered by the unilateral editing of the material). Instead, the film's use of images (whether photographs, newsclips, or sequences from preexisting films) is governed by the principle of *détournement*, which the situationists have defined as "communication that includes a critique of itself." The images through which spectacular society presents itself to itself are taken and turned against it: the spectacle's means should be treated with insolence. As a result, in a certain sense this film, coming at the end of the cinema's pseudo-autonomous history, incorporates all the memories of that history. It can thus be seen simultaneously as a historical film, a Western, a love story, a war movie, etc. Like the society it examines, it also presents a number of comical aspects. In talking about the spectacular order, and about the commodity domination that it serves, one is also talking about what this order hides: class struggles and strivings toward real historical life, revolution and its past failures, and the responsibilities for those failures. Nothing in this film is made to please the fashionable blockheads of leftist cinema: it has equal contempt for what they respect and for the style in which they express that respect. One who is capable of understanding and denouncing an entire socio-economic formation will denounce it even in a film. Objections to our "extremism" are meaningless, because current history is already on the verge of going beyond the most extreme possibilities imagined.

Theses that have never before been presented in the cinema will now appear there in a never before seen form, simply because for the first time a filmmaker has undertaken an *uncompromising critique.*

In the socio-economic context, the total freedom required to create such a film obviously means that the producer must renounce any claim to exert any preliminary control over the director, whether by insisting that he present a synopsis or by seeking to obtain from him any other sort of meaningless commitment. This has been recognized in the contract between the film-maker and the producer, Simar Films: "It is understood that the filmmaker will carry out his work in complete freedom, without any control or supervision whatsoever, and without even being obliged to pay the slightest attention to any comment that the producer might make regarding any aspect of the content or of the cinematic form that the filmmaker feels appropriate for his film."

Considering that this film itself expresses its meaning in a sufficiently comprehensible manner, the producer and the filmmaker believe that it is unnecessary to provide any further explanations.

From a brochure announcing the opening of the film (Paris, April 1974).

The Use of Stolen Films

On the question of stolen films, that is, of fragments of preexisting films incorporated into my films—notably in *The Society of the Spectacle*—(I'm talking here primarily about the films that *interrupt* and punctuate with their own dialogues the text of the spoken "commentary" derived from the book), the following should be noted:

In "A User's Guide to Détournement" (*Lèvres Nues* #8) we already noted that "It is thus necessary to conceive of a parodic-serious stage in which detourned elements are combined . . . in order to create a certain sublimity."

"Détournement" is not an enemy of art. The enemies of art are those who have not wanted to take into account the positive lessons of the "degeneration of art."

Thus, in the film *The Society of the Spectacle* the (fiction) films detourned by me are not used as critical *illustrations* of an art of spectacular society (in contrast to the documentaries and news footage, for example). On the contrary, these stolen fiction films, external to my film but brought into it, are used, *regardless of whatever their original meaning may have been,* to represent *the rectification of the "artistic inversion of life."*

The spectacle has deported real life behind the screen. I have tried to "expropriate the expropriators." *Johnny Guitar* evokes real memories of love, *The Shanghai Gesture* other adventurous ambiences, *For Whom the Bell Tolls* the vanquished revolution. The *Rio Grande* sequence is intended to evoke historical action and reflection in general. *Mr. Arkadin* is at first brought in to evoke Poland, but then hints at authentic life, life as it should be. The Russian films also in a sense evoke revolution. The American films on the Civil War and Custer are intended to evoke all the class struggles of the nineteenth century; and even their potential future.

The situation shifts in *In girum* due to several important differences: I directly shot a portion of the images; I wrote the text specifically for this particular film; and the theme of the film is not the spectacle, but real life. The films that interrupt the discourse do so primarily to support it positively, even if there is an element of irony (Lacenaire, the Devil, the fragment from Cocteau, or Custer's last stand). *The Charge of the Light Brigade* is intended to crudely and eulogistically "represent" a dozen years of the SI's actions!

As for the use of *music,* even though it is detourned like everything else, it will be felt by everyone in the normal way; it is never distanciated and always has a positive, "lyrical" aim.

Manuscript note, May 31, 1989. From the critical edition of In girum.

The Themes of *In girum*

The entire film (including the images, but already in the text of the spoken "commentary") is based on the theme of *water*. Hence the quotations from poets evoking the *evanescence* of everything (Li Po, Omar Khayyam, Heraclitus, Bossuet, Shelley?), who all used water as a metaphor for the flowing of *time*.

Secondarily, there is the theme of *fire; of momentary brilliance*—revolution, Saint-Germain-des-Prés, youth, love, *negation in the night,* the Devil, battles and "unfulfilled missions" where spellbound "passing travelers" meet their doom; and *desire within this night of the world* ("nocte consumimur igni").

But the water of time remains, and ultimately overwhelms and extinguishes the fire. Thus the brilliant youth of Saint-Germain-des-Prés, the fire of the ardent Charge of the Light Brigade, advancing "under the cannon fire of time," were drowned in the flowing water of their century. . . .

Manuscript fragment, December 22, 1977. From the critical edition of In girum.

Instructions to the *In girum* Sound Engineer

Throughout the film you should equalize the loudness of the spoken commentary, not only between different sentences, but even within each sentence. I am not striving for any oratorical effect by stressing any particular words. Try to produce a tone that is cold, monotonous, and slightly distant (though obviously not so distant that it becomes inaudible).

The few phrases that are spoken over a blank screen (excerpts from *Howls for Sade*) should be distinctly less loud than the spoken commentary, as if coming from farther away.

As for the dialogues in the sequences from other films, respect their internal variations of volume, but tone them down *slightly* so that they don't contrast too much with the commentary.

The music should be normal, relatively loud. Bring it to an abrupt halt at the end of each passage.

1977. From the critical edition of In girum.

Collaboration Conditions for the Final Video

Dear Brigitte,

This is to confirm the conclusions of our recent conversation in Normandy. I approve, under these precise conditions, your project of directing a one-hour historical program concerning my art and my time.

I will indicate to you—or in some cases I will furnish to you directly—all the visual and audio elements that will be specifically necessary to carry out this project. I will guarantee the pertinence of these elements and the authenticity of their use to treat this subject effectively—an important point, considering how much this subject has been polluted by so many legends. Answering to me alone, you will be completely responsible for determining the appropriate means to carry out this project, without accepting any intervention, restriction, or commentary from anyone else. I don't want to hear—and I don't want you to pay any attention to—any comments whatsoever from anyone else, *even laudatory ones*. It is in fact inconceivable that I would recognize anyone else as having the slightest competence or qualification to judge any aspect of my work or my conduct.

You will also see to it that the production deals with copyright matters with an appropriate precision and firmness.

Best regards,
Guy Debord

Letter from Guy Debord to Brigitte Cornand, March 17, 1993 (reproduced in Debord's Oeuvres, *pp. 1877–1878).*

Notes

HOWLS FOR SADE

General Note: *Howls for Sade* contains no images whatsoever. During the spoken dialogues the screen remains blank white. During the silences it remains blank black. For more information on this film, see pp. 220–221.

Page 2. *Treatise on Slime and Eternity* (Isidore Isou) and *The Anticoncept* (Gil J Wolman) are lettrist films. The other films listed are all well-known classics, respectively by Georges Méliès, Robert Wiene, René Clair, Sergei Eisenstein, Luis Buñuel, and Charlie Chaplin. **"Just as the projection . . . discussion":** quotation from Isou's *Esthétique du cinéma.* **Property is either real or personal:** literally, "movable or immovable"—French legal terminology for personal property and real estate. **She is ugliness and beauty—like everything we love today:** passage from Apollinaire's *The Poet Assassinated.*

3. Happiness is a new idea in Europe: quotation from French Revolution leader Louis-Antoine de Saint-Just. **"I know people . . . our works":** letter from Isou to Debord.

5. The cold of interstellar space . . . proximate dawn: quotation from Joyce's *Ulysses* (chap. 17). **The rapid passage of Jacques Vaché . . . Arthur Cravan . . .:** quotation from the last chapter of André Breton's *Lost Steps* (Breton is evoking Vaché and Cravan as precursors of dadaism). Jacques Vaché, a friend of Breton's during World War I, committed suicide in 1919. Arthur Cravan—poet, boxer, perpetrator of scandals, and "deserter of seventeen nations"—disappeared in the Gulf of Mexico in 1920. "Arthur Cravan is a prototype of these people [i.e. cultural saboteurs who refused to play along with the usual social games] glimpsed passing through the most radioactive zones of the cultural disaster without leaving behind them any commodities or memories" (*Situationist International Anthology: Revised and Expanded Edition,* PM Press, 2024, p. 140). **Article 1793:** Unlike the other excerpts from the French Civil Code, which Debord seems to have chosen for their content (themes of insanity, disappearance, etc.), this article was probably picked simply because 1793 was the year of the "Reign of Terror" during the French Revolution.

6. Order reigns but does not govern: Cf. the British constitutional doctrine: "The King [or Queen] reigns but does not govern."

7. Voice 4: Telephones, they're funny: Voice 4 is a "little girl" (actually a teenage lover of Debord's with a rather little-girlish voice). Her statements are sometimes childlike and a bit ungrammatical. **What a love-challenge** [*Quel amour-défi*]**, as Madame de Ségur said:** Probably a humorous play on the title *Quel amour d'enfant* by the Comtesse de

Ségur, nineteenth-century author of popular children's books. **Ivich:** This name (derived from a neurotic and rebellious female character in Sartre's *Roads to Freedom* trilogy) became an in-term among the lettrists for a charmingly unpredictable fantasy girl. There are some obscure allusions to her in the first few issues of *Potlatch.* **Gun Crazy:** title of an American B film (1949). **We won't forget this cursed planet:** purportedly (but probably not actually) the last words of the decadent writer Auguste Villiers de l'Isle-Adam.

8. Serge Berna: lettrist who organized the Easter 1950 scandal in which another lettrist (Michel Mourre) disguised himself as a Catholic priest, made his way onto the altar of Notre-Dame cathedral, and solemnly proclaimed to the audience of believers that the Catholic Church was a fraud and that God was dead. **Jean-Isidore:** Isidore Isou, the founder of lettrism. **Gabriel Pomerand:** another lettrist. The sentences containing these last two names are grammatically incomplete as in the original French text.

9. "Poetic worlds . . . forgotten": quotation from Isou's *Précisions sur ma poésie et moi.* **"When we were on the Shenandoah":** quotation from the film *Rio Grande.* The voice in Debord's film actually says "on the Chattanooga," but Debord corrected it to "on the Shenandoah" in the published script. Probably he intended to evoke the Shenandoah film passage (which he later used in *The Society of the Spectacle;* see p. 78), but misremembered the name during the original recording of the 1952 film. **down the hatch:** an attempt to render the French play on words: *couler* can mean either "to flow" (like the gin, etc.) or "to sink" (like the Spanish Armada of 1588).

10. Europe Quarter: Although Debord probably intends this phrase as a sort of poetic evocation of the continent of Europe, he is also drawing on the fact that Paris and Grenoble (home of Madelaine Reineri) each have a "Europe Quarter": a district in which most of the streets are named for various cities of Europe.

ON THE PASSAGE OF A FEW PERSONS THROUGH A RATHER BRIEF UNITY OF TIME

General Note: For more information on this film, see pp. 222 and 224.

13. *Unity of Time* (*unité de temps*): The French phrase can mean either "unit of time" or "unity of time." In the present context it suggests a period of time that forms a coherent whole, recalling the "unities" of time, place, and action in classical drama. **Saint-Germain-des-Prés:** Paris district frequented by the lettrists in the early 1950s. It was famous as the scene of postwar bohemianism and existentialism (Camus, Sartre, Simone de Beauvoir, etc.), but less visibly, in less trendy cafés and less reputable bars, Debord and his friends pursued their own adventures, evoked in this film and in *In girum,* hinted at in Debord's *Mémoires,* and recounted in detail in Jean-Michel Mension's *The Tribe.* **two couples . . . table:** The people in the photo (reproduced on p. 25) are Michèle Bernstein, Asger Jorn, Collette Gaillard, and Debord.

14. Human beings are not fully conscious . . . outcomes they had not intended: quotation from Henri Lefebvre's *Problèmes actuels du marxisme.* **masters and possessors of their own lives:** Cf. Descartes's *Discourse on Method* (Part 6): "we may find a practical philosophy by means of which . . . we may render ourselves the masters and possessors of nature." **Just as we do not judge . . . production:** quotation from the Preface to Marx's *Contribution to the Critique of Political Economy.*

15. Les Halles: labyrinthine food distribution center in the heart of Paris, destroyed in the 1960s to make way for posh malls and the Centre Pompidou museum—a glaring example of the "assassination of Paris" that Debord later laments in *In girum.*

16. "Our life is a journey . . . seek our passage": song of the Swiss Guards, quoted as an epigraph in Céline's novel *Journey to the End of the Night*. **trompe-l'oeil** ("deceiving the eye"): art in which objects are portrayed in such realistic detail that they seem to be real.

17. "In the process of movement and consequently by their ephemeral side": paraphrase of part of the Marx passage quoted in Note 50.

20. People can see . . . landscape is animated: Debord quotes the same passage (from Marx) in "Theory of the Dérive" (*SI Anthology*, p. 63).

20–21. The dictatorship of the proletariat . . . old society: quotation from Lenin's *"Left-Wing" Communism: An Infantile Disorder* (chap. 5).

21. Algiers, May 1958. General Massu and General Salan: Algeria had been in revolt against French domination since 1954. In May 1958 Salan and Massu, commanders of the French Army in Algeria, led a massive demonstration calling for a more authoritarian regime in France that would enable them to carry out a more vigorous repression of the Algerian revolt. Their favored candidate for this role, General Charles de Gaulle, distanced himself from their implied threat of a coup d'état, but declared that he would be ready to take power "if called." The French parliamentary government caved in to the pressure and allowed de Gaulle to "legally" take power and rewrite the constitution largely as he wished. The SI's on-the-spot analysis of the situation can be found in *Internationale Situationniste* #1 (p. 32).

22. swish pan shot: pan shot so rapid that the images become blurred.

24. in the Bois de Boulogne: The script only says "au Bois" ("in the Woods"), but French readers would understand this to mean the Bois de Boulogne, a posh park on the western edge of Paris.

CRITIQUE OF SEPARATION

General Note: For more information on this film, see p. 223.

29. Midway on the journey . . . was lost: opening lines of Dante's *Divine Comedy*.

31–32. If man is shaped by circumstances, it is necessary to create human circumstances: quotation from Marx and Engels's *The Holy Family* (VI.3.d).

32. Unitary urbanism: "theory of the combined use of arts and techniques as means contributing to the construction of a unified milieu in dynamic relation with experiments in behavior" (*SI Anthology*, p. 52). See the various articles on urbanism and psychogeography in the same volume (pp. 1–14, 62–66, 69–73, 86–89). **Until the environment . . . of boredom:** slightly modified passage from "Preliminary Problems in Constructing a Situation" (*SI Anthology*, p. 51).

34. Djamila Bouhired: Algerian rebel captured by French authorities in 1957. Under torture she confessed to bombing a café and was condemned to death, but was reprieved and later freed due to public pressure. The photograph (reproduced in *Internationale Situationniste* #2, p. 33) is cut off at the top so that only Lartéguy's hands are visible. **Jean Lartéguy,** a right-wing army officer and journalist, was presumably involved in Bouhired's interrogation or reporting on it.

35. lost children (*enfants perdus*): soldiers or scouts assigned to particularly dangerous missions. A comic strip frame included in Debord's *Mémoires* contains a picturesque description: "As an adventurer, or 'lost child,' he flits around the troop, a lone vanguard scout, exploring everywhere and ferreting out hidden dangers." Debord was obviously fond of this term, with its multiple evocative connotations: it also occurs in the last line of *Howls for Sade,* in the song from *Les Visiteurs du Soir* included in *In girum* (p. 189), and in several other places in his works.

36. Who would wish . . . could he serve?: quotation from Pascal's *Pensées* (#194). **Already farther away than India or China:** line from Baudelaire's poem "Moesta et Errabunda" ("Sad and Restless"). **idiotic spectacle . . . full of sound and fury:** Cf. the famous passage in Shakespeare's *Macbeth* (V.v): "Life . . . is a tale told by an idiot, full of sound and fury, signifying nothing."

37. "The production . . . but the scene": The three sentence fragments (along with the *Macbeth* line on p. 38) are from Debord's 1958 *Mémoires*—a book which itself consists entirely of fragmentary elements detourned from other sources. In this case, "It has all the elements of an American detective novel—violence, sex, cruelty—but the scene" is from a review of Albert Bester's science-fiction novel *The Demolished Man*.

38. The wine of life . . . dregs remain: Cf. "The wine of life is drawn, and the mere lees is left this vault to brag of" (*Macbeth*, II, iii).

39. Asger Jorn: Danish artist who was one of the key figures in the post–World War II radical avant-garde (Cobra, etc.) and in the early years of the SI. Although Jorn resigned from the SI in 1961, he and Debord remained close friends until his death in 1973. ***The Mysteries of New York*:** a 1915 movie serial.

THE SOCIETY OF THE SPECTACLE

General Note: The voice-over text of this film consists entirely of excerpts from Debord's book of the same name. The bracketed numbers at the end of each paragraph (not in the original script) indicate the paragraph number in the book.

The opening credits include the following statement: "In the détournement of preexisting films, use has been made of works by John Ford (*Rio Grande*), Nicolas Ray (*Johnny Guitar*), Josef von Sternberg (*The Shanghai Gesture*), Raoul Walsh

(*They Died With Their Boots On*), Orson Welles (*Mr. Arkadin*), and Sam Wood (*For Whom the Bell Tolls*), as well as works by a certain number of bureaucratic filmmakers of the so-called 'socialist' countries."

Although the following notes are extensive, I have focused mainly on matters that seem most relevant to the film. See my annotated edition of the book (PM Press, 2024) for more detailed information on Debord's allusions and détournements.

43. Since each particular feeling . . . the living: quotation from Hegel's "Love" (a manuscript fragment included in his *Early Theological Writings*). **Alice Becker-Ho** (Alice Debord): Guy Debord's partner and then wife for the last thirty years of his life. **In societies dominated . . . accumulation of spectacles:** The opening sentence (of both the book and the film) echoes the opening sentence of Marx's *Capital*: "The wealth of societies in which the capitalist mode of production prevails presents itself as an immense accumulation of commodities." (Marx is in turn giving a nod to *The Wealth of Nations* by his great predecessor, Adam Smith.)

44. The spectacle presents itself simultaneously as society itself, as a part of society, and as a *means of unification*: The first example among many revealing that "the spectacle" is not some fixed, objective entity that could be defined once and for all, but a multifaceted process or tendency within the present society that must be seen and examined from different angles. **Giscard d'Estaing:** Valéry Giscard d'Estaing, President of France (1974–1981). **Servan-Schreiber:** another French politician. **Séguy:** Georges Séguy, head of the CGT, France's largest labor union, dominated by the Communist Party. Séguy is attempting to justify the May 27, 1968 "Grenelle Accords" between the government, the employers, and the labor unions, which agreed to a large package of wage and benefit increases for the workers if they would abandon their nationwide wildcat strike and factory occupations. (The following day rank-and-file workers all over the country overwhelmingly rejected those Accords.) With exquisite irony Debord is detourning Séguy's mealy-mouthed prevarications into a totally opposite sense, since the May revolt did indeed have many "positive" aspects while nevertheless leaving "much to be done" (above all, learning how to do without bureaucrats like Séguy).

45. The spectacle is not a collection . . . mediated by images: Cf. *Capital* (chap. 33): "Capital is not a thing; it is a social relation between people that is mediated by things."

46. the true is a moment of the false: Cf. Hegel's *Phenomenology of Spirit* (Preface): "The false (though no longer *as* false) is a moment of the true." **What appears is good; what is good appears:** Cf. Hegel's *Philosophy of Right* (Preface): "What is rational is real, and what is real is rational."

47. When the real world is transformed into mere images, mere images become real beings: Cf. Marx and Engels's *The Holy Family* (chap. 8.3): "For one to whom the sensuously perceptible world becomes a mere idea, mere ideas are transformed into sensuously perceptible beings. The figments of his brain assume corporeal form." **The spectacle is the bad dream . . . guardian of that sleep:** Cf. Freud's *The Interpretation of Dreams* (chap. 5.C), which contends that dreams reflect "the wish for sleep" and that "dreams are the guardians of sleep." **The fact that the practical power . . . in contradiction with itself:** Cf. Marx's "Theses on Feuerbach": "But the fact that the secular basis detaches itself from itself and establishes itself as an independent realm in the clouds can only be explained by the divisions and contradictions within this secular basis."

48. In the spectacle, a part of the world . . . is superior to it: Cf. Marx's "Theses on Feuerbach": "It thus tends to divide society into two parts, one of which is superior to society."

48–49. Workers do not produce themselves . . . excluded from that life: Cf. various passages from the "Alienated Labor" section of Marx's *Manuscripts of 1844,* e.g. "The worker is related to the *product* of his labor as to an *alien* object. The more the worker exerts himself in his work, the more powerful becomes the world of objects that he brings into being over against himself, and the poorer his inner world becomes, and the less he belongs to himself. . . . The greater his activity, the less he possesses. What is embodied in the product of his labor is no longer his own. The greater this product, the less he is himself. The *alienation* of the worker in his product means not only that his labor becomes an *object,* an external existence, but that it exists *outside him,* independently of him and alien to him, and begins to confront him as an autonomous power; that the life he has bestowed on the object confronts him as a hostile and alien force."

49. "zero degree of writing": title of a book by Roland Barthes (translated into English as *Writing Degree Zero*). It means writing totally stripped of substance and meaning, leaving nothing but the bare skeleton: writing "as such." Its "reversal" is thus writing that has the fullest possible substance and significance.

50. The very style of dialectical theory . . . inevitable destruction: Cf. Marx's Afterword to the Second German Edition of *Capital:* "In its rational form dialectics is a scandal and abomination to bourgeois society and its doctrinaire professors, because in comprehending the existing state of things it simultaneously recognizes the negation of that state, its inevitable destruction; because it regards every historically developed social form as in fluid movement, and thus takes into account its transitory nature as well as its momentary existence." **"Truth is not like some finished product . . . made it":** quotation from the Preface to Hegel's *Phenomenology of Spirit.* **reversal:** The French word *renversement* can mean reversal or inversion, but it also has a more active connotation of overthrowing or overturning. **détournement:** See "A User's Guide to Détournement" (pp. 217–220).

50–51. Ideas improve . . . Plagiarism is necessary . . . right one: This paragraph is a verbatim plagiarism from Isidore Ducasse's *Poésies*.

51. Détournement has grounded its cause on nothing but . . . critique: Cf. the opening of Max Stirner's *The Ego and His Own:* "I have founded my cause on nothing."

52. The spectacular expropriators must be expropriated: allusion to the expropriation of the capitalist expropriators envisaged in Marx's *Capital* (end of chap. 22). **The world has already been filmed. The point now is to change it:** Cf. Marx's "Theses on Feuerbach": "The philosophers have only interpreted the world. The point is to change it." **Two harbors . . . by Claude Lorrain:** *Port Scene with the Villa Medici* (1637) and *Ulysses Returns Chryseis to Her Father* (1648). Debord mentions Lorrain's harbor paintings (he did several others along the same lines) in *Potlatch #2* and *Les Lèvres Nues #6* and *#9*. He liked them because of their splendidly nonfunctionalist juxtaposition of palaces and harbors, and said that nothing could rival them in beauty but a Paris metro map: "I am not, of course, talking about mere physical beauty —the new beauty can only be a beauty of situations—but simply about the particularly moving presentation, in both cases, of a *sum of possibilities*" (*SI Anthology*, p. 11). **When art becomes independent . . . the dusk of life:** Cf. Hegel's *Philosophy of Right* (Preface): "When philosophy paints its gray on gray, a form of life has grown old. Gray philosophy can understand it, but it cannot rejuvenate it. The owl of Minerva [a.k.a Athena, the goddess of wisdom] takes flight only at dusk."

52–53. Johnny Guitar: Here and in the other *Johnny Guitar* sequence (pp. 74–75) I have reproduced the film's original dialogue (the clips included in Debord's film are dubbed in French).

53. Cieszkowski's *Prolegomena to Historiosophy* (1838) applied Hegel's dialectic to the Hegelian system itself, envisioning future historical transformations that would transcend that system and stressing the preeminence of practice over theory. **Marchais:** Georges Marchais, head of the French Communist Party. **Mitterrand:** François Mitterrand, Socialist Party leader, later President of France (1981–1995). **conflict is at the origin of everything in its world:** Cf. Heraclitus: "Conflict is the origin of all things."

54. our old enemy the commodity . . . metaphysical subtleties . . . "imperceptible as well as perceptible things": Cf. "The Fetishism of the Commodity" (*Capital*, chap. 1, sec. 4): "A commodity appears at first glance to be something very trivial and obvious. Analysis reveals that it is in reality a very strange thing, abounding in metaphysical subtleties and theological abstrusities. . . . A commodity is therefore a mysterious thing, simply because in it the social character of men's labor appears to them as an objective character stamped on the product of that labor; because the relation of the producers to the sum total of their own labor is presented to them as a social relation, existing not between themselves, but between the products of their labor. This is the reason why the products of labor become commodities, social things whose qualities are at the same time perceptible and imperceptible by the senses." **Pompidou:** Georges Pompidou, President of France (1969–1974).

55. remaining unknown precisely because it was so familiar: Cf. Hegel's *Phenomenology of Spirit* (Preface): "What is familiarly known is not really known, precisely because it is so familiar." **opium war:** allusion to the Opium Wars of 1839–1842 and 1857–1860. China wanted to ban the British opium trade, and England went to war against China to force it to accept that trade, which at the time was one of the main sources of the British Empire's wealth. England (joined by France in the second one) won both wars and gained Hong Kong and several other port districts as free-trade areas (referred to as "Concessions"—see pp. 66–67). On the **Watts riot** (1965), see Debord's article "The Decline and Fall of the Spectacle-Commodity Economy" (*SI Anthology*, pp. 194–203). **survival:**

For in-depth analysis of the situationists' distinction between real life and mere "survival," see Raoul Vaneigem's "Basic Banalities" (*SI Anthology*, pp. 117–130, 154–173) and his book *The Revolution of Everyday Life*.

56. *condottiere* . . . for its own sake: *Condottieri* were mercenary leaders in Renaissance Italy who often ended up taking over the small states they were hired to fight for.

59. Johnny Hallyday, Eddy Mitchell, Dick Rivers: popular French singers.

60. The spectacle exists in a *concentrated* form or a *diffuse* form: In chapter 4 of his 1988 book *Comments on the Society of the Spectacle* (translated by Malcolm Imry; Verso, 1990) Debord updates his analysis: "In 1967 I distinguished two rival and successive forms of spectacular power, the concentrated and the diffuse. . . . The former, presenting an ideology concentrated around a dictatorial personality, had accompanied the Nazi and Stalinist totalitarian counterrevolutions. The latter, inciting wage-earners to apply their freedom of choice to a vast range of new commodities now on offer, had represented the Americanization of the world. . . . Since then a third form has been established—a calculated combination of the two preceding forms, based on the victory of the form that had proven the stronger of the two: the diffuse. This is the *integrated spectacle*, which has since tended to impose itself globally." Debord's *Comments* book is largely concerned with examining the implications of this new form of spectacular power. **bureaucratic capitalism** (a.k.a. "state capitalism"): Although Western "free enterprise" capitalism has also become increasingly bureaucratized, when Debord uses the terms "bureaucratic capitalism," "the bureaucracy," "the bureaucratic class," etc., he is referring to the "Communist" parties' evolution into a new type of totalitarian bureaucratic ruling class. See *The Society of the Spectacle* ##103–113.

62–63. The spectacle does not sing of men and their arms: Cf. the opening line of Virgil's *The Aeneid:* "I sing of arms and of the man who . . ."

63. In this blind struggle each commodity . . . absolute realization: Cf. Hegel's *Reason in History* (the introduction to his *Philosophy of History*): "Particular interests contend with one another, and some are destroyed in the process. But it is from this very conflict and destruction of particular things that the universal emerges. The universal Idea does not itself enter into conflict and danger; it remains in the background, untouched and unharmed, and sends forth the particular interests of passion to fight and wear themselves out in its stead. With what we may call the *cunning of reason,* it sets the passions to work in its service, so that the agents by which it gives itself existence must pay the penalty and suffer the loss."

64. Lin Biao: During the Chinese "Cultural Revolution" Lin Biao (Lin Piao) was Mao's designated successor—until there was a sudden turnabout and he was reported killed in a plane crash while trying to leave the country. The third person in the photo (reproduced on p. 104) is Zhou Enlai (Chou En-lai), one of the few bureaucrats who managed to stay on top through all the party-line zigzags. See Debord's article "The Explosion Point of Ideology in China" (*SI Anthology,* pp. 240–251) and Simon Leys's *The Chairman's New Clothes: Mao and the Cultural Revolution,* online at www.bopsecrets.org/CF/leys.htm.

65. Nothing stands still for it. . . . inclination: Cf. Pascal's *Pensées* (#72): "When we try to anchor ourselves to any point, it wavers and leaves us; and if we pursue it, it eludes our grasp and vanishes forever. Nothing stands still for us. This is our natural condition, yet it is completely contrary to our inclination."

66. Buenaventura Durruti (1896–1936): Spanish revolutionary anarchist; leader of an anarchist militia column during the Spanish Civil War. See

Abel Paz's *Durruti: The People Armed.* **Fellow prole-tarians, are we really living . . . birth?:** Although the montage makes it seem as if Durruti is saying these words, they are actually a quotation from Bossuet's *Funeral Oration for Maria-Theresa of Austria* (1683), except that the word "Christians" is re-placed with "proletarians." ***Ten Days That Shook the World*** (a.k.a. *October*): 1928 film about the 1917 Russian Revolution by Sergei Eisenstein.

67. This homogenizing power . . . walls of China: Cf. Marx and Engels's *Communist Mani-festo:* "The cheapness of its commodities is the heavy artillery that batters down all the walls of China."

68. *Manuscripts of 1844* (a.k.a. "Economic and Philosophical Manuscripts of 1844"): The quota-tion is from the Third Manuscript, part 3: "Human Needs and the Division of Labor."

70. *The Shanghai Gesture:* In this and in the later scene from the same film (p. 76) I have reproduced the actual English dialogue. Debord's script quotes the slightly different French subtitles.

73. Women lovers, as memories: The French (*Des amoureuses, comme souvenirs*) is equally vague. One guesses that the women shown are former lovers of Debord's.

75. The bird of Minerva: the owl. **And therefore . . . spoil the idle pleasures of these days:** lines from the opening scene of Shakespeare's *Richard III.* I have changed a couple of words to match the sense of the French translation used by Debord.

78. "Herodotus . . . the deeds of men": opening sentence of Herodotus's *History of the Persian Wars.* **"Tennis Court Oath":** At the beginning of the French Revolution, June 20, 1789, the represen-tatives of the Third Estate (the nonprivileged classes), locked out of the national meeting hall in Versailles, assembled in a nearby indoor tennis court and took an oath never to separate until a

written constitution was established for France. The image is from a black-and-white sketch by Jacques-Louis David, in preparation for his classic oil painting of the event.

79. Professionals of values: i.e. professional stock traders. **"Once there was history, but not any more":** quotation from Marx's *The Poverty of Philosophy* (chap. 2.7).

81: the consciousness that always arrives too late: Cf. Hegel's *Philosophy of Right* (Preface): "As for trying to teach the world what it ought to be, for this purpose philosophy always arrives too late."

82. Kronstadt sailors: This sequence (from Dzigan's 1936 film *We From Kronstadt*) has no con-nection with the 1921 revolt against the Bolshe-viks. It depicts the sailors' 1919 defense of Petro-grad against the Whites during the Russian Civil War. The caption for the still from this sequence (p. 107) is from the revolutionary song they are singing: "The Internationale."

83. Winter Palace: palace of the Czars, captured during the Russian revolution of October 1917. **Tuileries Palace:** palace of the French monarchy, taken over during the French Revolution.

84. "immensity of its own tasks": Marx uses this phrase in several places, e.g. "Proletarian revolu-tions . . . recoil again and again before the immen-sity of their tasks, until a situation is finally cre-ated that goes beyond the point of no return" (*The Eighteenth Brumaire of Louis Bonaparte*).

85. The soviet . . . was not a theoretical discov-ery: The first soviet (Russian for "council") was formed by striking workers during the 1905 Rus-sian revolution. No previous radical theorists had envisaged this form of popular self-organization, however obvious it may have seemed in retrospect. **the most advanced theoretical truth . . . was its own existence in practice:** Cf. Marx's *The Civil War in France:* "The greatest social measure of the Paris Commune was its own working existence."

Vendôme Column: Erected by Napoleon as a monument to the victories of French imperialism, it was pulled down during the Paris Commune (1871). **You will learn . . . party of one:** The subtitle about the bitterness of exile is from Dante's *Paradise* (Canto 17). Marx and Bakunin both spent most of their life in exile. On the split between the two, see *The Society of the Spectacle* #91.

86. Those who . . . hierarchical parties: Cf. Machiavelli's *Discourses* (III.3): "Whoever makes himself tyrant of a state and does not kill Brutus will not last long; nor will he who restores the liberty to a state and does not kill the sons of Brutus." **On the Odessa steps . . . demonstrators:** the famous scene from Eisenstein's *Potemkin*, dramatizing the Russian revolution of 1905. **Bruno Rizzi:** author of *The Bureaucratization of the World* (1939), which includes what can be considered the first in-depth analysis of the class nature of the "Soviet" Union.

89–90. Stalin: The description of Stalin's power quotes or echoes Hegel's description of the power of the Roman emperors over their subjects in *The Phenomenology of Spirit* (VI.A.c): "This lord and master of the world holds himself in this way to be the absolute person who embraces within himself the whole of existence and for whom there exists no superior Spirit. He is a person, but the solitary person who stands over against all the rest. . . . In this knowledge of himself as the sum and substance of all actual powers, this lord and master of the world is the titanic self-consciousness that thinks of itself as an actual living god. . . . The lord of the world becomes really conscious of what he is—the universal power of the actual world—through the destructive power he exerts against the self of his subjects."

90. the Reichstag burns: The February 1933 arson of the German national government building was almost certainly perpetrated or orchestrated by the Nazis themselves. In any case, it was exploited to give them an excuse to outlaw the Communist Party and expand their dictatorial powers. Debord's script sums up the scene without giving the full dialogue. The French subtitles of this 1954 East German film (Slatan Dudow's *Stärker als die nacht*) read: "Comrades! Alarming news: the Reichstag is in flames! Fascist Radio claims that the Communists started it—a monstrous provocation by the Nazi government!" Police officer: "This meeting is now closed!" The militant continues: "They want to outlaw our party! To choke off the voice of the working class! As long as there are Communists in Germany the fight against Hitler will never end! Fight for peace among all peoples. Hitler means war!" On fascism, see *The Society of the Spectacle* #109. **There's a valley in Spain called Jarama . . . as well:** Debord quotes a French translation of these original English lyrics by Alex McDade, a volunteer in the Abraham Lincoln Brigade, one of the international contingents that went to fight the Francoists during the Spanish Civil War (1936-1939). The song is also known in a somewhat different version by Woody Guthrie. On the Spanish civil war and revolution, see the next note and also Note 121.

91. Spanish partisans: The situationists saw the Spanish revolution (1936-1937) as the final act of the classic proletarian revolutionary movement, which everywhere else had already been defeated and destroyed by the combined forces of Stalinism, fascism, and reformism. "The classic workers' movement can be considered to have begun a couple decades before the official formation of the International [1864] with the first linking up of communist groups of several countries that Marx and his friends organized from Brussels in 1845. And it was completely finished after the defeat of the Spanish revolution, that is, after the Barcelona May days of 1937" (*SI Anthology*, p. 110). The **Nazi concentration camp** scene (1930s) and the **Place de la Concorde** scene (ca. 1960s) mark the boundaries of the "social peace" established over the dead body of the old revolutionary movement, before the beginning of a new era of revolt heralded by the situationists in the early 1960s and exemplified most dramatically and undeniably by May 1968.

92. the proletariat cannot truly recognize itself in any particular wrong . . . real life: Cf. Marx's *Introduction to the Critique of Hegel's Philosophy of Right,* which describes the proletariat as "a sector of society that has a general character because its sufferings are general, a sector that does not claim any *particular right* because the wrong it suffers is not any *particular wrong* but a *general wrong*." **May 1968:** On the May revolt see René Viénet's *Enragés and Situationists in the Occupation Movement* and the articles, documents, and graffiti in the *SI Anthology* (pp. 288–325, 435–458).

93. From this day . . . we band of brothers: Cf. Shakespeare's *Henry V* (IV.iii): "And Crispin Crispian shall ne'er go by, from this day to the ending of the world, but we in it shall be remembered—we few, we happy few, we band of brothers." Debord cites the last nine words in English. **Christian Sebastiani** and **Patrick Cheval:** May 1968 rebels who subsequently became members of the SI. **"humanity won't be happy until the . . .":** The graffitist was presumably interrupted. The complete text of this notorious slogan goes: "Humanity won't be happy until the last capitalist is hung with the guts of the last bureaucrat."

96. In a café in Tangiers . . .: This is the actual English dialogue (from *Mr. Arkadin*). Debord's script slightly abridges the French subtitles. The references to **Poland** evoke the then-recent workers' insurrectionary strike in Poland (December 1970–January 1971), crushed by the Stalinist regime.

97. East Berlin: 1953 workers' uprising, which opposed the Stalinist bureaucracy with a demand for "a government of steelworkers." **But if we consider . . . it negates:** quotation from Hegel's *Phenomenology of Spirit* (V.C.a). **"It would obviously be easy . . . success was guaranteed":** quotation from Marx, letter to Kugelmann (April 17, 1871).

98. Mr. Arkadin: This is the actual English dialogue of Orson Welles's film *Mr. Arkadin* (a.k.a. *Confidential Report*). Debord's script reproduces the slightly abridged French subtitles. **Ivan Chtcheglov:** See Note 170. **Asger Jorn:** See Note 39. **Arkadin concludes another story:** His story began as follows: A scorpion asks a frog to carry him across a stretch of water. The frog hesitates, fearing that the scorpion will sting him. The scorpion replies that it would be illogical for the scorpion to sting the frog while being carried, because he himself would then be drowned. So the frog starts carrying him, and half way across the water the scorpion very illogically stings the frog. . . .

REFUTATION OF ALL THE JUDGMENTS . . .

General Note: During the opening credits there is a soundtrack from a French traffic report (not mentioned in Debord's script), which runs roughly as follows: "Access to the route to Narbonne via the Central Highway is still very difficult. Same thing for the A9 tollbooth, with a bottleneck on the approach and afterward. For those heading toward Spain, a bottleneck of 15 kilometers continues. On National 9 there's a 14-kilometer bottleneck extending to Dijon—a total of 30 kilometers of bottlenecks from Narbonne to Dijon. The bottleneck at Pertuis still extends 26 kilometers, and the hot, stormy weather there and the gusty winds in the middle of the vineyards at Roussillon reminded me of other bottlenecks. . . . In Charente, firemen came to the aid of motorists stuck in the bottlenecks at La Rochelle–La Pallice. The motorists had to wait there for five hours under the hot sun. Firemen brought them water and sympathetic local residents sprinkled their vehicles with garden hoses. Now I'll turn you over to Bernard Avali and those bottlenecks at Bordeaux. . . . The litany begins—on National 10, Montbazon 2 kilometers . . ."

At the end of the credits, the following notice

appears: "The reviews most specifically discussed in the present film appeared in 1974 in *Le Nouvel Observateur* (April 29), *Le Quotidien de Paris* (May 2), *Le Monde* (May 9), *Télérama* (May 11), *Le Nouvel Observateur* (May 13), *Charlie-Hebdo* (May 13), *Le Point* (May 20), and *Cinéma 74* (June)."

The film then begins with the Chateaubriand epigraph on p. 111.

113. radio announcer reporting . . . traffic jams: This traffic report (mentioned but not quoted in Debord's script) runs roughly as follows: "And on National 9 traffic is backed up to Tariac. For those of you coming home, there is still 4 kilometers of nonstop bumper-to-bumper traffic in one lane. The jam at Pertuis has only gotten worse and already goes for 5 kilometers. . . . Everything's fine on National 10 and National 12—we flew over that just a moment ago—as well as on Autoroute West. Whatever problems remain are on Autoroute South. As we said earlier, there are two jams, one just before . . ."

114. The spectacle does not debase people to the point of making them love it: Cf. Vauvenargues's Maxim #22: "Servitude debases people to the point of making them love it."

115. the woods of history . . . march against their castle: allusion to the march of the Birnam Wood in the last act of Shakespeare's *Macbeth*.

117. the wisdom of President Giscard (*la pensée du président Giscard*): In French this phrase is humorously reminiscent of *la pensée du président Mao* ("Chairman Mao thought"), the exotic form of Stalinism that was fashionable at that time.

118. as Machiavelli put it: The reference is probably to *The Discourses* (I.25): "He who desires to alter the government of a state, and wishes to have it accepted by everyone, must at least retain the semblance of the old forms, so that it may seem to the people that there has been no change in the institutions, even though they are in fact entirely different from the old ones. . . . And if the number,

authority, and duration of the terms of service of the magistrates are changed, the titles at least ought to be preserved." **the class struggle in Portugal:** allusion to the Portuguese revolution of 1974-1975, which was continuing as Debord was making this film. The best account is Phil Mailer's *Portugal: The Impossible Revolution?* **Cunhal:** Alvaro Cunhal, head of the Portuguese Communist Party. **Soares:** Mário Soares, head of the Portuguese Socialist Party, later prime minister and then president of Portugal.

119. It seeks to understand . . . before our very eyes: Cf. the *Communist Manifesto:* "The theoretical conclusions of the communists are in no way based on ideas or principles that have been invented or discovered by this or that would-be universal reformer. They merely express, in general terms, actual relations springing from an existing class struggle, from a historical movement that is developing before our very eyes."

121. Budapest not so long ago: allusion to the Hungarian revolution of 1956, crushed by the Russian army. **Historic Compromise:** proposed alliance between the Italian Communist Party and the other Italian parties during the 1970s. **Popular Front governments:** coalitions of centrist and leftist parties during the late 1930s. The French Popular Front held power from 1936–1938. Its election was accompanied by widespread strikes and factory occupations (May–June 1936), but the workers were maneuvered into returning to work by the promise of reforms. The Spanish Popular Front was elected in February 1936. General Francisco Franco's fascistic military uprising against that government (July 1936) triggered a popular movement to defend it which rapidly developed into a widespread and predominately anarchist revolution. While the Popular Front government and the anarchists maintained an uneasy alliance in the civil war against the fascists, the government (and in particular the Stalinists) actually devoted much of their efforts to sabotaging the revolution; after which they were in turn defeated by the Francoists in 1939. See *The Society of the Spectacle* #94.

124. magazine of . . . Mitterrand's electoral constituency: *Charlie-Hebdo.* **Chirac:** Jacques Chirac, French Prime Minister (1974–1976) and later President (1995–2007). **Vincennes University:** post-1968 university on the outskirts of Paris noted for its permissive administrative policies and its trendy "postmodernist" professors such as Foucault, Lyotard, and Deleuze.

126. Lyotard, Castoriadis: Jean-François Lyotard and Cornelius Castoriadis (a.k.a. Paul Cardan), participants in the ultraleftist *Socialisme ou Barbarie* group during the 1950s who later took up careers as authors and academics. The SI acknowledged the radical contributions of *Socialisme ou Barbarie* (Debord himself even collaborated with the group for a few months in 1960–1961), but called attention to its increasing degeneration into incoherence in the early sixties. (See *Internationale Situationniste* #9, pp. 34–35, and #10, pp. 78–79.)

128. The specialists . . . bad cinema: Debord is echoing the Foreword to Marx's *The Poverty of Philosophy:* "In France, Proudhon has the right to be a bad economist because he is reputed to be a good German philosopher. In Germany, he has the right to be a bad philosopher because he is reputed to be one of the ablest of French economists. But being both a German and an economist, I wish to protest against this double error."

IN GIRUM IMUS NOCTE
ET CONSUMIMUR IGNI

General Note: The notes below set in ***bold italics*** are by Debord himself, published in the "critical edition" of *In girum* (Lebovici, 1990; Gallimard, 1999). In cases where Debord merely noted the source of a quotation or détournement, however, they have not been so indicated, but have been

silently incorporated with the other notes by the translator.

133. In girum . . . igni: The title (a medieval Latin palindrome of unknown authorship) means "We turn in the night and are consumed by fire." **in this film:** ***In 1978 this discourse was illustrated by a film. This sort of film never really had any place in "the cinema," just as it can now be seen that the cinema itself no longer has much of a place in this society. But the text alone (with a few notes to help clarify the meaning) should be instructive enough. Our time will have left few other writings that consider so bluntly the immense transformations it has gone through. What insights about it could we expect from those who have shared any of its interlinked ambitions and illusions?*** [Debord refers to this film in the past tense here because these notes of his originally appeared in a printed edition of the spoken text (without the image descriptions) published several years after he had withdrawn *In girum* and all his other films from circulation.]

134. "People who love life go to the cinema": ***A publicity campaign had just been based on this idiotic slogan. It did not persuade the public to start going to the movies again.*** **A modern employee:** The French word *employé(e)* is roughly equivalent to "white-collar worker." In this film Debord is talking more specifically about "the stratum of low-level skilled employees in the various 'service' occupations that are so necessary to the present production system: management, control, maintenance, research, teaching, propaganda, entertainment, and pseudocritique," which he goes on to criticize in scathing detail. (This stratum seems to be much the same as the "cadre" that Debord analyzed in *The Real Split in the International:* see "Theses on the SI and Its Time" ##34–38.) For the sake of consistency, I have translated the term as "employee" throughout, although in some contexts it might be more usual to refer to the people in the images as "a yuppie couple," "a middle-class woman," etc. It should also be noted that Debord's characterization of the "class composition" of film audiences naturally applies more to 1978 France than to other times and places. In the United States, for example, the increasingly moronic quality of Hollywood films over the last several decades has catered to increasingly juvenile and illiterate audiences, whatever their class origins or social pretentions might be.

135. They share poverties . . . without sharing in the revolts: Debord is echoing Marx's *Introduction to a Critique of Hegel's Philosophy of Right:* "We Germans have shared in the restorations of modern nations without having shared in their revolutions." **modernized illiteracy:** *When this film was made, that phrase was simply a figurative way of referring to the general ignorance produced by spectacular culture. A few years later it had become evident that that culture was also beginning to produce a new form of illiteracy in the literal sense of the word.*

137. those possessing nothing: *This was the original Roman sense of the word "proletarius."*

139–140. hope of distracting attention . . . destitution: *This social need is specifically catered to by a large portion of present-day news reportage and by the commercial campaigns of "charitable" organizations.*

142. the only one of its habits that seems to have been respected: *This is no longer the case. After abolishing so many other things, economic progress has now abolished the cinema to which these spectators were rather simple-mindedly devoted. New imperatives, to which these same spectators are totally subordinate, have managed to force them to love a more precise expression of the ruling rationality: the video clip.*

143–144. The cinema I am talking about . . . time sweeps away: Cf. Bossuet's *Funeral Oration for Henrietta-Anna of England:* "The wisdom he is talking about here is that deranged sort of wisdom, skilled in self-torment and self-deceit, which consumes itself in the present and loses itself in

the future. Its mass of reasonings and grand efforts amounts to nothing but a useless accumulation of things the wind sweeps away."

144. The latest fashion in intellectual lackeydom: *Referred to during a brief period by the media as "the New Philosophers."*

144–145. the real movement that dissolves existing conditions: Cf. Marx and Engels's *The German Ideology* (I.ii.5): "Communism is for us not a state of affairs which is to be established, an *ideal* to which reality will have to adjust itself. What we call communism is the *real movement* that is dissolving existing conditions."

145. Dramatized anecdotes have been the building blocks of the cinema: Cf. "Prisons are built with stones of Law, Brothels with bricks of Religion" (Blake, *The Marriage of Heaven and Hell*).

146. This film disdains the image-scraps of which it is composed: Cf. one of Saint-Just's last speeches before he was guillotined: "I disdain the dust of which I am composed and which is speaking to you." **troops landing on a beach, June 6, 1944:** i.e. in Normandy during the Allied invasion on D-Day.

146–147. I have even been plagiarized much less . . . until now at least: *Some people wanted to start doing so in 1982; but by then it was too late to launch a career in this art before its collapse.*

147. "It is no small satisfaction . . ." follows the French translation quoted by Debord. Swift's actual words (from the final chapter of *Gulliver's Travels*) are: "I am not a little pleased that this Work of mine can possibly meet with no Censurers."

148. no real opposition . . . refraining: *There are no exceptions to this historical law. It constitutes the central difficulty of anticapitalist revolutions, as Robert Michels pointed out as long* *ago as 1912 in his book "Political Parties: A Sociological Study of the Oligarchical Tendencies of Modern Democracy."*

149. Kriegspiel ("War Game"): a board game invented by Debord, based on military strategy in the era of Clausewitz and Napoleon. See the book on this game by Debord and Alice Becker-Ho: *Le "Jeu de la Guerre".*

151. Jomini: Antoine-Henri Jomini, one of Napoleon's generals. **level of competence (or even a little above it):** allusion to the Peter Principle: "Employees tend to rise to their level of incompetence" (because if they are competent at a particular job they are likely to be promoted, until they reach a position where they are not competent and are thus no longer promoted).

152. "the knights and ladies . . . bold adventures": first two lines of Ariosto's *Orlando Furioso.* **in the middle of the century:** *1951.*

153. "Here was the abode . . . into the sea": poem by Li Po. **driven out and dispersed:** Cf. Machiavelli's *The Prince* (chap. 5): "Whoever becomes the ruler of a city that is accustomed to freedom and does not destroy it can expect to be destroyed by it, for it can always find a pretext for rebellion in the name of its former freedom and age-old customs, which are never forgotten despite the passage of time or any benefits it has received. No matter what the ruler does or what precautions he takes, the inhabitants will never forget that freedom or those customs—*unless they are driven out and dispersed.*" (italics added). Debord used this passage as the epigraph to chapter 7 of *The Society of the Spectacle.*

154. The houses . . . done to a street: Cf. Canto 15 of *Paradise,* where Dante speaks of Florence as it used to be: "The houses were not yet deserted. Sardanapalus had not yet come to show what could be done in a chamber." The first sentence also contains a sarcastic allusion to the modern fashion for antique styles such as exposed-beam ceilings.

155. *The Man Without Qualities* (Robert Musil): The quote is from vol. 1, part 2, chap. 61.

156. Bliss it was to be young . . .: Cf. "Bliss was it in that dawn to be alive / But to be young was very heaven!" (Wordsworth, *The Prelude,* Book XI, referring to the French Revolution). **you cannot enter the same river twice:** Heraclitus. **a neighborhood where the negative held court:** *In 1952, in the middle of the 6th Arrondissement.* **"Cave of Time"** (*Cave du Temps*): Although the French word *cave* usually means cellar or underground nightclub, the sense here is indeed "cave." In this episode of *Prince Valiant* (April 23, 1939) the hero has come across this cave in the woods; the young woman is a benevolent witch and the "Time" referred to is Father Time himself, with whom Valiant unsuccessfully wrestles. **"Never work!":** This graffiti was written by Debord himself in 1953.

157. Arthur Cravan: See Note 5. **Lacenaire:** Pierre-François Lacenaire (1803–1836), "the dandy of crime": thief, murderer, and author, whose *Memoirs* were published following his execution. The Lacenaire clips are all from Marcel Carné's film *Children of Paradise* (1943–1945).

158. "Article 488 . . .": This paragraph and the seven that follow are excerpts from *Howls for Sade.*

159–160. Why should someone . . . remained the same: Cf. Pascal's *Pensées* (#88): "How can one who was so weak in his childhood become really strong when he grows older? . . . What has been weak can never become absolutely strong. People may say, 'He has grown, he has changed'; but he is also the same."

161. "highest of time": *Phrase used by Thomas Hobbes to describe a period of troubles.* [Debord is probably referring to the opening sentence of Hobbes's *Behemoth: The History of the Causes of the Civil Wars of England:* "If in time, as in place, there were degrees of high and low, I verily believe that the highest of time would be that which passed between 1640 and 1660."]

163. Andreas Baader and Gudrun Enslin: members of the Baader–Meinhof Group (a.k.a. the Red Army Faction), killed in a German prison in 1977. **announcing . . . that God was dead:** allusion to the lettrist Notre-Dame scandal of 1950. See Note 8.

163–164. I drank their wine and I remain faithful to them: *The feudal oath of fidelity included the phrase: "I have eaten his bread."*

164. "Drink and the devil had done for the rest": song from Robert Louis Stevenson's *Treasure Island.* **Midway on the journey . . .** echoes the opening lines of Dante's *Divine Comedy* (quoted more fully on p. 29). **lost youth** (*la jeunesse perdue*) has the same ambiguity in French as in English. Debord specified that he meant it in the sense of irredeemably disaffected young people, not in the sense of losing one's youth by growing older.

164–165. " 'Tis all a checkerboard . . . lays": quatrain by Omar Khayyam. I have used the classic Edward Fitzgerald translation.

165. "How many ages . . . yet unknown!": lines from Shakespeare's *Julius Caesar* (III.i). **"What is writing . . . equality of friends":** quotation from Alcuin's *The Tale of the Good Child.* **"Bernard, what do you want . . . will not last forever":** quotation from Bossuet's *Panegyric on Saint Bernard of Clairvaux.* **She vanishes** (*Elle fuit*): This phrase would normally be translated as "It vanishes"—*Elle* refers to the feminine noun *félicité* (happiness) in the previous, unquoted sentence of Bossuet's text. Debord's montage, however, takes advantage of the ambiguity in French to make it seem to refer to the woman in the accompanying image ("she who was the most beautiful that year): Éliane Papaï (later Éliane Brau), one of Debord's lovers from the early 1950s (see illustration on p. 198).

166. The same woman reappears: i.e. Éliane Papaï. **"One generation passes away . . . like a shadow":** quotation from Ecclesiastes. I have mostly followed the Revised Standard Version,

though the French version quoted by Debord has slightly different senses for the last two sentences. **"No, let us cross over . . . trees":** last words of General Stonewall Jackson, dying in battle.

167. as if with a knife in my hand: Cf. Machiavelli's *The Prince* (chap. 8): "Whoever acts otherwise, either through timidity or bad counsels, can never rest but is always obliged to stand with knife in hand . . ."

169. As for myself . . . done anything any differently: *It has been vainly debated whether this conclusion is modest or arrogant. I believe I have considered my defects and vices quite objectively.*

170. As Clausewitz amusingly remarks, "Whoever has genius . . .": The remark is amusing because of an untranslatable play on words: in both German and French the word for "genius" (*Genie/génie*) also refers to the "engineer corps" of an army. The quotation is from Clausewitz's "Remarks on the Strategy of Bülow." The **Baltasar Gracián** quotation is from *The Art of Worldly Wisdom* (#55). **But can I ever forget the one whom I see everywhere in the greatest moment of our adventures:** *This paragraph and the following one are a eulogy to Ivan Vladimirovitch Chtcheglov.* Chtcheglov was one of Debord's fellow "psychogeographical" explorers and visionaries during the early 1950s. See his "Formulary for a New Urbanism" (*SI Anthology,* pp. 1–8). His few other writings are collected in *Écrits retrouvés* (Allia, 2006). See also Jean-Marie Apostolidès and Boris Donné's study, *Ivan Chtcheglov, profil perdu* (Allia, 2006). The sentence "But can I ever forget . . ." is detourned from Bossuet's *Funeral Oration for Messire Le Tellier.*

171. "The Third Man": Orson Welles playing the title character in Carol Reed's 1939 film. **writ in water:** Cf. *"Here lies one whose name was writ in water." Percy Shelley, who disappeared at sea, had written this as an epitaph for himself.* [Actually, it was written by Shelley's friend John Keats, and appears on Keats's tombstone.]

171–172. Comic strip sequence: My translation follows the French version shown in Debord's film. The original *Prince Valiant* comic (May 7, 1939) had slightly different words.

172. Ceaselessly drifting: allusion to the practice of *dérives.* See Debord's article "Theory of the Dérive" (*SI Anthology,* pp. 62–66). **finest player . . . forests of madness:** Chtcheglov became insane and spent several years in a mental hospital. **Ludwig II:** eccentric king of Bavaria from 1864–1886 who built an unfinished fairy-tale castle situated precariously on a crag and decorated with scenes from Wagner's operas. Like Chtcheglov, he eventually became insane. *Potlatch* #4 contains some brief remarks in praise of Ludwig and of that other proto-psychogeographical architect, Ferdinand Cheval.

173. the Devil's party: Cf. Blake's *The Marriage of Heaven and Hell:* "The reason Milton wrote in fetters when he wrote of Angels & God, and at liberty when of Devils & Hell, is because he was a true Poet and of the Devil's party without knowing it." **the "bad side" that makes history:** Cf. Marx's *The Poverty of Philosophy* (II.1) where, in response to Proudhon's simplistic distinction between the "good" and "bad" sides of various historical periods, Marx notes that "it is the bad side that makes history by provoking struggles." *Les Visiteurs du Soir:* film by Marcel Carné (1942).

174. a happy, eternally present unity: *This unitary image obviously only serves to cover up a miserable process of division and constant disintegration.* **to strike with the time** *(frapper avec le temps):* In the most direct sense the French means to strike "with time": to use time as a weapon (as one would strike with a club). But as contrasted with the previously mentioned people who are only waiting for something good to happen, it also suggests striking with *the* time (i.e. in accordance with the time in which one finds oneself)—striking at the right moment, while there's still time, before it's too late. **"he who has been wronged":** *Certain millenarian sects used this euphemism to*

refer to the Devil; later Bakunin's Italian partisans used it for him because of the way he had been treated by the International Working Men's Association. **Asger Jorn, Giuseppe Pinot-Gallizio, Attila Kotányi, Donald Nicholson-Smith:** members of the Situationist International.

175. no other revolutionary endeavor . . . transformation of the world: *This has been a century of counterrevolution and of new refinements in slavery. Undertakings truly determined to push it in the other direction have been rare. Most of them, combining theoretical nullity with practical nullity, did not understand how class society was developing nor what its new weak points would be.*

177. "O wretchedness . . . trembling": line at the end of a poem in Victor Hugo's *Châtiments* ("In the ghastly cemetery . . ."). **seize it by brute force:** *Allusion to May 1968.*

178. It's a beautiful moment . . . set in motion: *This paragraph and the four following ones sum up the history of the Situationist International (1957–1972).*

179. "good old cause": *Expression used by the Levellers during the English Revolution of the seventeenth century.*

180. The strategist Sun Tzu . . . aware of everything: The quotations are from Sun Tzu's *The Art of War* (chap. 7) and Clausewitz's *Observations on Prussia in Her Great Catastrophe.* **you have to pay up front to see what comes next:** *This phrase simultaneously evokes the game of poker, where you sometimes have to pay to see the opponent's hand, and Clausewitz's discussion of the "commerce" of war, where he describes the moment of battle as the point when there's no more credit and you have to pay up front, with blood.* [Debord is probably referring to Clausewitz's *On War* (I.2): "The decision by arms is, for all operations in war, great and small, what cash payment is in bill transactions."]

181. to have enlivened their time without outliving it: an attempt to translate the double meaning of *"avoir fait leur temps."* In the most literal sense it means to have *made* one's time (thus to have marked it, influenced it, inspired it, etc.). More idiomatically it means to have done or served one's time (e.g. to have completed one's prison term or military service), or that one's time is up.

182. The particular wears itself out fighting: See Note 63. **"Yet your bones . . . mission unfulfilled":** lines from *The Iliad* (Book 4).

184. as poor in power and prestige as before (what I have had on a purely personal level from the beginning has always been enough for me): *A kind of long-standing personal authority, which has certainly never been exposed to the risk of being increased by any form of social approval.* **I have also refused . . . on their own:** *Definitive judgment of the "pro-situs" and of the years when they imagined they might be capable of imitating the SI.* [*pro-situs:* derogatory term referring to the numerous would-be imitators of the SI who emerged in the aftermath of May 1968. See "Theses on the SI and Its Time" ##25–38 in *The Real Split in the International.*]

184–185. These people were unaware . . . not enough: Cf. Machiavelli's *Discourses* (III.30): "But he forgot that in such matters nothing is to be expected from time, that goodness does not suffice, and that benefits will not placate envious malignity."

185. a field which no one can ever master: *This was Admiral Coligny's conclusion about the science of factions and political disturbances (quoted in Cardinal de Retz's "Memoirs").* **The results . . . will not be presented in cinematic form:** *Thus, in 1978 I had already declared that this film was going to be my last one.*

186. one of the best cities that ever was: *Florence.*

186–187. "Each of us . . . exile in Italy": quotation from Dante's *Purgatory* (Canto 13).

187. "the banks . . . farewells": quotation from Musset's *Lorenzaccio.* **Dogana promontory:** in Venice. **"When we were young . . . like the wind":** quatrain by Omar Khayyam. **Cardinal de Retz** (Jean-François-Paul de Gondi): leading figure in the Fronde, a complex series of revolts and social conflicts in seventeenth-century France (1648–1653). A note in *Potlatch #26* praises the playfulness of Retz's intrigues, and he would undoubtedly have been prominently featured in Debord's unrealized film on the Fronde (see p. 263).

188. "Where are those merry companions of times gone by?": lines from François Villon's *Testament* (stanza 29). For some remarks on Villon and his world, see chapter 2 of Debord's *Panegyric.*

189. remake of the old film: The previous Light Brigade sequences were from Michael Curtiz's *The Charge of the Light Brigade* (1936). The remake was by Tony Richardson (1968). **because the enemy has pushed its mistakes so far:** *The commentators have not yet dared to assess just how much the Chernobyl nuclear disaster of 1986 contributed to the collapse of the totalitarian bureaucracy in Russia that began three years later; nor the extent to which the growing powers of spectacular-democratic methods of government, and the excessive use that has been made of them, have contributed to the astonishing atrophy in the strategic sense of those who rule over these conditions.*

190. brought them to this cesspit: *This pollution is generally attributed to accidental mishaps; but it is in fact the inevitable consequence of the kind of "happiness" chosen by spectacle-commodity society, its secret but constantly present accompaniment.*

191. a poet of the T'ang period: Wang Wei.

192. Marx wrote to Ruge: in May 1843.

193. reflections on violence: title of a book by Georges Sorel. **No wising up and no settling down:** *La sagesse ne viendra jamais* literally means "Wisdom will never come." In this context, however, Debord is talking about himself, continuing from the preceding sentence ("for me there will be no turning back and no reconciliation") and using *sagesse* in the more colloquial French sense of "sensibleness, moderation, good behavior." (An *enfant sage*, for example, is a "well-behaved child.") Debord is saying that he will never "wise up" in this sense, never "mature" or "settle down." **To be gone through again from the beginning:** *In contrast to the traditional indications of conclusion, "The End" or "To Be Continued," this phrase should be understood in all senses of the French verb "reprendre"* [i.e., to repeat, resume, recommence, start over, go through again, return, reconsider, rectify, etc.]. *First of all it means that the film, whose title is a palindrome, warrants immediately being seen again in order to achieve its fullest despair-producing effect—when you know how it ends, you will have a better idea of how to make sense of the beginning. It also means that everything will have to be recommenced—the actions evoked as well as the comments on them. Finally, it means that everything must be reconsidered from the beginning, corrected, and perhaps blamed, in order to eventually achieve more favorable results.*

GUY DEBORD: HIS ART AND HIS TIME

General Note: This "antitelevisual" video was created in collaboration with Brigitte Cornand (see p. 235). It was completed in 1994 and broadcast by the French television channel Canal + on January 9, 1995. Meanwhile, suffering from an incurable and increasingly painful illness, Debord committed suicide on November 30, 1994. Alice Debord communicated the following final note from him to Cornand, asking her to append it to the end of the video:

"Illness known as alcoholic polyneuropathy, first noticed in autumn 1990. Almost imperceptible at first, then progressively worse. Only became really painful toward the end of November 1994. As with any incurable malady, it's wiser to neither seek nor accept treatment. It's the contrary of a malady that one might contract due to a regret-

table imprudence. On the contrary, one should remain stubbornly faithful to one's whole life."

Unlike Debord's six films, this video has no spoken voice-over. Instead, it presents a series of silent text titles which alternate with the visual material (photos, newsclips, etc.). I have thus followed the different layout style used in the script included in Debord's *Oeuvres* (Gallimard, 2006, pp. 1870–1878), in which the text titles are indicated by large type and other material by smaller type. That script is much more minimal than the film scripts: newsclips that may run for some time and include substantial spoken content are indicated very briefly. I have translated such brief indications as they appear in the original script, but have in many cases added much more detailed summaries or explanations in these notes.

207. Franz-Olivier Giesbert: During a televised book-review program, Giesbert speaks roughly as follows (with interruptions from his fellow commentators in parentheses): "I find it a very odd book because it talks at length about a pathology. He speaks about spectacle as if there was no history. History? What about Napoleon? That was a real spectacle. Or Louis XIV!" ("Wait a minute! We haven't read the same book!") "So he demonizes the spectacle, which is supposedly all-powerful and falsifies everything! He tells us . . ." ("That's not what I read!") "Please, I read the book, I can even quote his exact words. He says secrecy is spreading. Whereas my impression is that things are becoming increasingly open and transparent. He tells us that history is disappearing. And why? Simply because it hasn't unfolded to his liking since May '68!" ("He tells us that truth is disappearing, as if it never had in 2000 years!" . . . "It's now conjured away by an economic system.") "Last but not least, he tells us that democracy is breaking down." ("He's right.") "He says that, whereas I have the impression that democracy is advancing all over the world. All you have to do is read the papers! In Yugoslavia, Algeria, Chile, and so on. So Monsieur Debord has written a very interesting book. But he hasn't read the history books. And he doesn't even read the papers! And . . . just let me finish! He puts it all down to one big conspiracy." ("Yes, that's the weakness of the book—his paranoia sees conspiracies everywhere.") "But why do I not like this talented though rather jargonistic book? Because, though he doesn't actually say so, because it legitimizes violence. It legitimizes violence because it tells us that the world, the conspiracy we're entering is horrible. That there is no democracy, so why not simply . . . And I can't accept that." **"I'll never work . . ."**: lines from Bruant's song "Lézard" ("Loafing"). **"The Paris of old is there no more (alas, the form of a city changes more rapidly than the heart of a mortal)"**: quotation from Baudelaire's poem "Le Cygne" ("The Swan"). **Pont Neuf recreated in a film by Leos Carax:** Video voice-over: "One thing I hate is the word 'commercial' applied to a film. You always hear: 'It only takes a stroke of the magic wand to commercialize a script.' A film works when it is made with the utmost sincerity and when that sincerity touches a significant number of people."

208. In 1952: Allusion to Debord's imageless film, *Howls for Sade*. **Page from *Mémoires*:** This "metagraphic" or collage work by Debord was issued as a thin booklet in 1958. It consists entirely of words or images cut out from books, magazines, advertisements, and other sources and arranged in a seemingly jumbled manner (interconnected with "supporting structures" painted by Asger Jorn). Among the more substantial text passages shown: "the arrangement of words that form a discourse transforms something in the world order by acting on consciousnesses: the consciousness that forms it and the consciousness that receives it. It is the breach through which a moment of eternity is engulfed in a world moving obscurely toward its ruin." . . . "How far away are we?" . . . "Note that at that time the characters' more pitiful aspects were not known as they have since been revealed by the admissions in these *Memoirs*." . . . "What a tragedy! And who can we rely on? I daresay that our side had ardor, good will, and good disposition. But within a half hour the Prussian king's maneuvers

forced our cavalry and infantry to give way; they retreated in good order, but without ever looking back." **Never work:** Graffiti by Debord (Paris, 1952). **Directives:** two painted slogans by Debord (1963). **Photos:** see Note 215.

209. Pont Neuf wrapped up by Christo: Newsclip voice-over: "We would never have seen the Pont Neuf so vividly as since the magician Christo made it appear by making it disappear: an ephemeral sculpture now carved in our memory." **The little that remains of the Aral Sea:** Newsclip voice-over: "2000 kilometers south of Moscow, in the heart of Soviet Central Asia, the Aral is the world's fourth largest landlocked sea. In 30 years its surface has diminished by one third, its volume by two thirds, and its level has dropped 14 meters. It's dying of thirst and if nothing halts the process, in the next ten years it will be wiped off the map." Within a few years the Aral Sea did indeed dry up almost completely, except for a few scattered lakes. **I shall write my thoughts in order . . . true order:** Quotation from Isidore Ducasse's *Poésies* (part 2). **A trapped Colombian girl:** News coverage of the slow death of 13-year-old Omayra Sánchez, whose legs were caught in wreckage in such a way that it was impossible to extricate her or to amputate her legs without killing her.

210. Women wrestling in Japan: Video of a brutal and very dangerous wrestling match between two young women, followed by an interview with the winner, who says that if she can continue to gain such victories she hopes to be able to move to a regular apartment. (The one she currently lives in is a tiny cubbyhole with barely room for her bed and TV.) **Prospecting for oil under the Paris Basin:** Newsclip voice-over: "Oil under the Paris Basin is nothing new, but in this case they're not prospecting in some ordinary wheatfield, but in the Arboretum just two kilometers from the Versailles Palace: an immense reserve of over 2000 species of trees, partly open to the public—a public that can now view the drilling team at work." **Sometimes, on Sunday . . .:** That title and the immediately following sequence of exploding buildings is from Luis Buñuel's surrealist film *L'Âge d'or* (1930). It is followed by clips of actual demolitions of huge modern housing projects. **1933 was one of the most sinister dates:** In January 1933 the Nazi Party won a 37% plurality of seats in the German parliamentary election and Hitler was appointed Chancelor. The burning of the Reichstag the following month (see Note 90) gave them an excuse to outlaw the Communist Party and then pass the "Enabling Act," which gave Hitler the power to rule through executive orders, effectively making him the national dictator. **Assassination of Kennedy in Dallas:** Clips of the 1963 assassination, including newscaster Walter Cronkite's announcement of Kennedy's death.

211. Repression of Tienanmen: The famous video of a young man standing in front of several tanks. **Tanks in the streets of Moscow:** Newsclip voice-over: "This disturbing scene reminds Muscovites of two years ago when the same tanks surrounded the same White House under orders from the putschists. Yet tonight it's Boris Yeltsin who's showing that he means business, calling out armored cars of Red Berets and crack commandos equipped with grenades and night-vision. . . . The Muscovites are preparing for crisis. . . . At the gates of this factory the workers are perplexed." **Tonton Macoute:** Haitian dictator "Papa Doc" Duvalier's paramilitary militia and secret police. Newsclip voice-over: "Army and police turn a blind eye. Every morning there are corpses on the sidewalks and houses torched. Most shops of the capital remain closed. Intimidation remains the sole arm of Duvalier's followers to prevent elections." **Gunshots during a demonstration in Algiers:** Newsclip voice-over: "Anger, indignation, crime, and above all incomprehension. A pro-democracy march turned into a nightmare." A young woman shouts: "In the face of death we will remain standing! Long live free Algeria! Down with fundamentalism!" **A Somali woman being lynched . . .:** She is probably about to be killed for breaking some sharia law. **Students in a professional high**

school . . . justifying all that: The extreme ignorance of the students (much of the class is unclear when the nineteenth century was) would be even more shocking if one did not at the same time notice the meaninglessness of the rote lessons they are being taught ("In what year was this Zola novel published?"). Interviewed afterwards, some of the students say that such lessons are necessary because they will enable them to pass exams. Another young man, asked what he thinks he can do in life if he doesn't know how to read, says he looks forward to joining the army. **"solitary, poor, nasty, brutish, and short":** The quote is from Hobbes's 1651 book *Leviathan* (part 1, chap. 13). **Nazi Time:** Daylight Saving Time was initiated in France during the Nazi occupation, then discontinued after the war. It was resumed in the 1970s and extended to all of Europe.

212. radioactive alert: Video voice-over: "Ladies and gentlemen, we interrupt this program to bring you important news. Word has just been received from the Atomic Energy Commission that due to a change in wind direction the residue from this morning's atomic detonation is drifting in the direction of St. George. It is suggested that everyone remain indoors for one hour or until further notice. There is no danger." **Chernobyl:** Location in Ukraine of the worst nuclear disaster in history (so far)—April 26, 1986. Video voice-over: "First there was Hiroshima. Everyone thought it did not concern us. It had no repercussions. Then there was Chernobyl. Everyone thought it would go away. The government told us: Everything's fine. Eat mushrooms [i.e. they're not contaminated], go for walks, there's no problem. Five years have passed. Chernobyl has entered every household." Immediate segue to a French newsclip a few years later: "Here's the G-7's new gift to Ukraine: the means to complete this new nuclear power plant. But to replace Chernobyl, which amounted to 7% of the national grid, more is needed, so Ukraine is driving a hard bargain. Mikhail Umanev says it will take 30 years to wipe Chernobyl off the map. The boss of Ukraine Nuclear thinks the rebuilding of the national energy policy will require at least $5 billion, and that saving Ukraine will require six new reactors. In today's declaration the G-7 has given Ukraine new loans amounting to $3.5 billion." See also Note 190. **Launching of a 24/7 news channel:** Note that three decades ago, when there was no Internet and only a few television channels, the very existence of such a thing could be seen as a rather shocking example of the spectacular domination of people's lives, though it is now business as usual all over the world. Much the same could of course be said regarding many of the other examples Debord cites in this video. **responsible but not guilty:** A French Health Department bureaucrat regrets, but justifies, having left French people in the dark about certain medical risks. When she mentions "evaluating" the comparative risks, Debord interjects the text comment: "And you'd evaluate how much each of you would stand to gain?" **Arthur Cravan:** See Note 5. **Buren Columns:** An ugly array of small pillars installed in the courtyard of the Palais Royal in Paris by the artist Daniel Buren (1985).

213. Silvio Berlusconi: Italian media tycoon and Prime Minister. **Funeral of Pierre Bérégovoy:** Bérégovoy was briefly Prime Minister under Mitterrand. The newsclip of his funeral notes the presence of "the entire French political establishment gathered in grief" at this "highly emotional ceremony," and includes a homily spoken by Bishop Moutel: "No one knows the heart of man. Only God fathoms the secret of our lives, and the mystery that dwells within each of us. . . ." **Long line waiting to get into the Louvre . . . Musée d'Orsay:** Newsclip voice-over: "Paris is overflowing, not with water from the Seine, but with enthusiasm for art." **Rue Daguerre . . . Rue de Buci:** streets in the Parisian neighborhoods of Montparnasse and Saint-Germain-des-Prés, formerly noted for their artistic qualities, but now culturally lifeless. **Bernard Tapie:** French businessman, politician, television host, and "media personality." In the interview he complains about his constant struggle against unfair harassment by the media, which are

constantly questioning his notoriously corrupt business practices. **Yasser Arafat:** leader of the Palestinian Liberation Organization. In his talk (following a recent "peace accord") he salutes his new "brothers": the ruling politicians of Israel. **Philippe Alexandre, Serge July, and Christine Ockrent:** French journalists. Their discussion of the current French political mood is interrupted by four sarcastic text comments by Debord. The last one, difficult to translate, implies that this is all meaningless verbiage.

214. ACT UP: AIDS Coalition To Unleash Power, an international grassroots organization formed in 1987 to address the AIDS pandemic. The group attempted to improve the lives of people with AIDS through direct actions, medical research, treatment, advocacy, and appeals for changed legislation and public policies. **Immunological prevention is a thing of the past:** Debord implies that new pandemics such as AIDS are becoming so widespread and varied that it is impossible to prevent them in advance. **Boutboul family . . . Fantastic Lottery Nights:** *La Famille Boutboul à Loose Vegas* and *Les Nuits Fantastiques du Loto* were popular theatrical shows that seem to have been almost as idiotic as most of their American counterparts. Coincidentally, there was a widely reported scandal about a real-life Boutboul family when a Madame Boutboul hired someone to murder her son-in-law. **ad for the DRSP:** The DRSP organizes the leasing of prison labor to private businesses. The video ad, addressed to such businesses, states: "Your advantages? They are threefold: cost, flexibility, and results. Regarding costs, I guarantee, for 1000 jobs, 50% reduction in social charges. I also guarantee you manpower paid exclusively according to yield. The quality of the finished products is also guaranteed. Flexibility? We can adapt to the tightest deadlines. I also guarantee zero absenteeism, and that they'll work all year round with no labor disputes with your company. As for results: I offer you very broad capabilities, from the most repetitive tasks to software development—whatever you need. I hope I've convinced you. So why not come see us and tell us your needs. DRSP advisors are at your disposal seven days a week, committed to your company's strategy and to meeting your deadlines with tailormade solutions." **Rwanda:** In the newsclip, the few foreign doctors and nurses on hand note that there are far too few of them to care for the thousands of sick people who are brought to them.

215. Portraits: Marbaix and Herbute were companions of Debord's from the 1950s; López-Pintor was a close friend from late in his life. **Clinton:** Bill Clinton, US president (1992–2000).

DOCUMENTS

217. Détournement: The French word means diversion, deflection, rerouting, distortion, misuse, misappropriation, hijacking, or otherwise turning something aside from its normal course or purpose. It has sometimes been translated as "diversion," but that word is confusing because of its more common meaning of idle entertainment. Like most other English-speaking people who have actually practiced détournement, I have chosen simply to anglicize the French word. For the complete Debord–Wolman article and other articles on détournement, see *SI Anthology*, pp. 14–21, 67–68, 273–277.

219. The cheapness of its products . . . Chinese walls of understanding: See Note 67.

220. one could have Robespierre say . . . governing of nations: In the first imagined scene a quotation from a Greek tragedy (Sophocles's *Oedipus at Colonus*) is put in the mouth of French Revolution leader Maximilien Robespierre. In the second, a quotation from Robespierre is put in the mouth of a truck driver.

221. supersession of Isou's conception of "discrepant cinema": Isou's notion of discrepant cinema implied separating the sound track from the image track, freeing sound from its dependence on the image so as to revive the autonomy of the text, which had been almost totally lost in the cinema. But whereas Isou still had a sort of aesthetic agenda (the use of those cinematic elements, in combination with other elements, to create new artistic forms), Debord was already aiming at the supersession of art, at transcending the creation of works of art through the creation of "situations."

222. *For Whom the Bell Tolls*: Debord was later able to use the passage he describes in *The Society of the Spectacle* (see p. 83). The soap ad actress who subsequently had a "brighter future" was Anna Karina.

227. facing a blank screen . . . belatedly plagiarized: Allusion to the lettrist films of the early 1950s, which frequently contained such blank-screen passages, culminating in Debord's first film, *Howls for Sade*. For numerous other examples of Godard's copying from Debord, see the last two pages of the Thomas Levin study mentioned on p. 264.

228. Jacopetti: Gualtiero Jacopetti, director of sensationalistic "shockumentaries."

230. famous analysis of the fetishism of the commodity: in *Capital* (chap. 1, section 4). **"bacchanalia of truth where no one remains sober":** quotation from the Preface to Hegel's *Phenomenology of Spirit*.

233. "expropriate the expropriators": See Note 52.

CHRONOLOGY

1931. Birth of Guy Debord in Paris, December 28.

1951. He takes up with the lettrists.

1952. *Howls for Sade*. Debord breaks from Isidore Isou's lettrist group and forms the Lettrist International. Other LI members include Gil J Wolman, Ivan Chtcheglov, and Michèle Bernstein (Debord's first wife). Publications include the bulletin *Potlatch* and several articles in the Belgian surrealist journal *Les Lèvres Nues*.

1957. The LI merges with radical avant-garde currents of other countries to form the Situationist International. Early SI members include Danish artist Asger Jorn, Italian painter Pinot-Gallizio, Dutch architect Constant, and Scottish novelist Alexander Trocchi. Debord edits the group's journal, *Internationale Situationniste*.

1958. *Mémoires*.

1959. *On the Passage of a Few Persons Through a Rather Brief Unity of Time*.

1961. *Critique of Separation*.

1962. Exclusion of opportunist artist members (German "Spurists" and Scandinavian "Nashists") marks the SI's development in a more radical political direction. New members during the following period include Raoul Vaneigem (Belgian), Attila Kotányi (Hungarian exile), René Viénet (French), Mustapha Khayati (Tunisian), and Gianfranco Sanguinetti (Italian).

1964. *Contre le Cinéma*. Debord begins living with Alice Becker-Ho, his partner and then wife for the rest of his life.

1966. "Strasbourg scandal": Khayati's pamphlet *On the Poverty of Student Life* published at the expense of Strasbourg University.

1967. Publication of Debord's *The Society of the Spectacle* and Vaneigem's *The Revolution of Everyday Life*.

1968. May 1968 revolt. Agitation by SI-influenced Enragés group triggers street fighting and occupation of universities, which in turn inspires a nationwide wildcat strike: within two weeks virtually all the factories of France are occupied by over ten million workers. Situationists and Enragés push for extension and radicalization of this movement (against the Communist Party and labor-union bureaucrats desperately trying to stop it). Following its defeat they escape to Belgium to avoid the temporary repression and write *Enragés and Situationists in the Occupations Movement.*

1969–1970. While post-May notoriety inspires the formation of numerous "pro-situationist" groups around the world, the SI itself goes through various internal crises.

1971. Debord meets Gérard Lebovici, who publishes his subsequent books and finances his last three films.

1972. *The Real Split in the International.* Dissolution of the SI.

1973. *The Society of the Spectacle* (film).

1975. *Refutation of All the Judgments . . .*

1978. *In girum imus nocte et consumimur igni. Complete Cinematic Works.*

1970s. Sojourns in Italy.

1980s. Sojourns in Spain.

1984. Assassination of Lebovici. Debord withdraws all his films from circulation.

1985. *Considerations on the Assassination of Gérard Lebovici.*

1987. *The Game of War.*

1988. *Comments on the Society of the Spectacle.*

1989. *Panegyric, Volume 1.*

1993. *This Bad Reputation.*

1994. Suffering from an incurable and increasingly painful illness, Debord commits suicide on November 30.

1995. Television broadcast of *Guy Debord: His Art and His Time.*

2001. Alice Debord begins the rerelease of all of Debord's films with a complete retrospective at the Venice Film Festival.

FILMOGRAPHY AND BIBLIOGRAPHY

Hurlements en faveur de Sade

France, 1952
Written and directed by Guy Debord
Voice 1: Gil J Wolman
Voice 2: Guy Debord
Voice 3: Serge Berna
Voice 4: Barbara Rosenthal
Voice 5: Jean-Isidore Isou
35mm, B&W, 75 minutes

Sur le passage de quelques personnes à travers une assez courte unité de temps

France, 1959
Written and directed by Guy Debord
Assistant Director: Ghislain de Marbaix
Cameraman: André Mrugalski
Assistant Cameraman: Jean Harnois
Editing: Chantal Delattre
Continuity: Michèle Vallon
Grip: Bernard Largemain
Voice 1: Jean Harnois
Voice 2: Guy Debord
Voice 3: Claude Brabant
Music: George Frederick Handel and
    Michel-Richard Delalande
Laboratory: GTC Joinville
Production: Dansk-Fransk Experimental-
    filmskompagni
35mm, B&W, 20 minutes

Critique de la séparation

France, 1961
Written and directed by Guy Debord
Cameraman: André Mrugalski
Assistant Cameraman: Bernard Davidson
Editing: Chantal Delattre
Continuity: Claude Brabant
Grip: Bernard Largemain
Music: François Couperin and Joseph Bodin de
    Boismortier
Voice: Guy Debord
Voice (during the credits): Caroline Rittener
Actress: Caroline Rittener
Laboratory: GTC Joinville
Production: Dansk-Fransk Experimental-
    filmskompagni
35mm, B&W, 20 minutes

La Société du Spectacle

France, 1973
Written and directed by Guy Debord
    (adapted from his 1967 book)
Assistant Directors: Jean-Jacques Raspaud and
    Gianfranco Sanguinetti
Cameraman: Antonis Georgakis
Assistant Cameraman: Philippe Delpont
Editing: Martine Barraqué
Editing Assistant: Manoela Ferreira
Documentalist: Suzanne Schiffmann

Sound: Antoine Bonfanti
Production Director: Christian Lentretien
Music: Michel Corrette
Laboratory: GTC Joinville
Production: Simar Films
Producer: Gérard Lebovici
Voice: Guy Debord
35mm, B&W, 90 minutes

Réfutation de tous les jugements, tant élogieux qu'hostiles, qui ont été jusqu'ici portés sur le film "La Société du Spectacle"
France, 1975
Written and directed by Guy Debord
Editing: Martine Barraqué
Editing Assistant: Paul Griboff
Sound Mixing: Paul Bertauld
Laboratory: GTC Joinville
Production: Simar Films
Producer: Gérard Lebovici
Voice: Guy Debord
35mm, B&W, 20 minutes

In girum imus nocte et consumimur igni
France, 1978
Written and directed by Guy Debord
Assistant Directors: Elisabeth Gruet and
    Jean-Jacques Raspaud
Cameraman: André Mrugalski
Assistant Cameraman: Richard Copans
Editing: Stéphanie Granel
Editing Assistant: Christine Noël
Grip: Bernard Largemain
Sound Mixing: Dominique Dalmasso
Sound Effects: Jérôme Levy
Documentalist: Joëlle Barjolin
Music: François Couperin; Benny Golson
    (*Whisper Not,* performed by Art Blakey and
    the Jazz Messengers)

Laboratory: GTC Joinville
Production: Simar Films
Producer: Gérard Lebovici
Voice: Guy Debord
35mm, B&W, 105 minutes

Guy Debord, son art et son temps
France, 1994
Written by Guy Debord
Directed by Brigitte Cornand
Editing: Jean-Pierre Baiesi
Documentalist: Geraldine Gauvin
Music: Lino Leonardi (excerpted from his album
    devoted to the poems of François Villon)
Production: Canal +, INA (Institut national
    d'audiovisuel)
Producer: Alain De Greef
Video, B&W, 60 minutes

All seven of these films were reissued in a three-DVD set: *Guy Debord: Oeuvres Cinématographiques Complètes* (Gaumont Video, 2005). That set (prepared by Olivier Assayas and including a 130-page booklet of documents) is no longer available, but various versions of the individual films can be found online, many of them dubbed or subtitled in English and other languages. For links to them and other information about Debord's films, see www.bopsecrets.org/SI/debord.films.

UNREALIZED FILM PROJECTS

Hurlements en faveur de Sade (first version)
    The initial script, published in the lettrist journal *Ion* #1 (April 1952), was somewhat different from the final version and also specified a number of images. Soon thereafter Debord revised the script and eliminated all the images, and this earlier version was never made.

La belle jeunesse [*Beautiful Youth*]

Mentioned, along with proposed films by other LI members, in *Internationale Lettriste #3*.

Portrait d'Ivan Chtcheglov [*Portrait of Ivan Chtcheglov*]

Les aspects ludiques manifestes et latents dans la Fronde [*Hidden and Manifest Playful Aspects in the Fronde*]

Éloge de ce que nous avons aimé dans les images d'une époque [*Homage to What We've Loved in the Images of an Era*]

Préface à une nouvelle théorie du mouvement révolutionnaire [*Preface to a New Theory of the Revolutionary Movement*]

The above four titles were listed on the back cover of *Contre le Cinéma* (1964) as films that Debord proposed to make if he could find a producer willing to grant him total artistic freedom. This did not happen until he met Gérard Lebovici several years later. (The more modest production expenses of Debord's earlier short films were covered by Asger Jorn.) Although none of these proposed films were ever realized, elements from them were incorporated into Debord's later films.

Traité de savoir-vivre à l'usage des jeunes générations [*Treatise on Living for the Young Generations*]

In an internal SI letter (April 27, 1970) Debord mentioned that in addition to filming his own book, *The Society of the Spectacle,* he would also like to film Raoul Vaneigem's *Traité* (known in English as *The Revolution of Everyday Life*). The bitter split between the two shortly thereafter made such a collaboration inconceivable.

De l'Espagne [*On Spain*]

Des Contrats includes a 1982 contract between Debord and Soprofilms (owned by Lebovici) granting Debord an allowance for an 18-month period during which he would investigate the feasibility of making a long film (2–4 hours) that would represent "an exhaustive and definitive examination of the spirit of modern Spain, from the fifteenth century to the present. Avoiding both exoticism and patriotism, this film will not express what foreigners (Europeans, Americans, Japanese, etc.) may imagine about this subject, nor even what Spaniards themselves may believe, but what Spain *really is*." The film would have examined contemporary Spain, but would also have included historical reenactments; and "for several obvious historical and cultural reasons" it would have been "centered on Andalusia." Following the assassination of Lebovici (March 1984) Debord abandoned this project.

RELATED BOOKS

Internationale Situationniste: 1958–1969 (Van Gennep, 1970; Champ Libre, 1975; Fayard, 1997). 700-page facsimile reprint of all twelve issues of the French SI journal. Selections are translated in Ken Knabb's *Situationist International Anthology* (revised and expanded edition, PM Press, 2024).

Guy Debord, *La Société du Spectacle* (Buchet-Chastel, 1967; Champ Libre, 1972; Gallimard, 1992). Translated by Fredy Perlman et al. (Black & Red, 1970; revised 1977; reprinted by AK Press, 2005); by Donald Nicholson-Smith (Zone, 1994); and by Ken Knabb (online 2002; Rebel Press, 2004; revised and annotated edition, Bureau of Public Secrets, 2014; new PM Press edition, 2024).

Contre le Cinéma (Institut Scandinave de Vandalisme Comparé, 1964). Illustrated scripts of the first three films, with an introduction by Asger Jorn.

Oeuvres cinématographiques complètes: 1952–1978 (Champ Libre, 1978; Gallimard, 1994). Illustrated scripts of all six films.

Ordures et décombres déballés à la sortie du film "In girum imus nocte et consumimur igni" par différentes sources autorisées (Champ Libre, 1982). Fourteen reviews of *In girum* reproduced in full without any comment.

In girum imus nocte et consumimur igni: Édition critique (Lebovici, 1990; Gallimard, 1999). Separate edition of the film's voice-over text with annotations by Debord. The Gallimard edition adds some other documents by Debord plus the reviews previously published in *Ordures et décombres* (including two additional reviews).

Des contrats (Le Temps Qu'il Fait, 1995). Three of Debord's film contracts with Gérard Lebovici.

The script of the 1994 video *Guy Debord, son art et son temps* was first published posthumously in Debord's *Oeuvres* (Gallimard, 2006), pp. 1870–1878.

* * *

In girum was first translated by Lucy Forsyth (Pelagian, 1991). Translations of the other five films (by Ken Knabb, Richard Parry, Fredy Perlman, and Keith Sanborn) were published in Richard Parry (ed.), *Society of the Spectacle and Other Films* (Rebel Press, 1992). An alternative photocopy edition of the *Society of the Spectacle* script (Not Bored, 1996) used the Nicholson-Smith translation instead of the Perlman one. Keith Sanborn used his own translations in preparing subtitled videotapes of *The Society of the Spectacle* (1996) and *Refutation of All the Judgments* (2001). Ken Knabb translated all six films plus related documents in *Complete Cinematic Works* (AK Press, 2003). The present revised and expanded edition (PM Press, 2026) has added the final video, *Guy Debord: His Art and His Time*.

* * *

Thomas Y. Levin's *Dismantling the Spectacle: The Cinema of Guy Debord* (1987) was the first serious and substantial study of Debord's films in any language, and it is still probably the best general introduction. It has been included in two or three print anthologies and is also online at www.bopsecrets.org/CF/levin.htm.

For more detailed articles on each of the films, see *Grey Room on Debord's Cinema* (MIT Press, 2013), online at https://1000littlehammers.wordpress.com/2013/08/28/grey-room-on-debords/.

There are also at least four books in French, all competent and informative:

Antoine Coppola, *Introduction au cinéma de Guy Debord et de l'avant-garde situationniste* (Sulliver, 2003).

Guy-Claude Marie, *Guy Debord: de son cinéma en son art et en son temps* (Vrin, 2009).

Fabien Danesi, *Le cinéma de Guy Debord, ou la négativité à l'oeuvre* (Paris Expérimental, 2011).

Fabien Danesi, Emmanuel Guy, and Fabrice Flahutez, *La fabrique du cinema de Guy Debord* (Actes Sud, 2013).

* * *

The above texts are more or less directly related to Debord's films. A far more extensive bibliography, with comments on more than a hundred books in French or English by or about Debord or the SI, is included in the latest edition of the *SI Anthology* (PM Press, 2024). The same bibliography, continually updated, can be found online at www.bopsecrets.org/SI/bibliog.htm.

INDEX

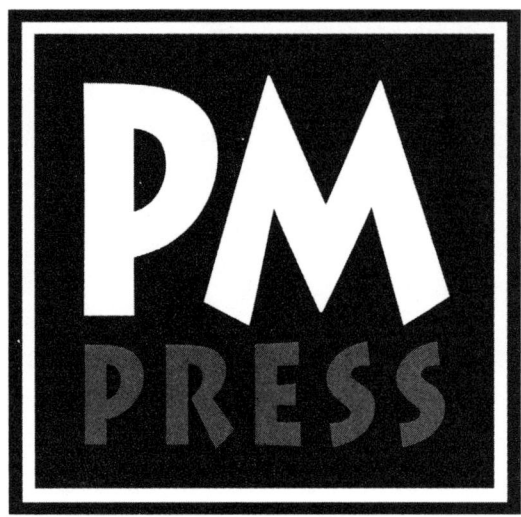

PM Press is an independent, radical publisher of critically necessary books for our tumultuous times. Our aim is to deliver bold political ideas and vital stories to all walks of life and arm the dreamers to demand the impossible. Founded in 2007 by a small group of people with decades of publishing, media, and organizing experience, we have sold millions of copies of our books, most often one at a time, face to face. We're old enough to know what we're doing and young enough to know what's at stake. Join us to create a better world.

PM Press
PO Box 23912
Oakland CA 94623
510-703-0327
www.pmpress.org

PM Press in Europe
europe@pmpress.org
www.pmpress.org.uk

Join the Friends of PM Press Book Club!

Help support radical, independent publishing and get PM Press titles shipped to you each month.

What?

A subscription bargain! You will automatically receive every new title delivered to your door each month and a 50% discount on all webstore purchases. On average we publish around thirty titles a year!

How Does it Work?

Your card is billed once a month and we ship you our new books, until you tell us to stop. Or until our efforts succeed in bringing the revolution around. Or the financial meltdown of Capital makes plastic redundant. Whichever comes first. There's no catch. No hidden fees. There is no minimum number of months required.

Why?

We are frequently asked why we offer such a great deal and how does it benefit PM Press. Your subscription fees provide us with a stable monetary platform that we can count on each month. All subscription fees go toward paying for the staggering cost of production. This steady source of income helps us to remain a truly independent publisher, unafraid to work with authors, artists, and activists who have traditionally been marginalized by mainstream publishers.

Options (all receive a 50% discount on purchases from our website)
- **$15 A MONTH** Get three e-Books each month
- **$30 A MONTH** Get all of our new books and pamphlets each month
- **$40 A MONTH** Get all PM Press releases (including CDs and DVDs)
- **$100 A MONTH** Everything plus PM merchandise and free downloads

For those who can't afford $30 or more a month, we have *Sustainer Rates* at $15, $10, and $5. Sustainers get a 50% discount on all purchases from our website.

pmpress.org/fopm

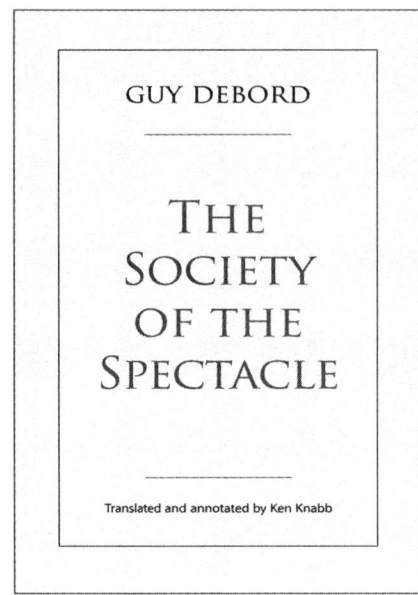

The Society of the Spectacle

Guy Debord

Translated and Annotated by Ken Knabb
ISBN: 979-8-88744-056-9
$19.95
5.25 x 8.25 • 160 pages

Guy Debord was the founder of the Situationist International, the radical avant-garde group that helped trigger the May 1968 revolt in France. His book *The Society of the Spectacle*, originally published in Paris in 1967, has been translated into more than twenty other languages and is arguably the most important radical work of the twentieth century. Ken Knabb's meticulous new translation is the first edition in any language to include extensive annotations, clarifying the historical allusions and revealing the sources of Debord's quotations and "détournements."

Contrary to popular misconceptions, Debord's book is neither an ivory-tower philosophical discourse nor a mere expression of "protest." It is a carefully considered effort to clarify the most fundamental tendencies and contradictions of the society in which we find ourselves—in order to facilitate its overthrow. This makes the book more of a challenge, but it is also why it remains so pertinent more than half a century after its original publication, while countless other social theories and intellectual fads have come and gone.

It has, in fact, become even more pertinent than ever, because the spectacle has become more all-pervading and glaringly obvious than ever. As Debord noted in his follow-up work, *Comments on the Society of the Spectacle*, "spectacular domination has succeeded in raising an entire generation molded to its laws."

Debord's book remains the key guidebook to understanding and breaking that mold.

Situationist International Anthology

REVISED AND EXPANDED EDITION

Edited and translated by Ken Knabb

ISBN: 979-8-88744-057-6

$29.95

6 x 9 • 544 pages

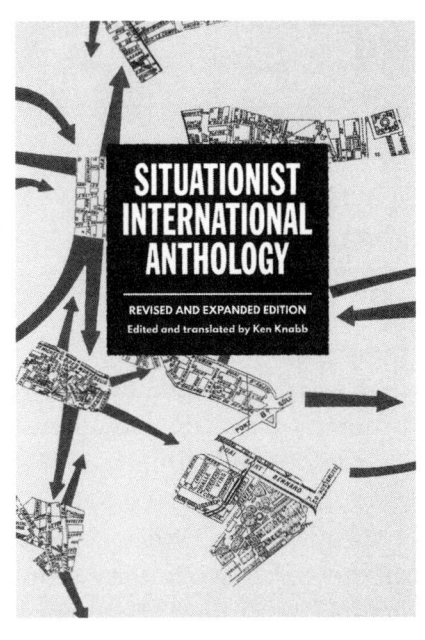

In 1957 a few European avant-garde groups came together to form the Situationist International. Picking up where the dadaists and surrealists had left off, the situationists challenged people's passive conditioning with carefully calculated scandals and the playful tactic of *détournement*. Seeking a more extreme social revolution than was dreamed of by most leftists, they developed an incisive critique of the global spectacle-commodity system and of its "Communist" pseudo-opposition, and their new methods of agitation helped trigger the May 1968 revolt in France, which brought the entire country to a standstill for several weeks. Since then situationist theories and tactics have continued to inspire radical currents all over the world.

The Situationist International Anthology is the most comprehensive and accurately translated collection of situationist writings in English. It presents a rich variety of articles, leaflets, graffiti, and internal documents, ranging from early experiments in "psychogeography" to lucid analyses of the Watts riots, the Vietnam War, the Prague Spring, the Chinese Cultural Revolution, and other crises and upheavals of the sixties.

For this revised and expanded edition more than one hundred pages of new material have been added, and the bibliography has been updated to include comments on dozens of newer books by and about the situationists.

Guy Debord

Anselm Jappe

Translated by Donald Nicholson-Smith
Foreword by T.J. Clark
ISBN: 978-1-62963-449-4
$21.95
6 x 9 • 224 pages

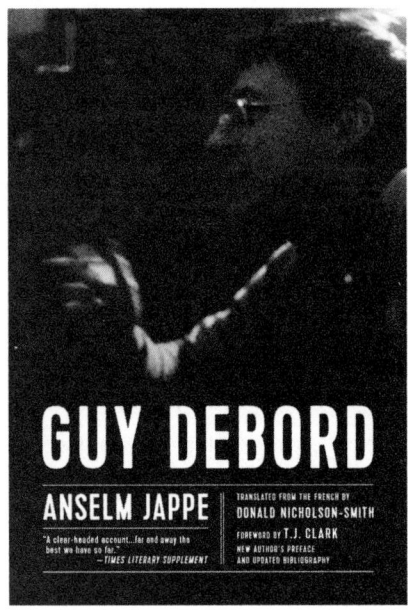

This is the first and best intellectual biography of Guy Debord, prime mover of the Situationist International (1957–1972) and author of *The Society of the Spectacle*, perhaps the seminal book of the May 1968 uprising in France. Anselm Jappe offers a powerful corrective to the continual attempts to incorporate Debord's theoretical work into "French theory." Jappe's focus, to the contrary, is on Debord's debt to the Hegelian-Marxist tradition, to Karl Korsch and Georg Lukács, and more generally to left-Marxist currents of council communism. His close reading of Debord's magnum opus supplies a superb gloss that has never been rivaled despite the great flood of writing on the Situationists in recent decades.

At the same time, Debord is placed squarely in context among the Letterist and Situationist anti-artists who, in the aftermath of World War II, sought to criticize and transcend the legacy of Dada and Surrealism. Jappe's book offers a lively account of the Situationists' theory and practice as this "last avant-garde" made its way from radical bohemianism to revolutionary theory and action.

Guy Debord has been translated into many languages. This PM Press reprint edition benefits from a new author's preface and a bibliographical update.

The Revolution of Everyday Life

Raoul Vaneigem

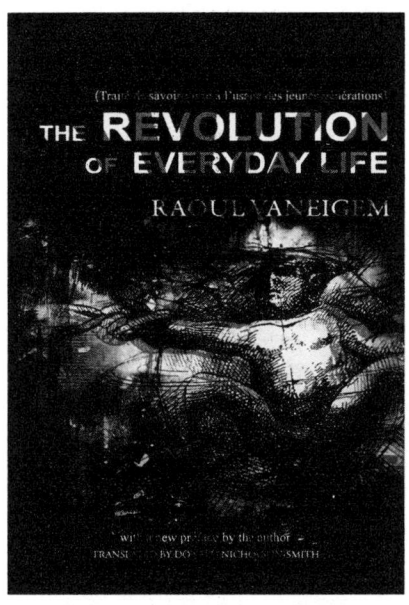

Translated by Donald Nicholson-Smith
ISBN: 978-1-60486-678-0
$20.00
6 x 9 • 288 pages

Originally published just months before the May 1968 upheavals in France, Raoul Vaneigem's *The Revolution of Everyday Life* offered a lyrical and aphoristic critique of the "society of the spectacle" from the point of view of individual experience. Whereas Debord's masterful analysis of the new historical conditions that triggered the uprisings of the 1960s armed the revolutionaries of the time with theory, Vaneigem's book described their feelings of desperation directly, and armed them with "formulations capable of firing point-blank on our enemies."

"I realise," writes Vaneigem in his introduction, "that I have given subjective will an easy time in this book, but let no one reproach me for this without first considering the extent to which the objective conditions of the contemporary world advance the cause of subjectivity day after day."

Vaneigem names and defines the alienating features of everyday life in consumer society: survival rather than life, the call to sacrifice, the cultivation of false needs, the dictatorship of the commodity, subjection to social roles, and above all the replacement of God by the Economy. And in the second part of his book, "Reversal of Perspective," he explores the countervailing impulses that, in true dialectical fashion, persist within the deepest alienation: creativity, spontaneity, poetry, and the path from isolation to communication and participation.

This new edition of *The Revolution of Everyday Life* has been reviewed and corrected by the translator and contains a new preface addressed to English-language readers by Raoul Vaneigem.

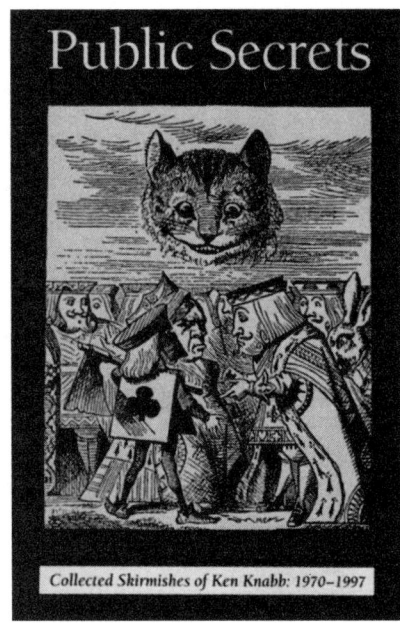

Public Secrets

Collected Skirmishes of Ken Knabb: 1970–1997

Public Secrets: Collected Skirmishes of Ken Knabb

ISBN: 978-0-93968-203-4
$15.00
5 x 7.5 • 408 pages

Ken Knabb is well known for his translations of works by Guy Debord and the Situationist International. *Public Secrets* is first comprehensive collection of his own writings.

The first half of the book consists of two substantial new texts. "The Joy of Revolution" is a series of observations on the problems and possibilities of a global antihierarchical revolution. Beginning with a brief overview of the failure of Bolshevism and the inadequacy of reformism, it examines the pros and cons of a wide range of radical tactics, then concludes with some provocative speculations about what a liberated society might be like. "Confessions of a Mild-Mannered Enemy of the State" is largely concerned with Knabb's situationist activities, but it also includes reminiscences of the sixties counterculture and accounts of his Zen practice and other later ventures.

The second half of the book presents Knabb's shorter writings, including a variety of pamphlets, posters, comics, and articles on Wilhelm Reich, Kenneth Rexroth, Gary Snyder, radical Buddhists, Japanese anarchists, Chinese dissidents, the 1970 Polish revolt, the 1979 Iranian uprising, and the 1991 Gulf war.

"Ken Knabb's two distinctive qualities, clarity and simplicity, distinguish him from the situationists yet at the same time mark him as one of their authentic successors. Does this mean that his work is a sort of 'Situationist International for Dummies'? No, but it could certainly serve as such—anyone who is unfamiliar with the SI should put this book at the very top of their reading list."
>   —Jean-Pierre Depétris (reviewing the French edition of *Public Secrets*)

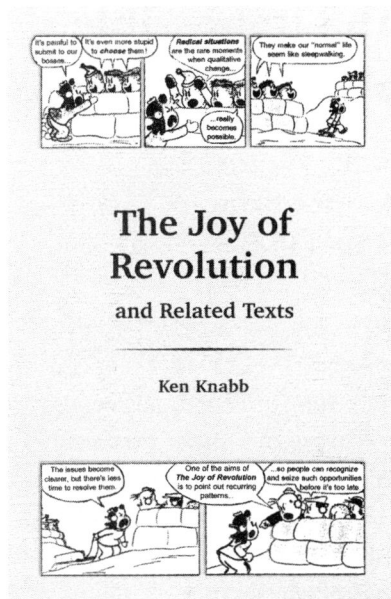

The Joy of Revolution
and Related Texts

Ken Knabb

ISBN: 979-8-88744-184-9
$21.95
5.5 x 8.5 • 272 pages

"It may seem absurd to talk about revolution. But all the alternatives assume the continuation of the present system, which is even more absurd."

Well known for his translations of works by Guy Debord and the Situationist International, Ken Knabb is also the author of numerous radical texts. *The Joy of Revolution* is widely considered his most significant work. While there have been countless histories of past revolutions and countless debates about the merits and drawbacks of different radical tactics, it would be difficult to name a single book that more clearly and concisely explores the overall problems and possibilities of a modern, situationist-type revolution.

Beginning with a brief overview of the absurdities of the present society and of the failures of various efforts to change it, it examines the pros and cons of a wide range of radical tactics, first in the context of "normal" or "ordinary" conditions, then in the very different context of radical situations—those rare breakthroughs where masses of people start to call everything into question and real change becomes possible. The book then concludes with some speculations on how a global liberated society might work, how it might deal with various problems, and what it might be like to live in.

For this new edition, Ken has updated his book and added several more recent texts, including a series of articles and talks on the Occupy movement, in which he was an enthusiastic participant.

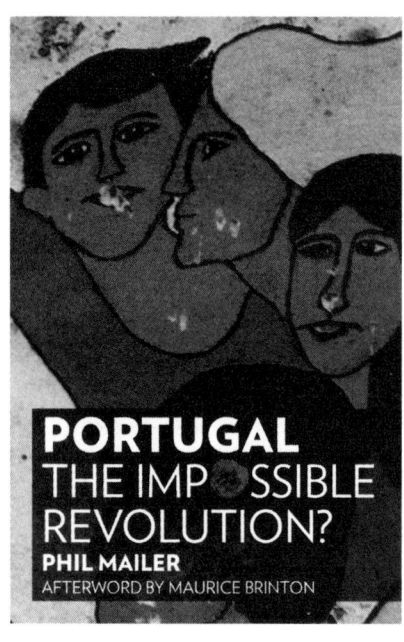

Portugal: The Impossible Revolution?

Phil Mailer

Afterword by Maurice Brinton
ISBN: 978-1-60486-336-9
$24.95
6 x 9 • 288 pages

After the military coup in Portugal on April 25th, 1974, the overthrow of almost fifty years of Fascist rule, and the end of three colonial wars, there followed eighteen months of intense, democratic social transformation which challenged every aspect of Portuguese society. What started as a military coup turned into a profound attempt at social change from the bottom up and became headlines on a daily basis in the world media. This was due to the intensity of the struggle as well as the fact that in 1974–75 the right-wing moribund Francoist regime was still in power in neighboring Spain and there was huge uncertainty as to how these struggles might affect Spain and Europe at large.

This is the story of what happened in Portugal between April 25, 1974, and November 25, 1975, as seen and felt by a deeply committed participant. It depicts the hopes, the tremendous enthusiasm, the boundless energy, the total commitment, the released power, even the revolutionary innocence of thousands of ordinary people taking a hand in the remolding of their lives. And it does so against the background of an economic and social reality which placed limits on what could be done.

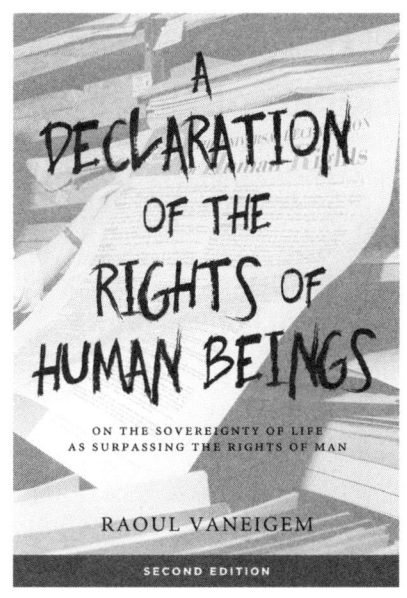

A Declaration of the Rights of Human Beings: On the Sovereignty of Life as Surpassing the Rights of Man, Second Edition

Raoul Vaneigem

Translated by Liz Heron
ISBN: 978-1-62963-155-4
$20.00
6 x 9 • 144 pages

"A declaration of rights is indispensable in order to halt the ravages of despotism." So wrote the revolutionary Antoine Barnave in support of the Declaration of the Rights of Man and of the Citizen (1789). Over two centuries after the Great French Revolution, Raoul Vaneigem writes that today, "in a situation comparable to the condition of France on the eve of its Revolution," we cannot limit ourselves to demanding liberties—the so-called bourgeois freedoms—that came into being with free trade, for now the free exchange of capital is the totalitarian form of a system which reduces human beings and the earth itself to merchandise. The time has come to give priority to the real individual rather than to Man in the abstract, the citizen answerable to the State and to the sole dictates of God's successor, the economy.

Sometimes playful or poetic, always provocative, Vaneigem reviews the history of bills of rights before offering his own call, with commentary, for fifty-eight rights yet to be won in a world where the "freedoms accorded to Man" are no longer merely "the freedoms accorded by man to the economy."

Every human being has the right, for example: to become human and to be treated as such; to dispose freely of their time; to comfort and luxury; to free modes of transport set up by and for the collectivity; to permanent control over scientific experimentation; to association by affinity; to bend toward life what was turned toward death; to the flux of passions and the freedoms of love; to a natural life and a natural death; to hold nothing sacred; to excess and to moderation; to desire what seems beyond the realm of the possible.

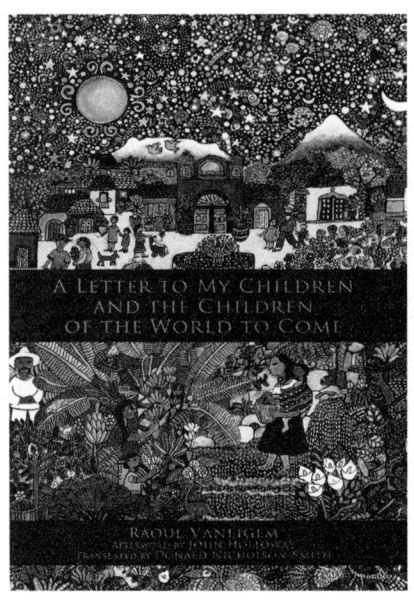

A Letter to My Children and the Children of the World to Come

Raoul Vaneigem

Afterword: John Holloway
Translated by Donald Nicholson-Smith
ISBN: 978-1-62963-512-5
$15.95
8 x 5 ♦ 128 pages

Readers of Vaneigem's now-classic work *The Revolution of Everyday Life*, which as one of the main contributions of the Situationist International was a herald of the May 1968 uprisings in France, will find much to challenge them in these pages written in the highest idiom of subversive utopianism.

Written some thirty-five years after the May "events," this short book poses the question of what kind of world we are going to leave to our children. "How could I address my daughters, my sons, my grandchildren and great-grandchildren," wonders Vaneigem, "without including all the others who, once precipitated into the sordid universe of money and power, are in danger, even tomorrow, of being deprived of the promise of a life that is undeniably offered at birth as a gift with nothing expected in return?"

A Letter to My Children provides a clear-eyed survey of the critical predicament into which the capitalist system has now plunged the world, but at the same time, in true dialectical fashion, and "far from the media whose job it is to ignore them," Vaneigem discerns all the signs of "a new burgeoning of life forces among the younger generations, a new drive to reinstate true human values, to proceed with the clandestine construction of a living society beneath the barbarity of the present and the ruins of the Old World."